CONRAD'S
SECRET SHARER
AND THE CRITICS

Wadsworth Guides to Literary Study

Maurice Beebe, General Editor

CONRAD'S
SECRET SHARER
AND THE CRITICS

EDITED BY BRUCE HARKNESS
University of Illinois

WADSWORTH PUBLISHING COMPANY, INC.
BELMONT, CALIFORNIA

Fifth printing, June 1969

L.C. Cat. Card No.: 62–13199

Printed in the United States of America.

TO

REH   *REEH*
MSW   *LAW*

PREFACE

This book is intended primarily for students in composition and literature courses, but it may prove interesting to many other readers as well. The critical selections included should add to a richer understanding of the tale—one that is generally held to be among Conrad's best. Further, the book may, in a small way, help toward a solution of one important problem—that of Conrad's text. The edition of "The Secret Sharer" printed in this volume is the first edition based on a collation of all important editions of the story and the first that reprints the proper copy-text—that of the Heinemann collected *Works,* the last separate edition published in Conrad's lifetime.

The Textual Note near the end of the book describes the basic publications of the story and lists a representative sample of variations in these editions. This collation permits the interested reader to trace the sample variations in the editions and to examine sample usages in the manuscript. More important, the Note suggests that a critical edition of Conrad's works is overdue.

The plan of this volume is simple. The text of "The Secret Sharer" is followed by two analogues of the story; these in turn are followed by critical selections. At the end of the book are sections containing materials for further study—the Textual Note, questions and suggested theme topics, and a short bibliography of works on Conrad.

Conrad tells us in his "Author's Note" that he heard "the basic fact of the tale" in the seaman's gossip of his sailing days. He was in Sydney, Australia, in November–December of 1880, less than two months after the crime had been committed, and doubtless heard a version of the murder there. Basil Lubbock's version, the first of the analogues printed here, is from his 1924 *Log of the "Cutty Sark"*: it is not Conrad's source, but an independent retelling of the crime. A second analogue—two accounts of the arrest and trial of the *Cutty Sark's* mate—is reprinted from the London *Times*. Conrad's "Author's Note" tells us that he read newspaper accounts of the trial. We do not know what paper Conrad read; but in July–August of 1882, when the *Times* published four items on the trial of Sidney Smith for the murder of John Francis, Conrad was lying idle at Falmouth, waiting for his ship, the *Palestine,* to be repaired before setting out on the ill-starred trip that was to become the source of "Youth." It was there that he must have read the newspaper accounts he refers to in his "Author's Note."

The critical section includes most of the significant current interpretations of the story. These critical selections, it will be seen, "question and answer" one another; compare "The Secret Sharer" to Conrad's *The Shadow-Line*; and raise larger issues of critical methodology. Thus, Albert Guerard, Daniel Curley, Carl Benson, and R. W. Stallman interpret the story as different kinds of myths or allegories, and disagree about the value of Leggatt, "the murderer." Marvin Mudrick and Jocelyn Baines implicitly and explicitly suggest non-allegorical approaches to the story. The selections by Walter Wright and by Royal Gettmann and myself tend toward a moral reading. Finally, Louis Leiter's article rounds off the critical section of this volume with a return to a mythic (and technical) analysis of "The Secret Sharer." The reader will readily discover, in spite of the extent and the intensity of comment evoked by the story, that many problems of detail, interpretation, and evaluation are far from settled. The intention here is not to supplant the story with criticism nor to present a "final" answer to the problems raised by the story, but to stimulate further study and a closer reading of the story itself.

In the main, the selections are full articles or self-contained sections from books on Conrad. For the reader's convenience, I have regularized all citation-references by the critics to "The Secret Sharer" (and to the Lubbock analogue) to match the pagination of the present volume. Page references to other works of Conrad are to the collected editions published by Dent and by Doubleday. I have indicated pagination of the original sources in raised numerals enclosed in brackets. Whenever the page of the original text ended with a divided word, I have placed the page reference at the end of the complete word. Original pagination is not given for "The Secret Sharer," since this volume presents a new critical text. Also, the article by Mr. Curley and the one by Mr. Gettmann and myself are in effect new publications and consequently do not have these numerals. The amount of material omitted from any article reprinted here can be ascertained by checking the original pagination. Unspaced ellipses (...) are the original author's; spaced ellipses (. . .) are mine.

I have, further, given new titles to some of the selections; and when the critic has had footnotes at the back of his book as well as at the foot of the page, I have worked these notes into one series, renumbering where necessary. One more word on footnotes is in order. Some of the critical selections are sections from books, and the critic often uses short titles in referring to other works by and about Conrad; he has, of course, given a full bibliographical reference earlier in his volume. I have let these short titles stand instead of expanding them in brackets; in most instances, the reader can determine a critic's reference by study of the bibliography at the end of this book. For example, *LL* stands for *Life and Letters*, G. Jean-Aubry's two-volume edition of Conrad's letters.

In addition to my thanks to the authors and publishers of the materials that make up this volume, I would like to record my gratitude to the following: to Professor S. Sterling McMillan of Western Reserve University, who permitted me to examine the manuscript; to the University of Illinois Research Board for travel funds; to the libraries of the University of Illinois and especially to Mr. Frank Rodgers, who helped me with interlibrary loans; to Miss Nina Logan and Mrs. Barbara Garrett, who helped to prepare the manuscript.

University of Illinois   *B. H.*

CONTENTS

CONTENTS

THE SECRET SHARER

from the volume

'TWIXT LAND & SEA

TALES

Life is a tragic folly
Let us laugh and be jolly
Away with melancholy
Bring me a branch of holly
Life is a tragic folly

A. SYMONS

TO
CAPTAIN C. M. MARRIS
LATE MASTER AND OWNER
OF THE
ARABY MAID: ARCHIPELAGO TRADER

IN MEMORY OF THOSE
OLD DAYS OF ADVENTURE

Joseph Conrad

"Author's Note" to *'Twixt Land & Sea* Volume*

The only bond between these three stories is, so to speak, geographical, for their scene, be it land, be it sea, is situated in the same region, which may be called the region of the Indian Ocean, with its offshoots and prolongations north of the Equator even as far as the Gulf of Siam. In point of time they belong to the period immediately after the publication of that novel with the awkward title, *Under Western Eyes*, and, as far as the life of the writer is concerned, their appearance in a volume marks a definite change in the fortunes of his fiction. For there is no denying the fact that *Under Western Eyes* found no favour in the public eye, whereas the novel called *Chance*, which followed *'Twixt Land and Sea*, was received on its first appearance by many more readers than any other of my books.

This volume of three tales was also well received, publicly and privately and from a publisher's point of view. This little success was a most timely tonic for my enfeebled bodily frame. For this may indeed be called the book of a man's convalescence, at least as to three-fourths of it; because "The Secret Sharer," the middle story, was written much earlier than the other two.

For in truth the memories of *Under Western Eyes* are associated with the memory of a severe illness which seemed to wait like a tiger in the jungle on the turn of a path to jump on me the moment the last words of that novel were written. The memory of an illness is very much like the memory of a nightmare. On emerging from it in a much enfeebled state I was inspired to direct my tottering steps toward the Indian Ocean, a complete change of surroundings and atmosphere from the Lake of Geneva, as nobody would deny. Begun so languidly and with such a fumbling hand that the first twenty pages or more had to be thrown into the wastepaper-basket, "A Smile of Fortune," the most purely Indian Ocean-story of the three, has ended by becoming what the reader will see. I will only say for myself that I have been patted on the back for it by most unexpected people, personally unknown to me, the chief of them of course being the editor of a popular illustrated magazine, who published it serially in one mighty instalment. Who will dare say after this that the change of air had not been an immense success?

---

* Reprinted from *'Twixt Land and Sea* with permission of the Trustees of the Joseph Conrad Estate, Doubleday & Co., Inc., New York, and J. M. Dent and Sons, Ltd., London.

The origins of the middle story, "The Secret Sharer," are quite other. It was written much earlier, and was published first in *Harper's Magazine* during the early part, I think, of 1911. Or perhaps the latter part? My memory on that point is hazy. The basic fact of the tale I had in my possession for a good many years. It was in truth the common possession of the whole fleet of merchant ships trading to India, China, and Australia: a great company, the last years of which coincided with my first years on the wider seas. The fact itself happened on board a very distinguished member of it, *Cutty Sark* by name and belonging to Mr. Willis, a notable shipowner in his day, one of the kind (they are all underground now) who used personally to see his ships start on their voyages to those distant shores where they showed worthily the honoured house-flag of their owner. I am glad I was not too late to get at least one glimpse of Mr. Willis on a very wet and gloomy morning watching from the pier-head of the New South Dock one of his clippers starting on a China voyage—an imposing figure of a man under the invariable white hat so well known in the Port of London, waiting till the head of his ship had swung downstream before giving her a digni-fied wave of a big gloved hand. For all I know it may have been the *Cutty Sark* herself, though certainly not on that fatal voyage. I do not know the date of the occurrence on which the scheme of "The Secret Sharer" is founded; it came to light and even got into newspapers about the middle eighties, though I had heard of it before, as it were privately, among the officers of the great wool fleet in which my first years in deep water were served. It came to light under circumstances dramatic enough, I think, but which have nothing to do with my story. In the more specially maritime part of my writings this bit of presenta-tion may take its place as one of my two Calm-pieces. For, if there is to be any classification by subjects, I have done two Storm-pieces, in *The Nigger of the Narcissus* and in *Typhoon;* and two Calm-pieces: this one and *The Shadow-Line,* a book which belongs to a later period.

Notwithstanding their autobiographical form the above two stories are not the record of personal experience. Their quality, such as it is, depends on something larger if less precise: on the character, vision, and sentiment of the first twenty independent years of my life. And the same may be said of the "Freya of the Seven Isles." I was consider-ably abused for writing that story, on the ground of its cruelty, both in public prints and in private letters. I remember one from a man in America who was quite furiously angry. He told me with curses and imprecations that I had no right to write such an abominable thing, which, he said, had gratuitously and intolerably harrowed his feelings. It was a very interesting letter to read. Impressive, too. I carried it for some days in my pocket. Had I the right? The sincerity of the anger impressed me. Had I the right? Had I really sinned as he said, or was

it only that man's madness? Yet there was a method in his fury. . . .
I composed in my mind a violent reply, a reply of mild argument, a
reply of lofty detachment; but they never got on paper in the end, and
I have forgotten their phrasing. The very letter of the angry man has
got lost somehow; and nothing remains now but the pages of the story,
which I cannot recall and would not recall if I could.

But I am glad to think that the two women in this book—Alice, the
sullen, passive victim of her fate, and the actively individual Freya, so
determined to be the mistress of her own destiny—must have evoked
some sympathies, because of all my volumes of short stories this was the
one for which there was the greatest immediate demand.

J. C.

1920.

THE SECRET SHARER

An Episode from the Coast

THE SECRET SHARER*
Joseph Conrad

I

On my right hand there were lines of fishing-stakes resembling a mysterious system of half-submerged bamboo fences, incomprehensible in its division of the domain of tropical fishes, and crazy of aspect as if abandoned for ever by some nomad tribe of fishermen now gone to the other end of the ocean; for there was no sign of human habitation as far as the eye could reach. To the left a group of barren islets, suggesting ruins of stone walls, towers, and blockhouses, had its foundations set in a blue sea that itself looked solid, so still and stable did it lie below my feet; even the track of light from the westering sun shone smoothly,
10 without that animated glitter which tells of an imperceptible ripple. And when I turned my head to take a parting glance at the tug which had just left us anchored outside the bar, I saw the straight line of the flat shore joined to the stable sea, edge to edge, with a perfect and unmarked closeness, in one levelled floor half brown, half blue under the enormous dome of the sky. Corresponding in their insignificance to the islets of the sea, two small clumps of trees, one on each side of the only fault in the impeccable joint, marked the mouth of the river Meinam we had just left on the first preparatory stage of our homeward journey;
and, far back on the inland level, a larger and loftier mass, the grove
20 surrounding the great Paknam pagoda, was the only thing on which the eye could rest from the vain task of exploring the monotonous sweep of the horizon. Here and there gleams as of a few scattered pieces of silver marked the windings of the great river; and on the nearest of them, just within the bar, the tug steaming right into the land became lost to my sight, hull and funnel and masts, as though the impassive earth had swallowed her up without an effort, without a tremor. My eye followed the light cloud of her smoke, now here, now there, above the plain, according to the devious curves of the stream, but always fainter and farther away, till I lost it at last behind the mitre-shaped hill of the
30 great pagoda. And then I was left alone with my ship, anchored at the head of the Gulf of Siam.

---

* Reprinted from *'Twixt Land and Sea* with permission of the Trustees of the Joseph Conrad Estate, Doubleday & Co., Inc., New York, and J. M. Dent and Sons, Ltd., London.

3

She floated at the starting-point of a long journey, very still in an immense stillness, the shadows of her spars flung far to the eastward by the setting sun. At that moment I was alone on her decks. There was not a sound in her—and around us nothing moved, nothing lived, not a canoe on the water, not a bird in the air, not a cloud in the sky. In this breathless pause at the threshold of a long passage we seemed to be measuring our fitness for a long and arduous enterprise, the appointed task of both our existences to be carried out, far from all human eyes, with only sky and sea for spectators and for judges.

10   There must have been some glare in the air to interfere with one's sight, because it was only just before the sun left us that my roaming eyes made out beyond the highest ridge of the principal islet of the group something which did away with the solemnity of perfect solitude. The tide of darkness flowed on swiftly; and with tropical suddenness a swarm of stars came out above the shadowy earth, while I lingered yet, my hand resting lightly on my ship's rail as if on the shoulder of a trusted friend. But, with all that multitude of celestial bodies staring down at one, the comfort of quiet communion with her was gone for good. And there were also disturbing sounds by this time—voices, foot-
20 steps forward; the steward flitted along the main deck, a busily ministering spirit; a hand-bell tinkled urgently under the poop deck....

I found my two officers waiting for me near the supper table, in the lighted cuddy. We sat down at once, and as I helped the chief mate, I said:

"Are you aware that there is a ship anchored inside the islands? I saw her mast-heads above the ridge as the sun went down."

He raised sharply his simple face, overcharged by a terrible growth of whisker, and emitted his usual ejaculations, "Bless my soul, sir! You
30 don't say so!"

My second mate was a round-cheeked, silent young man, grave beyond his years, I thought; but as our eyes happened to meet I detected a slight quiver on his lips. I looked down at once. It was not my part to encourage sneering on board my ship. It must be said, too, that I knew very little of my officers. In consequence of certain events of no particular significance, except to myself, I had been appointed to the command only a fortnight before. Neither did I know much of the hands forward. All these people had been together for eighteen months or so, and my position was that of the only stranger on board. I men-
40 tion this because it has some bearing on what is to follow. But what I felt most was my being a stranger to the ship; and if all the truth must be told, I was somewhat of a stranger to myself. The youngest man on board (barring the second mate), and untried as yet by a position of the fullest responsibility, I was willing to take the adequacy of the others

for granted. They had simply to be equal to their tasks; but I wondered how far I should turn out faithful to that ideal conception of one's own personality every man sets up for himself secretly.

Meantime the chief mate, with an almost visible effect of collaboration on the part of his round eyes and frightful whiskers, was trying to evolve a theory of the anchored ship. His dominant trait was to take all things into earnest consideration. He was of a painstaking turn of mind. As he used to say, he "liked to account to himself" for practically everything that came in his way, down to a miserable scorpion he had
10 found in his cabin a week before. The why and the wherefore of that scorpion—how it got on board and came to select his room rather than the pantry (which was a dark place and more what a scorpion would be partial to), and how on earth it managed to drown itself in the inkwell of his writing-desk—had exercised him infinitely. The ship within the islands was much more easily accounted for; and just as we were about to rise from table he made his pronouncement. She was, he doubted not, a ship from home lately arrived. Probably she drew too much water to cross the bar except at the top of spring tides. Therefore she went into that natural harbour to wait for a few days in preference
20 to remaining in an open roadstead.

"That's so," confirmed the second mate suddenly, in his slightly hoarse voice. "She draws over twenty feet. She's the Liverpool ship *Sephora* with a cargo of coal. Hundred and twenty-three days from Cardiff."

We looked at him in surprise.

"The tugboat skipper told me when he come on board for your letters, sir," explained the young man. "He expects to take her up the river the day after to-morrow."

After thus overwhelming us with the extent of his information he
30 slipped out of the cabin. The mate observed regretfully that he "could not account for that young fellow's whims." What prevented him telling us all about it at once, he wanted to know.

I detained him as he was making a move. For the last two days the crew had had plenty of hard work, and the night before they had very little sleep. I felt painfully that I—a stranger—was doing something unusual when I directed him to let all hands turn in without setting an anchor-watch. I proposed to keep on deck myself till one o'clock or thereabouts. I would get the second mate to relieve me at that hour.

"He will turn out the cook and the steward at four," I concluded,
40 "and then give you a call. Of course at the slightest sign of any sort of wind we'll have the hands up and make a start at once."

He concealed his astonishment. "Very well, sir." Outside the cuddy he put his head in the second mate's door to inform him of my unheard-of caprice to take a five hours' anchor-watch on myself. I heard the other raise his voice incredulously—"What? The captain himself?" Then a few more murmurs, a door closed, then another. A few moments later I went on deck.

My strangeness, which had made me sleepless, had prompted that unconventional arrangement, as if I had expected in those solitary hours of the night to get on terms with the ship of which I knew nothing, manned by men of whom I knew very little more. Fast alongside a wharf, littered like any ship in port with a tangle of unrelated
10 things, invaded by unrelated shore people, I had hardly seen her yet properly. Now, as she lay cleared for sea, the stretch of her main deck seemed to me very fine under the stars. Very fine, very roomy for her size, and very inviting. I descended the poop and paced the waist, my mind picturing to myself the coming passage through the Malay Archipelago, down the Indian Ocean, and up the Atlantic. All its phases were familiar enough to me, every characteristic, all the alternatives which were likely to face me on the high seas—everything! ... except the novel responsibility of command. But I took heart from the reasonable thought that the ship was like other ships, the men like
20 other men, and that the sea was not likely to keep any special surprises expressly for my discomfiture.

Arrived at that comforting conclusion, I bethought myself of a cigar and went below to get it. All was still down there. Everybody at the after end of the ship was sleeping profoundly. I came out again on the quarter-deck, agreeably at ease in my sleeping suit on that warm, breathless night, barefooted, a glowing cigar in my teeth, and, going forward, I was met by the profound silence of the fore end of the ship. Only as I passed the door of the forecastle I heard a deep, quiet, trustful sigh of some sleeper inside. And suddenly I rejoiced in the great security
30 of the sea as compared with the unrest of the land, in my choice of that untempted life presenting no disquieting problems, invested with an elementary moral beauty by the absolute straightforwardness of its appeal and by the singleness of its purpose.

The riding-light in the fore-rigging burned with a clear, untroubled, as if symbolic, flame, confident and bright in the mysterious shades of the night. Passing on my way aft along the other side of the ship, I observed that the rope side-ladder, put over, no doubt, for the master of the tug when he came to fetch away our letters, had not been hauled in as it should have been. I became annoyed at this, for exacti-
40 tude in small matters is the very soul of discipline. Then I reflected that I had myself peremptorily dismissed my officers from duty, and by my own act had prevented the anchor-watch being formally set and things properly attended to. I asked myself whether it was wise ever to interfere with the established routine of duties even from the kindest

of motives. My action might have made me appear eccentric. Goodness only knew how that absurdly whiskered mate would "account" for my conduct, and what the whole ship thought of that informality of their new captain. I was vexed with myself.

Not from compunction certainly, but, as it were mechanically, I proceeded to get the ladder in myself. Now a side-ladder of that sort is a light affair and comes in easily, yet my vigorous tug, which should have brought it flying on board, merely recoiled upon my body in a totally unexpected jerk. What the devil! ... I was so astounded by the
10 immovableness of that ladder that I remained stock-still, trying to account for it to myself like that imbecile mate of mine. In the end, of course, I put my head over the rail.

The side of the ship made an opaque belt of shadow on the darkling glassy shimmer of the sea. But I saw at once something elongated and pale floating very close to the ladder. Before I could form a guess a faint flash of phosphorescent light, which seemed to issue suddenly from the naked body of a man, flickered in the sleeping water with the elusive, silent play of summer lightning in a night sky. With a gasp I saw revealed to my stare a pair of feet, the long legs, a broad livid back
20 immersed right up to the neck in a greenish cadaverous glow. One hand, awash, clutched the bottom rung of the ladder. He was complete but for the head. A headless corpse! The cigar dropped out of my gaping mouth with a tiny plop and a short hiss quite audible in the absolute stillness of all things under heaven. At that I suppose he raised up his face, a dimly pale oval in the shadow of the ship's side. But even then I could only barely make out down there the shape of his black-haired head. However, it was enough for the horrid, frost-bound sensation which had gripped me about the chest to pass off. The moment of vain exclamations was past too. I only climbed on the spare
30 spar and leaned over the rail as far as I could, to bring my eyes nearer to that mystery floating alongside.

As he hung by the ladder, like a resting swimmer, the sea-lightning played about his limbs at every stir; and he appeared in it ghastly, silvery, fish-like. He remained as mute as a fish, too. He made no motion to get out of the water, either. It was inconceivable that he should not attempt to come on board, and strangely troubling to suspect that perhaps he did not want to. And my first words were prompted by just that troubled incertitude.

"What's the matter?" I asked in my ordinary tone, speaking down
40 to the face upturned exactly under mine.

"Cramp," it answered, no louder. Then slightly anxious, "I say, no need to call any one."

"I was not going to," I said.

"Are you alone on deck?"

"Yes."

I had somehow the impression that he was on the point of letting go the ladder to swim away beyond my ken—mysterious as he came. But, for the moment, this being appearing as if he had risen from the bottom of the sea (it was certainly the nearest land to the ship) wanted only to know the time. I told him. And he, down there, tentatively:

"I suppose your captain's turned in?"

"I am sure he isn't," I said.

He seemed to struggle with himself, for I heard something like the
10 low, bitter murmur of doubt. "What's the good?" His next words came out with a hesitating effort.

"Look here, my man. Could you call him out quietly?"

I thought the time had come to declare myself.

"*I* am the captain."

I heard a "By Jove!" whispered at the level of the water. The phosphorescence flashed in the swirl of the water all about his limbs, his other hand seized the ladder.

"My name's Leggatt."

The voice was calm and resolute. A good voice. The self-possession
20 of that man had somehow induced a corresponding state in myself. It was very quietly that I remarked:

"You must be a good swimmer."

"Yes. I've been in the water practically since nine o'clock. The question for me now is whether I am to let go this ladder and go on swimming till I sink from exhaustion, or—to come on board here."

I felt this was no mere formula of desperate speech, but a real alternative in the view of a strong soul. I should have gathered from this that he was young; indeed, it is only the young who are ever confronted by such clear issues. But at the time it was pure intuition on
30 my part. A mysterious communication was established already between us two—in the face of that silent, darkened tropical sea. I was young, too; young enough to make no comment. The man in the water began suddenly to climb up the ladder, and I hastened away from the rail to fetch some clothes.

Before entering the cabin I stood still, listening in the lobby at the foot of the stairs. A faint snore came through the closed door of the chief mate's room. The second mate's door was on the hook, but the darkness in there was absolutely soundless. He, too, was young and could sleep like a stone. Remained the steward, but he was not likely
40 to wake up before he was called. I got a sleeping suit out of my room, and, coming back on deck, saw the naked man from the sea sitting on the main-hatch, glimmering white in the darkness, his elbows on his knees and his head in his hands. In a moment he had concealed his damp body in a sleeping suit of the same grey-stripe pattern as the one

I was wearing, and followed me like my double on the poop. Together we moved right aft, barefooted, silent.

"What is it?" I asked in a deadened voice, taking the lighted lamp out of the binnacle, and raising it to his face.

"An ugly business."

He had rather regular features; a good mouth; light eyes under somewhat heavy, dark eyebrows; a smooth, square forehead; no growth on his cheeks; a small, brown moustache, and a well-shaped, round chin. His expression was concentrated, meditative, under the inspecting
10 light of the lamp I held up to his face; such as a man thinking hard in solitude might wear. My sleeping suit was just right for his size. A well-knit young fellow of twenty-five at most. He caught his lower lip with the edge of white, even teeth.

"Yes," I said, replacing the lamp in the binnacle. The warm, heavy tropical night closed upon his head again.

"There's a ship over there," he murmured.

"Yes, I know. The *Sephora*. Did you know of us?"

"Hadn't the slightest idea. I am the mate of her——" He paused and corrected himself. "I should say I *was*."

20 "Aha! Something wrong?"

"Yes. Very wrong indeed. I've killed a man."

"What do you mean? Just now?"

"No, on the passage. Weeks ago. Thirty-nine south. When I say a man——"

"Fit of temper," I suggested confidently.

The shadowy, dark head, like mine, seemed to nod imperceptibly above the ghostly grey of my sleeping suit. It was, in the night, as though I had been faced by my own reflection in the depths of a sombre and immense mirror.

30 "A pretty thing to have to own up to for a Conway boy," murmured my double distinctly.

"You're a Conway boy?"

"I am," he said, as if startled. Then, slowly..."Perhaps you too..."

It was so; but being a couple of years older I had left before he joined. After a quick interchange of dates a silence fell; and I thought suddenly of my absurd mate with his terrific whiskers and the "Bless my soul—you don't say so" type of intellect. My double gave me an inkling of his thoughts by saying:

40 "My father's a parson in Norfolk. Do you see me before a judge and jury on that charge? For myself I can't see the necessity. There are fellows that an angel from heaven—— And I am not that. He was one of those creatures that are just simmering all the time with a silly sort of wickedness. Miserable devils that have no business to live at all. He

wouldn't do his duty and wouldn't let anybody else do theirs. But what's the good of talking! You know well enough the sort of ill-conditioned snarling cur . . ."

He appealed to me as if our experiences had been as identical as our clothes. And I knew well enough the pestiferous danger of such a character where there are no means of legal repression. And I knew well enough also that my double there was no homicidal ruffian. I did not think of asking him for details, and he told me the story roughly in brusque, disconnected sentences. I needed no more. I saw it all going
10 on as though I were myself inside that other sleeping suit.

"It happened while we were setting a reefed foresail, at dusk. Reefed foresail! You understand the sort of weather. The only sail we had left to keep the ship running; so you may guess what it had been like for days. Anxious sort of job, that. He gave me some of his cursed insolence at the sheet. I tell you I was overdone with this terrific weather that seemed to have no end to it. Terrific, I tell you—and a deep ship. I believe the fellow himself was half crazed with funk. It was no time for gentlemanly reproof, so I turned round and felled him like an ox. He up and at me. We closed just as an awful sea made for
20 the ship. All hands saw it coming and took to the rigging, but I had him by the throat, and went on shaking him like a rat, the men above us yelling. 'Look out! Look out!' Then a crash as if the sky had fallen on my head. They say that for over ten minutes hardly anything was to be seen of the ship—just the three masts and a bit of the forecastle head and of the poop all awash driving along in a smother of foam. It was a miracle that they found us, jammed together behind the fore-bits. It's clear that I meant business, because I was holding him by the throat still when they picked us up. He was black in the face. It was too much for them. It seems they rushed us aft together, gripped as we
30 were, screaming 'Murder!' like a lot of lunatics, and broke into the cuddy. And the ship running for her life, touch and go all the time, any minute her last in a sea fit to turn your hair grey only a-looking at it. I understand that the skipper, too, started raving like the rest of them. The man had been deprived of sleep for more than a week, and to have this sprung on him at the height of a furious gale nearly drove him out of his mind. I wonder they didn't fling me overboard after getting the carcass of their precious shipmate out of my fingers. They had rather a job to separate us, I've been told. A sufficiently fierce story to make an old judge and a respectable jury sit up a bit. The first thing
40 I heard when I came to myself was the maddening howling of that endless gale, and on that the voice of the old man. He was hanging on to my bunk, staring into my face out of his sou'wester.

" 'Mr. Leggatt, you have killed a man. You can act no longer as chief mate of this ship.' "

His care to subdue his voice made it sound monotonous. He rested a hand on the end of the skylight to steady himself with, and all that time did not stir a limb, so far as I could see. "Nice little tale for a quiet tea-party," he concluded in the same tone.

One of my hands, too, rested on the end of the skylight; neither did I stir a limb, so far as I knew. We stood less than a foot from each other. It occurred to me that if old "Bless my soul—you don't say so" were to put his head up the companion and catch sight of us, he would think he was seeing double, or imagine himself come upon a scene of
10 weird witchcraft: the strange captain having a quiet confabulation by the wheel with his own grey ghost. I became very much concerned to prevent anything of the sort. I heard the other's soothing undertone:

"My father's a parson in Norfolk," it said. Evidently he had forgotten he had told me this important fact before. Truly a nice little tale.

"You had better slip down into my stateroom now," I said, moving off stealthily. My double followed my movements; our bare feet made no sound; I let him in, closed the door with care, and, after giving a call to the second mate, returned on deck for my relief.
20 "Not much sign of any wind yet," I remarked when he approached.

"No, sir. Not much," he assented sleepily in his hoarse voice, with just enough deference, no more, and barely suppressing a yawn.

"Well, that's all you have to look out for. You have got your orders."

"Yes, sir."

I paced a turn or two on the poop and saw him take up his position face forward with his elbow in the ratlines of the mizzen-rigging before I went below. The mate's faint snoring was still going on peacefully. The cuddy lamp was burning over the table on which stood a
30 vase with flowers, a polite attention from the ship's provision merchant —the last flowers we should see for the next three months at the very least. Two bunches of bananas hung from the beam symmetrically, one on each side of the rudder-casing. Everything was as before in the ship —except that two of her captain's sleeping suits were simultaneously in use, one motionless in the cuddy, the other keeping very still in the captain's stateroom.

It must be explained here that my cabin had the form of the capital letter L, the door being within the angle and opening into the short part of the letter. A couch was to the left, the bedplace to the
40 right; my writing-desk and the chronometers' table faced the door. But any one opening it, unless he stepped right inside, had no view of what I call the long (or vertical) part of the letter. It contained some lockers surmounted by a bookcase; and a few clothes, a thick jacket or two, caps, oilskin coat, and such-like, hung on hooks. There was at the

bottom of that part a door opening into my bathroom, which could be entered also directly from the saloon. But that way was never used.

The mysterious arrival had discovered the advantage of this particular shape. Entering my room, lighted strongly by a big bulkhead lamp swung on gimbals above my writing-desk, I did not see him anywhere till he stepped out quietly from behind the coats hung in the recessed part.

"I heard somebody moving about, and went in there at once," he whispered.

10   I, too, spoke under my breath.

"Nobody is likely to come in here without knocking and getting permission."

He nodded. His face was thin and the sunburn faded, as though he had been ill. And no wonder. He had been, I heard presently, kept under arrest in his cabin for nearly nine weeks. But there was nothing sickly in his eyes or in his expression. He was not a bit like me, really; yet, as we stood leaning over my bedplace, whispering side by side, with our dark heads together and our backs to the door, anybody bold enough to open it stealthily would have been treated to the uncanny

20   sight of a double captain busy talking in whispers with his other self.

"But all this doesn't tell me how you came to hang on to our side-ladder," I inquired, in the hardly audible murmurs we used, after he had told me something more of the proceedings on board the *Sephora* once the bad weather was over.

"When we sighted Java Head I had had time to think all those matters out several times over. I had six weeks of doing nothing else, and with only an hour or so every evening for a tramp on the quarter-deck."

He whispered, his arms folded on the side of my bedplace, staring

30   through the open port. And I could imagine perfectly the manner of this thinking out—a stubborn if not a steadfast operation; something of which I should have been perfectly incapable.

"I reckoned it would be dark before we closed with the land," he continued, so low that I had to strain my hearing, near as we were to each other, shoulder touching shoulder almost. "So I asked to speak to the old man. He always seemed very sick when he came to see me—as if he could not look me in the face. You know, that foresail saved the ship. She was too deep to have run long under bare poles. And it was I that managed to set it for him. Anyway, he came. When I had him in

40   my cabin—he stood by the door looking at me as if I had the halter round my neck already—I asked him right away to leave my cabin door unlocked at night while the ship was going through Sunda Straits. There would be the Java coast within two or three miles, off Anjer Point. I wanted nothing more. I've had a prize for swimming my second year in the Conway."

"I can believe it," I breathed out.

"God only knows why they locked me in every night. To see some of their faces you'd have thought they were afraid I'd go about at night strangling people. Am I a murdering brute? Do I look it? By Jove! if I had been he wouldn't have trusted himself like that into my room. You'll say I might have chucked him aside and bolted out, there and then—it was dark already. Well, no. And for the same reason I wouldn't think of trying to smash the door. There would have been a rush to stop me at the noise, and I did not mean to get into a confounded
10 scrimmage. Somebody else might have got killed—for I would not have broken out only to get chucked back, and I did not want any more of that work. He refused, looking more sick than ever. He was afraid of the men, and also of that old second mate of his who had been sailing with him for years—a grey-headed old humbug; and his steward, too, had been with him devil knows how long—seventeen years or more—a dogmatic sort of loafer who hated me like poison, just because I was the chief mate. No chief mate ever made more than one voyage in the *Sephora*, you know. Those two old chaps ran the ship. Devil only knows what the skipper wasn't afraid of (all his nerve went to pieces altogether
20 in that hellish spell of bad weather we had)—of what the law would do to him—of his wife, perhaps. Oh yes! she's on board. Though I don't think she would have meddled. She would have been only too glad to have me out of the ship in any way. The 'brand of Cain' business, don't you see? That's all right. I was ready enough to go off wandering on the face of the earth—and that was price enough to pay for an Abel of that sort. Anyhow, he wouldn't listen to me. 'This thing must take its course. I represent the law here.' He was shaking like a leaf. 'So you won't?' 'No!' 'Then I hope you will be able to sleep on that,' I said, and turned my back on him. 'I wonder that *you* can,' cries he, and locks the door.
30 "Well, after that, I couldn't. Not very well. That was three weeks ago. We have had a slow passage through the Java Sea; drifted about Carimata for ten days. When we anchored here they thought, I suppose, it was all right. The nearest land (and that's five miles) is the ship's destination; the consul would soon set about catching me; and there would have been no object in bolting to these islets there. I don't suppose there's a drop of water on them. I don't know how it was, but to-night that steward, after bringing me my supper, went out to let me eat it, and left the door unlocked. And I ate it—all there was, too. After I had finished I strolled out on the quarter-deck. I don't know
40 that I meant to do anything. A breath of fresh air was all I wanted, I believe. Then a sudden temptation came over me. I kicked off my slippers and was in the water before I had made up my mind fairly. Somebody heard the splash and they raised on awful hullabaloo. 'He's gone! Lower the boats! He's committed suicide! No, he's swimming.' Certainly I was swimming. It's not so easy for a swimmer like me to com-

mit suicide by drowning. I landed on the nearest islet before the boat left the ship's side. I heard them pulling about in the dark, hailing, and so on, but after a bit they gave up. Everything quieted down and the anchorage became as still as death. I sat down on a stone and began to think. I felt certain they would start searching for me at daylight. There was no place to hide on those stony things—and if there had been, what would have been the good? But now I was clear of that ship, I was not going back. So after a while I took off all my clothes, tied them up in a bundle with a stone inside, and dropped them in the deep water on the outer side of that islet. That was suicide enough for me. Let them think what they liked, but I didn't mean to drown myself. I meant to swim till I sank—but that's not the same thing. I struck out for another of these little islands, and it was from that one that I first saw your riding-light. Something to swim for. I went on easily, and on the way I came upon a flat rock a foot or two above water. In the daytime, I dare say, you might make it out with a glass from your poop. I scrambled up on it and rested myself for a bit. Then I made another start. That last spell must have been over a mile."

His whisper was getting fainter and fainter, and all the time he stared straight out through the porthole, in which there was not even a star to be seen. I had not interrupted him. There was something that made comment impossible, in his narrative, or perhaps in himself; a sort of feeling, a quality, which I can't find a name for. And when he ceased, all I found was a futile whisper, "So you swam for our light?"

"Yes—straight for it. It was something to swim for. I couldn't see any stars low down because the coast was in the way, and I couldn't see the land, either. The water was like glass. One might have been swimming in a confounded thousand feet deep cistern with no place for scrambling out anywhere; but what I didn't like was the notion of swimming round and round like a crazed bullock before I gave out; and as I didn't mean to go back ... No. Do you see me being hauled back, stark naked, off one of these little islands by the scruff of the neck and fighting like a wild beast? Somebody would have got killed for certain, and I did not want any of that. So I went on. Then your ladder——"

"Why didn't you hail the ship?" I asked, a little louder.

He touched my shoulder lightly. Lazy footsteps came right over our heads and stopped. The second mate had crossed from the other side of the poop and might have been hanging over the rail, for all we knew.

"He couldn't hear us talking—could he?" My double breathed into my very ear anxiously.

His anxiety was an answer, a sufficient answer, to the question

I had put to him. An answer containing all the difficulty of that situation. I closed the porthole quietly, to make sure. A louder word might have been overheard.

"Who's that?" he whispered then.

"My second mate. But I don't know much more of the fellow than you do."

And I told him a little about myself. I had been appointed to take charge while I least expected anything of the sort, not quite a fortnight ago. I didn't know either the ship or the people. Hadn't
10 had the time in port to look about me or size anybody up. And as to the crew, all they knew was that I was appointed to take the ship home. For the rest, I was almost as much of a stranger on board as himself, I said. And at the moment I felt it most acutely. I felt that it would take very little to make me a suspect person in the the eyes of the ship's company.

He had turned about meantime; and we, the two strangers in the ship, faced each other in identical attitudes.

"Your ladder——" he murmured, after a silence. "Who'd have thought of finding a ladder hanging over at night in a ship
20 anchored out here! I felt just then a very unpleasant faintness. After the life I've been leading for nine weeks, anybody would have got out of condition. I wasn't capable of swimming round as far as your rudder-chains. And, lo and behold! there was a ladder to get hold of. After I gripped it I said to myself, 'What's the good?' When I saw a man's head looking over I thought I would swim away presently and leave him shouting—in whatever language it was. I didn't mind being looked at. I—I liked it. And then you speaking to me so quietly—as if you had expected me—made me hold on a little longer. It had been a confounded lonely time—I don't mean
30 while swimming. I was glad to talk a little to somebody that didn't belong to the *Sephora*. As to asking for the captain, that was a mere impulse. It could have been no use, with all the ship knowing about me and the other people pretty certain to be round here in the morning. I don't know—I wanted to be seen, to talk with somebody, before I went on. I don't know what I would have said.... 'Fine night, isn't it?' or something of the sort."

"Do you think they will be round here presently?" I asked, with some incredulity.

"Quite likely," he said faintly.
40 He looked extremely haggard all of a sudden. His head rolled on his shoulders.

"H'm. We shall see then. Meantime get into that bed," I whispered. "Want help? There."

It was a rather high bedplace with a set of drawers underneath.

This amazing swimmer really needed the lift I gave him by seizing his leg. He tumbled in, rolled over on his back, and flung one arm across his eyes. And then, with his face nearly hidden, he must have looked exactly as I used to look in that bed. I gazed upon my other self for a while before drawing across carefully the two green serge curtains which ran on a brass rod. I thought for a moment of pinning them together for greater safety, but I sat down on the couch, and once there I felt unwilling to rise and hunt for a pin. I would do it in a moment. I was extremely tired, in a peculiarly 10 intimate way, by the strain of stealthiness, by the effort of whispering, and the general secrecy of this excitement. It was three o'clock by now, and I had been on my feet since nine, but I was not sleepy; I could not have gone to sleep. I sat there, fagged out, looking at the curtains, trying to clear my mind of the confused sensation of being in two places at once, and greatly bothered by an exasperating knocking in my head. It was a relief to discover suddenly that it was not in my head at all, but on the outside of the door. Before I could collect myself, the words "Come in" were out of my mouth, and the steward entered with a tray, bringing in my morning coffee. 20 I had slept, after all, and I was so frightened that I shouted, "This way! I am here, steward," as though he had been miles away. He put down the tray on the table next the couch and only then said, very quietly, "I can see you are here, sir." I felt him give me a keen look, but I dared not meet his eyes just then. He must have wondered why I had drawn the curtains of my bed before going to sleep on the couch. He went out, hooking the door open as usual.

I heard the crew washing decks above me. I knew I would have been told at once if there had been any wind. Calm, I thought, and I was doubly vexed. Indeed, I felt dual more than ever. The 30 steward reappeared suddenly in the doorway. I jumped up from the couch so quickly that he gave a start.

"What do you want here?"

"Close your port, sir—they are washing decks."

"It is closed," I said, reddening.

"Very well, sir." But he did not move from the doorway and returned my stare in an extraordinary, equivocal manner for a time. Then his eyes wavered, all his expression changed, and in a voice unusually gentle, almost coaxingly:

"May I come in to take the empty cup away, sir?"

40 "Of course!" I turned my back on him while he popped in and out. Then I unhooked and closed the door and even pushed the bolt. This sort of thing could not go on very long. The cabin was as hot as an oven, too. I took a peep at my double, and discovered that he had not moved; his arm was still over his eyes; but his chest

heaved, his hair was wet, his chin glistened with perspiration. I reached over him and opened the port.

"I must show myself on deck," I reflected.

Of course, theoretically, I could do what I liked, with no one to say nay to me within the whole circle of the horizon; but to lock my cabin door and take the key away I did not dare. Directly I put my head out of the companion I saw the group of my two officers, the second mate barefooted, the chief mate in long indiarubber boots, near the break of the poop, and the steward half-way down the
10 poop ladder talking to them eagerly. He happened to catch sight of me and dived, the second ran down on the main deck shouting some order or other, and the chief mate came to meet me, touching his cap.

There was a sort of curiosity in his eye that I did not like. I don't know whether the steward had told them that I was "queer" only, or downright drunk, but I know the man meant to have a good look at me. I watched him coming with a smile which, as he got into point-blank range, took effect and froze his very whiskers. I did not give him time to open his lips.

20 "Square the yards by lifts and braces before the hands go to breakfast."

It was the first particular order I had given on board that ship; and I stayed on deck to see it executed too. I had felt the need of asserting myself without loss of time. That sneering young cub got taken down a peg or two on that occasion, and I also seized the opportunity of having a good look at the face of every foremast man as they filed past me to go to the after braces. At breakfast time, eating nothing myself, I presided with such frigid dignity that the two mates were only too glad to escape from the cabin as soon as decency
30 permitted; and all the time the dual working of my mind distracted me almost to the point of insanity. I was constantly watching myself, my secret self, as dependent on my actions as my own personality, sleeping in that bed, behind that door which faced me as I sat at the head of the table. It was very much like being mad, only it was worse, because one was aware of it.

I had to shake him for a solid minute, but when at last he opened his eyes it was in the full possession of his senses, with an inquiring look.

"All's well so far," I whispered. "Now you must vanish into
40 the bathroom."

He did so, as noiseless as a ghost, and I then rang for the steward, and facing him boldly, directed him to tidy up my stateroom while I was having my bath—"and be quick about it." As my tone admitted of no excuses, he said, "Yes, sir," and ran off to fetch his dust-pan and brushes. I took a bath and did most of my dressing, splashing, and whistling softly for the steward's edification, while the secret sharer of my life stood drawn bolt upright in that little space, his face looking very sunken in daylight, his eyelids lowered under the stern, dark line of his eyebrows drawn together by a slight frown.

When I left him there to go back to my room the steward was finishing dusting. I sent for the mate and engaged him in some insignificant conversation. It was, as it were, trifling with the terrific
10 character of his whiskers; but my object was to give him an opportunity for a good look at my cabin. And then I could at last shut, with a clear conscience, the door of my stateroom and get my double back into the recessed part. There was nothing else for it. He had to sit still on a small folding stool, half smothered by the heavy coats hanging there. We listened to the steward going into the bathroom out of the saloon, filling the water-bottles there, scrubbing the bath, setting things to rights, whisk, bang, clatter—out again into the saloon—turn the key—click. Such was my scheme for keeping my second self invisible. Nothing better could be contrived under the
20 circumstances. And there we sat: I at my writing-desk ready to appear busy with some papers, he behind me, out of sight of the door. It would not have been prudent to talk in daytime; and I could not have stood the excitement of that queer sense of whispering to myself. Now and then, glancing over my shoulder, I saw him far back there, sitting rigidly on the low stool, his bare feet close together, his arms folded, his head hanging on his breast—and perfectly still. Anybody would have taken him for me.

I was fascinated by it myself. Every moment I had to glance over my shoulder. I was looking at him when a voice outside the
30 door said:

"Beg pardon, sir."

"Well!" . . . I kept my eyes on him, and so when the voice outside the door announced, "There's a ship's boat coming our way, sir," I saw him give a start—the first movement he had made for hours. But he did not raise his bowed head.

"All right. Get the ladder over."

I hesitated. Should I whisper something to him? But what? His immobility seemed to have been never disturbed. What could I tell him he did not know already? . . . Finally I went on deck.

II

40   The skipper of the *Sephora* had a thin, red whisker all round his face, and the sort of complexion that goes with hair of that colour; also the particular, rather smeary shade of blue in the eyes.

He was not exactly a showy figure; his shoulders were high, his stature but middling—one leg slightly more bandy than the other. He shook hands, looking vaguely around. A spiritless tenacity was his main characteristic, I judged. I behaved with a politeness which seemed to disconcert him. Perhaps he was shy. He mumbled to me as if he were ashamed of what he was saying; gave his name (it was something like Archbold—but at this distance of years I hardly am sure), his ship's name, and a few other particulars of that sort, in the manner of a criminal making a reluctant and doleful con-
10 fession. He had had terrible weather on the passage out—terrible— terrible—wife aboard, too.

By this time we were seated in the cabin and the steward brought in a tray with a bottle and glasses. "Thanks! No." Never took liquor. Would have some water, though. He drank two tumbler- fuls. Terrible thirsty work. Ever since daylight had been exploring the islands round his ship.

"What was that for—fun?" I asked, with an appearance of polite interest.

"No!" He sighed. "Painful duty."
20 As he persisted in his mumbling and I wanted my double to hear every word, I hit upon the notion of informing him that I regretted to say I was hard of hearing.

"Such a young man, too!" he nodded, keeping his smeary, blue, unintelligent eyes fastened upon me. "What was the cause of it— some disease?" he inquired, without the least sympathy and as if he thought that, if so, I'd got no more than I deserved.

"Yes; disease," I admitted in a cheerful tone which seemed to shock him. But my point was gained, because he had to raise his voice to give me his tale. It is not worth while to record that
30 version. It was just over two months since all this had happened, and he had thought so much about it that he seemed completely muddled as to its bearings, but still immensely impressed.

"What would you think of such a thing happening on board your own ship? I've had the *Sephora* for these fifteen years. I am a well-known shipmaster."

He was densely distressed—and perhaps I should have sympathised with him if I had been able to detach my mental vision from the unsuspected sharer of my cabin as though he were my second self. There he was on the other side of the bulkhead, four or five feet
40 from us, no more, as we sat in the saloon. I looked politely at Captain Archbold (if that was his name), but it was the other I saw, in a grey sleeping suit, seated on a low stool, his bare feet close together, his arms folded, and every word said between us falling into the ears of his dark head bowed on his chest.

"I have been at sea now, man and boy, for seven and thirty years, and I've never heard of such a thing happening in an English ship. And that it should be my ship. Wife on board, too."

I was hardly listening to him.

"Don't you think," I said, "that the heavy sea which, you told me, came aboard just then might have killed the man? I have seen the sheer weight of a sea kill a man very neatly, by simply breaking his neck."

"Good God!" he uttered impressively, fixing his smeary blue
10 eyes on me. "The sea! No man killed by the sea ever looked like that." He seemed positively scandalised at my suggestion. And as I gazed at him, certainly not prepared for anything original on his part, he advanced his head close to mine and thrust his tongue out at me so suddenly that I couldn't help starting back.

After scoring over my calmness in this graphic way he nodded wisely. If I had seen the sight, he assured me, I would never forget it as long as I lived. The weather was too bad to give the corpse a proper sea burial. So next day at dawn they took it up on the poop, covering its face with a bit of bunting; he read a short
20 prayer, and then, just as it was, in its oilskins and long boots, they launched it amongst those mountainous seas that seemed ready every moment to swallow up the ship herself and the terrified lives on board of her.

"That reefed foresail saved you," I threw in.

"Under God—it did," he exclaimed fervently. "It was by a special mercy, I firmly believe, that it stood some of those hurricane squalls."

"It was the setting of that sail which——" I began.

"God's own hand in it," he interrupted me. "Nothing less
30 could have done it. I don't mind telling you that I hardly dared give the order. It seemed impossible that we could touch anything without losing it, and then our last hope would have been gone."

The terror of that gale was on him yet. I let him go on for a bit, then said casually—as if returning to a minor subject:

"You were very anxious to give up your mate to the shore people, I believe?"

He was. To the law. His obscure tenacity on that point had in it something incomprehensible and a little awful; something, as it were, mystical, quite apart from his anxiety that he should not be
40 suspected of "countenancing any doings of that sort." Seven and thirty virtuous years at sea, of which over twenty of immaculate command, and the last fifteen in the *Sephora,* seemed to have laid him under some pitiless obligation.

"And you know," he went on, groping shamefacedly amongst

his feelings, "I did not engage that young fellow. His people had some interest with my owners. I was in a way forced to take him on. He looked very smart, very gentlemanly, and all that. But do you know—I never liked him, somehow. I am a plain man. You see, he wasn't exactly the sort for the chief mate of a ship like the *Sephora*."

I had become so connected in thoughts and impressions with the secret sharer of my cabin that I felt as if I, personally, were being given to understand that I, too, was not the sort that would have
10 done for the chief mate of a ship like the *Sephora*. I had no doubt of it in my mind.

"Not at all the style of man. You understand," he insisted superfluously, looking hard at me.

I smiled urbanely. He seemed at a loss for a while.

"I suppose I must report a suicide."

"Beg pardon?"

"Sui—cide! That's what I'll have to write to my owners directly I get in."

"Unless you manage to recover him before to-morrow," I assented
20 dispassionately.... "I mean, alive."

He mumbled something which I really did not catch, and I turned my ear to him in a puzzled manner. He fairly bawled:

"The land—I say, the mainland is at least seven miles off my anchorage."

"About that."

My lack of excitement, of curiosity, of surprise, of any sort of pronounced interest, began to arouse his distrust. But except for the felicitous pretence of deafness I had not tried to pretend anything. I had felt utterly incapable of playing the part of ignorance
30 properly, and therefore was afraid to try. It is also certain that he had brought some ready-made suspicions with him, and that he viewed my politeness as a strange and unnatural phenomenon. And yet how else could I have received him? Not heartily! That was impossible for psychological reasons, which I need not state here. My only object was to keep off his inquiries. Surlily? Yes, but surliness might have provoked a point-blank question. From its novelty to him and from its nature, punctilious courtesy was the manner best calculated to restrain the man. But there was the danger of his breaking through my defence bluntly. I could not, I think, have met
40 him by a direct lie, also for psychological (not moral) reasons. If he had only known how afraid I was of his putting my feeling of identity with the other to the test! But, strangely enough (I thought of it only afterward), I believe that he was not a little disconcerted by the reverse side of that weird situation, by something in me that

reminded him of the man he was seeking—suggested a mysterious similitude to the young fellow he had distrusted and disliked from the first.

However that might have been, the silence was not very prolonged. He took another oblique step.

"I reckon I had no more than a two-mile pull to your ship. Not a bit more."

"And quite enough, too, in this awful heat," I said.

Another pause full of mistrust followed. Necessity, they say, is
10 mother of invention, but fear, too, is not barren of ingenious suggestions. And I was afraid he would ask me point-blank for news of my other self.

"Nice little saloon, isn't it?" I remarked, as if noticing for the first time the way his eyes roamed from one closed door to the other. "And very well fitted out, too. Here, for instance," I continued, reaching over the back of my seat negligently and flinging the door open, "is my bathroom."

He made an eager movement, but hardly gave it a glance. I got up, shut the door of the bathroom, and invited him to have a look
20 round, as if I were very proud of my accommodation. He had to rise and be shown round, but he went through the business without any raptures whatever.

"And now we'll have a look at my stateroom," I declared, in a voice as loud as I dared to make it, crossing the cabin to the starboard side with purposely heavy steps.

He followed me in and gazed around. My intelligent double had vanished. I played my part.

"Very convenient—isn't it?"

"Very nice. Very comf . . ." He didn't finish, and went out
30 brusquely as if to escape from some unrighteous wiles of mine. But it was not to be. I had been too frightened not to feel vengeful; I felt I had him on the run, and I meant to keep him on the run. My polite insistence must have had something menacing in it, because he gave in suddenly. And I did not let him off a single item: mates' rooms, pantry, storerooms, the very sail-locker, which was also under the poop—he had to look into them all. When at last I showed him out on the quarter-deck he drew a long, spiritless sigh, and mumbled dismally that he must really be going back to his ship now. I desired my mate, who had joined us, to see to the
40 captain's boat.

The man of whiskers gave a blast on the whistle which he used to wear hanging round his neck, and yelled, *"Sephora's* away!" My double down there in my cabin must have heard, and certainly could not feel more relieved than I. Four fellows came running out from somewhere forward and went over the side, while my own men, appearing on deck too, lined the rail. I escorted my visitor to the gangway ceremoniously, and nearly overdid it. He was a tenacious beast. On the very ladder he lingered, and in that unique, guiltily conscientious manner of sticking to the point:

"I say ... you ... you don't think that——"

I covered his voice loudly:

"Certainly not.... I am delighted. Goodbye."

I had an idea of what he meant to say, and just saved myself
10 by the privilege of defective hearing. He was too shaken generally to insist, but my mate, close witness of that parting, looked mystified and his face took on a thoughtful cast. As I did not want to appear as if I wished to avoid all communication with my officers, he had the opportunity to address me.

"Seems a very nice man. His boat's crew told our chaps a very extraordinary story, if what I am told by the steward is true. I suppose you had it from the captain, sir?"

"Yes. I had a story from the captain."

"A very horrible affair—isn't it, sir?"
20   "It is."

"Beats all these tales we hear about murders in Yankee ships."

"I don't think it beats them. I don't think it resembles them in the least."

"Bless my soul—you don't say so! But of course I've no acquaintance whatever with American ships, not I, so I couldn't go against your knowledge. It's horrible enough for me.... But the queerest part is that those fellows seemed to have some idea the man was hidden aboard here. They had really. Did you ever hear of such a thing?"
30   "Preposterous—isn't it?"

We were walking to and fro athwart the quarter-deck. No one of the crew forward could be seen (the day was Sunday), and the mate pursued:

"There was some little dispute about it. Our chaps took offence. 'As if we would harbour a thing like that,' they said. 'Wouldn't you like to look for him in our coal-hole?' Quite a tiff. But they made it up in the end. I suppose he did drown himself. Don't you, sir?"

"I don't suppose anything."
40   "You have no doubt in the matter, sir?"

"None whatever."

I left him suddenly. I felt I was producing a bad impression, but with my double down there it was most trying to be on deck. And it was almost as trying to be below. Altogether a nerve-trying situation. But on the whole I felt less torn in two when I was with him. There was no one in the whole ship whom I dared take into my confidence. Since the hands had got to know his story, it would have been impossible to pass him off for any one else, and an accidental discovery was to be dreaded now more than ever....

The steward being engaged in laying the table for dinner, we could talk only with our eyes when I first went down. Later in the afternoon we had a cautious try at whispering. The Sunday quietness of the ship was against us; the stillness of air and water around
10 her was against us; the elements, the men were against us—everything was against us in our secret partnership; time itself—for this could not go on for ever. The very trust in Providence was, I supposed, denied to his guilt. Shall I confess that this thought cast me down very much? And as to the chapter of accidents which counts for so much in the book of success, I could only hope that it was closed. For what favourable accident could be expected?

"Did you hear everything?" were my first words as soon as we took up our position side by side, leaning over my bedplace.

He had. And the proof of it was his earnest whisper, "The man
20 told you he hardly dared to give the order."

I understood the reference to be to that saving foresail.

"Yes. He was afraid of it being lost in the setting."

"I assure you he never gave the order. He may think he did, but he never gave it. He stood there with me on the break of the poop after the maintopsail blew away, and whimpered about our last hope—positively whimpered about it and nothing else—and the night coming on! To hear one's skipper go on like that in such weather was enough to drive any fellow out of his mind. It worked me up into a sort of desperation. I just took it into my own hands and went
30 away from him, boiling, and—— But what's the use telling you? You know!... Do you think that if I had not been pretty fierce with them I should have got the men to do anything? Not it! The boss'en perhaps? Perhaps! It wasn't a heavy sea—it was a sea gone mad! I suppose the end of the world will be something like that; and a man may have the heart to see it coming once and be done with it—but to have to face it day after day... I don't blame anybody. I was precious little better than the rest. Only—I was an officer of that old coal-waggon, anyhow...."

"I quite understand," I conveyed that sincere assurance into
40 his ear. He was out of breath with whispering; I could hear him pant slightly. It was all very simple. The same strung-up force which had given twenty-four men a chance, at least, for their lives had, in a sort of recoil, crushed an unworthy mutinous existence.

But I had no leisure to weigh the merits of the matter—footsteps in the saloon, a heavy knock. "There's enough wind to get under way with, sir." Here was the call of a new claim upon my thoughts and even upon my feelings.

"Turn the hands up," I cried through the door. "I'll be on deck directly."

I was going out to make the acquaintance of my ship. Before I left the cabin our eyes met—the eyes of the only two strangers on board. I pointed to the recessed part where the little camp-stool awaited him and laid my finger on my lips. He made a gesture— somewhat vague—a little mysterious, accompanied by a faint smile,
10 as if of regret.

This is not the place to enlarge upon the sensations of a man who feels for the first time a ship move under his feet to his own independent word. In my case they were not unalloyed. I was not wholly alone with my command; for there was that stranger in my cabin. Or, rather, I was not completely and wholly with her. Part of me was absent. That mental feeling of being in two places at once affected me physically as if the mood of secrecy had penetrated my very soul. Before an hour had elapsed since the ship had begun to move, having occasion to ask the mate (he stood by my side) to
20 take a compass bearing of the Pagoda, I caught myself reaching up to his ear in whispers. I say I caught myself, but enough had escaped to startle the man. I can't describe it otherwise than by saying that he shied. A grave, preoccupied manner, as though he were in pos- session of some perplexing intelligence, did not leave him henceforth. A little later I moved away from the rail to look at the compass with such a stealthy gait that the helmsman noticed it—and I could not help noticing the unusual roundness of his eyes. These are trifling instances, though it's to no commander's advantage to be suspected of ludicrous eccentricities. But I was also more seriously
30 affected. There are to a seaman certain words, gestures, that should in given conditions come as naturally, as instinctively, as the winking of a menaced eye. A certain order should spring on to his lips without thinking; a certain sign should get itself made, so to speak, without reflection. But all unconscious alertness had abandoned me. I had to make an effort of will to recall myself back (from the cabin) to the conditions of the moment. I felt that I was appearing an irresolute commander to those people who were watching me more or less critically.

And, besides, there were the scares. On the second day out, for
40 instance, coming off the deck in the afternoon (I had straw slippers on my bare feet) I stopped at the open pantry door and spoke to the steward. He was doing something there with his back to me. At the sound of my voice he nearly jumped out of his skin, as the saying is, and incidentally broke a cup.

"What on earth's the matter with you?" I asked, astonished.

He was extremely confused. "Beg your pardon, sir. I made sure you were in your cabin."

"You see I wasn't."

"No, sir. I could have sworn I had heard you moving in there not a moment ago. It's most extraordinary . . . very sorry, sir."

I passed on with an inward shudder. I was so identified with my secret double that I did not even mention the fact in those scanty, fearful whispers we exchanged. I suppose he had made some slight noise of some kind or other. It would have been miraculous
10 if he hadn't at one time or another. And yet, haggard as he appeared, he looked always perfectly self-controlled, more than calm—almost invulnerable. On my suggestion he remained almost entirely in the bathroom, which, upon the whole, was the safest place. There could be really no shadow of an excuse for any one ever wanting to go in there, once the steward had done with it. It was a very tiny place. Sometimes he reclined on the floor, his legs bent, his head sustained on one elbow. At others I would find him on the camp-stool, sitting in his grey sleeping suit and with his cropped dark hair like a patient, unmoved convict. At night I would smuggle him into my
20 bedplace, and we would whisper together, with the regular footfalls of the officer of the watch passing and repassing over our heads. It was an infinitely miserable time. It was lucky that some tins of fine preserves were stowed in a locker in my stateroom; hard bread I could always get hold of; and so he lived on stewed chicken, pâté de foie gras, asparagus, cooked oysters, sardines—on all sorts of abominable sham-delicacies out of tins. My early morning coffee he always drank; and it was all I dared do for him in that respect.

Every day there was the horrible manœuvring to go through so that my room and then the bathroom should be done in the usual
30 way. I came to hate the sight of the steward, to abhor the voice of that harmless man. I felt that it was he who would bring on the disaster of discovery. It hung like a sword over our heads.

The fourth day out, I think (we were then working down the east side of the Gulf of Siam, tack for tack, in light winds and smooth water)—the fourth day, I say, of this miserable juggling with the unavoidable, as we sat at our evening meal, that man, whose slightest movement I dreaded, after putting down the dishes ran up on deck busily. This could not be dangerous. Presently he came down again; and then it appeared that he had remembered a coat of mine which
40 I had thrown over a rail to dry after having been wetted in a shower which had passed over the ship in the afternoon. Sitting stolidly at the head of the table I became terrified at the sight of the garment on his arm. Of course he made for my door. There was no time to lose.

"Steward!" I thundered. My nerves were so shaken that I could not govern my voice and conceal my agitation. This was the sort of thing that made my terrifically whiskered mate tap his forehead with his forefinger. I had detected him using that gesture while talking on deck with a confidential air to the carpenter. It was too far to hear a word, but I had no doubt that this pantomime could only refer to the strange new captain.

"Yes, sir," the pale-faced steward turned resignedly to me. It was this maddening course of being shouted at, checked without 10 rhyme or reason, arbitrarily chased out of my cabin, suddenly called into it, sent flying out of his pantry on incomprehensible errands, that accounted for the growing wretchedness of his expression.

"Where are you going with that coat?"

"To your room, sir."

"Is there another shower coming?"

"I'm sure I don't know, sir. Shall I go up again and see, sir?"

"No! never mind."

My object was attained, as of course my other self in there would have heard everything that passed. During this interlude my 20 two officers never raised their eyes off their respective plates; but the lip of that confounded cub, the second mate, quivered visibly.

I expected the steward to hook my coat on and come out at once. He was very slow about it; but I dominated my nervousness sufficiently not to shout after him. Suddenly I became aware (it could be heard plainly enough) that the fellow for some reason or other was opening the door of the bathroom. It was the end. The place was literally not big enough to swing a cat in. My voice died in my throat and I went stony all over. I expected to hear a yell of surprise and terror, and made a movement, but had not the strength 30 to get on my legs. Everything remained still. Had my second self taken the poor wretch by the throat? I don't know what I could have done next moment if I had not seen the steward come out of my room, close the door, and then stand quietly by the sideboard.

"Saved," I thought. "But, no! Lost! Gone! He was gone!"

I laid my knife and fork down and leaned back in my chair. My head swam. After a while, when sufficiently recovered to speak in a steady voice, I instructed my mate to put the ship round at eight o'clock himself.

"I won't come on deck," I went on. "I think I'll turn in, and 40 unless the wind shifts I don't want to be disturbed before midnight. I feel a bit seedy."

"You did look middling bad a little while ago," the chief mate remarked without showing any great concern.

They both went out, and I stared at the steward clearing the table. There was nothing to be read on that wretched man's face. But why did he avoid my eyes? I asked myself. Then I thought I should like to hear the sound of his voice.

"Steward!"

"Sir!" Startled as usual.

"Where did you hang up that coat?"

"In the bathroom, sir." The usual anxious tone. "It's not quite dry yet, sir."

For some time longer I sat in the cuddy. Had my double vanished as he had come? But of his coming there was an explanation, whereas his disappearance would be inexplicable. . . . I went slowly into my dark room, shut the door, lighted the lamp, and for a time dared not turn round. When at last I did I saw him standing bolt upright in the narrow recessed part. It would not be true to say I had a shock, but an irresistible doubt of his bodily existence flitted through my mind. Can it be, I asked myself, that he is not visible to other eyes than mine? It was like being haunted. Motionless, with a grave face, he raised his hands slightly at me in a gesture which meant clearly, "Heavens! what a narrow escape!" Narrow indeed. I think I had come creeping quietly as near insanity as any man who has not actually gone over the border. That gesture restrained me, so to speak.

The mate with the terrific whiskers was now putting the ship on the other tack. In the moment of profound silence which follows upon the hands going to their stations I heard on the poop his raised voice: "Hard alee!" and the distant shout of the order repeated on the main deck. The sails, in that light breeze, made but a faint fluttering noise. It ceased. The ship was coming round slowly; I held my breath in the renewed stillness of expectation; one wouldn't have thought that there was a single living soul on her decks. A sudden brisk shout, "Mainsail haul!" broke the spell, and in the noisy cries and rush overhead of the men running away with the main brace we two, down in my cabin, came together in our usual position by the bedplace.

He did not wait for my question. "I heard him fumbling here and just managed to squat myself down in the bath," he whispered to me. "The fellow only opened the door and put his arm in to hang the coat up. All the same. . . ."

"I never thought of that," I whispered back, even more appalled than before at the closeness of the shave, and marvelling at that something unyielding in his character which was carrying him through so finely. There was no agitation in his whisper. Whoever was being driven distracted, it was not he. He was sane. And the proof of his sanity was continued when he took up the whispering again.

"It would never do for me to come to life again."

It was something that a ghost might have said. But what he
was alluding to was his old captain's reluctant admission of the
theory of suicide. It would obviously serve his turn—if I had understood at all the view which seemed to govern the unalterable purpose
of his action.

"You must maroon me as soon as ever you can get amongst these
islands off the Cambodje shore," he went on.

"Maroon you! We are not living in a boy's adventure tale," I
protested. His scornful whispering took me up.

10 "We aren't indeed! There's nothing of a boy's tale in this. But
there's nothing else for it. I want no more. You don't suppose I
am afraid of what can be done to me? Prison or gallows or whatever
they may please. But you don't see me coming back to explain such
things to an old fellow in a wig and twelve respectable tradesmen,
do you? What can they know whether I am guilty or not—or of
what I am guilty, either? That's my affair. What does the Bible say?
'Driven off the face of the earth.' Very well. I am off the face of the
earth now. As I came at night so I shall go."

"Impossible!" I murmured. "You can't."

20 "Can't?... Not naked like a soul on the Day of Judgement. I
shall freeze on to this sleeping suit. The Last Day is not yet—and...
you have understood thoroughly. Didn't you?"

I felt suddenly ashamed of myself. I may say truly that I understood—and my hesitation in letting that man swim away from my
ship's side had been a mere sham sentiment, a sort of cowardice.

"It can't be done now till next night," I breathed out. "The
ship is on the offshore tack and the wind may fail us."

"As long as I know that you understand," he whispered. "But
of course you do. It's a great satisfaction to have got somebody to
30 understand. You seem to have been there on purpose." And in the
same whisper, as if we two whenever we talked had to say things
to each other which were not fit for the world to hear, he added,
"It's very wonderful."

We remained side by side talking in our secret way—but sometimes silent or just exchanging a whispered word or two at long
intervals. And as usual he stared through the port. A breath of wind
came now and again into our faces. The ship might have been moored
in dock, so gently and on an even keel she slipped through the water,
that did not murmur even at our passage, shadowy and silent like
40 a phantom sea.

At midnight I went on deck, and to my mate's great surprise put
the ship round on the other tack. His terrible whiskers flitted round
me in silent criticism. I certainly should not have done it if it had been
only a question of getting out of that sleepy gulf as quickly as

possible. I believe he told the second mate, who relieved him, that it was a great want of judgement. The other only yawned. That intolerable cub shuffled about so sleepily and lolled against the rails in such a slack, improper fashion that I came down on him sharply.

"Aren't you properly awake yet?"

"Yes, sir! I am awake."

"Well, then, be good enough to hold yourself as if you were. And keep a look out. If there's any current we'll be closing with some islands long before daylight."

10   The east side of the gulf is fringed with islands, some solitary, others in groups. On the blue background of the high coast they seem to float on silvery patches of calm water, arid and grey, or dark green and rounded like clumps of evergreen bushes, with the larger ones, a mile or two long, showing the outlines of ridges, ribs of grey rock under the dank mantle of matted leafage. Unknown to trade, to travel, almost to geography, the manner of life they harbour is an unsolved secret. There must be villages—settlements of fishermen at least—on the largest of them, and some communication with the world is probably kept up by native craft. But all that
20   forenoon, as we headed for them, fanned along by the faintest of breezes, I saw no sign of man or canoe in the field of the telescope I kept on pointing at the scattered group.

At noon I gave no orders for a change of course, and the mate's whiskers became much concerned and seemed to be offering themselves unduly to my notice. At last I said:

"I am going to stand right in. Quite in—as far as I can take her."

The stare of extreme surprise imparted an air of ferocity also to his eyes, and he looked truly terrific for a moment.

"We're not doing well in the middle of the gulf," I continued
30   casually. "I am going to look for the land breezes to-night."

"Bless my soul! Do you mean, sir, in the dark amongst the lot of all them islands and reefs and shoals?"

"Well, if there are any regular land breezes at all on this coast one must get close inshore to find them—mustn't one?"

"Bless my soul!" he exclaimed again under his breath. All that afternoon he wore a dreamy, comtemplative appearance which in him was a mark of perplexity. After dinner I went into my stateroom as if I meant to take some rest. There we two bent our dark heads over a half-unrolled chart lying on my bed.
40   "There," I said. "It's got to be Koh-ring. I've been looking at it ever since sunrise. It has got two hills and a low point. It must be inhabited. And on the coast opposite there is what looks like the mouth of a biggish river—with some town, no doubt, not far up. It's the best chance for you that I can see."

"Anything. Koh-ring let it be."

He looked thoughtfully at the chart as if surveying chances
and distances from a lofty height—and following with his eyes his own
figure wandering on the blank land of Cochin-China, and then passing
off that piece of paper clean out of sight into uncharted regions. And
it was as if the ship had two captains to plan her course for her.
I had been so worried and restless running up and down that I
had not had the patience to dress that day. I had remained in my
sleeping suit, with straw slippers and a soft floppy hat. The closeness
10 of the heat in the gulf had been most oppressive, and the crew were
used to see me wandering in that airy attire.

"She will clear the south point as she heads now," I whispered
into his ear. "Goodness only knows when, though—but certainly after
dark. I'll edge her in to half a mile, as far as I may be able to judge
in the dark..."

"Be careful," he murmured warningly—and I realised suddenly
that all my future, the only future for which I was fit, would perhaps
go irretrievably to pieces in any mishap to my first command.

I could not stop a moment longer in the room. I motioned him
20 to get out of sight and made my way on the poop. That unplayful
cub had the watch. I walked up and down for a while thinking things
out, then beckoned him over.

"Send a couple of hands to open the two quarter-deck ports,"
I said mildly.

He actually had the impudence, or else so forgot himself in his
wonder at such an incomprehensible order, as to repeat:

"Open the quarter-deck ports! What for, sir?"

"The only reason you need concern yourself about is because
I tell you to do so. Have them opened wide and fastened properly."

30 He reddened and went off, but I believe made some jeering
remark to the carpenter as to the sensible practice of ventilating a
ship's quarter-deck. I know he popped into the mate's cabin to
impart the fact to him, because the whiskers came on deck, as it
were by chance, and stole glances at me from below—for signs of
lunacy or drunkenness, I suppose.

A little before supper, feeling more restless than ever, I rejoined,
for a moment, my second self. And to find him sitting so quietly
was surprising, like something against nature, inhuman.

I developed my plan in a hurried whisper.
40 "I shall stand in as close as I dare and then put her round. I
shall presently find means to smuggle you out of here into the sail-
locker, which communicates with the lobby. But there is an opening,
a sort of square for hauling the sails out, which gives straight on
the quarter-deck and which is never closed in fine weather, so as to

give air to the sails. When the ship's way is deadened in stays and all
the hands are aft at the main braces you shall have a clear road to slip
out and get overboard through the open quarter-deck port. I've had
them both fastened up. Use a rope's end to lower yourself into the
water so as to avoid a splash—you know. It could be heard and cause
some beastly complication."

He kept silent for a while, then whispered, "I understand."

"I won't be there to see you go," I began with an effort. "The
rest . . . I only hope I have understood too."

10   "You have. From first to last"—and for the first time there
seemed to be a faltering, something strained in his whisper. He
caught hold of my arm, but the ringing of the supper bell made me
start. He didn't, though; he only released his grip.

After supper I didn't come below again till well past eight
o'clock. The faint, steady breeze was loaded with dew; and the wet,
darkened sails held all there was of propelling power in it. The
night, clear and starry, sparkled darkly, and the opaque, lightless
patches shifting slowly amongst the low stars were the drifting islets.
On the port bow there was a big one more distant and shadowily im-
20   posing by the great space of sky it eclipsed.

On opening the door I had a back view of my very own self
looking at a chart. He had come out of the recess and was standing
near the table.

"Quite dark enough," I whispered.

He stepped back and leaned against my bed with a level, quiet
glance. I sat on the couch. We had nothing to say to each other.
Over our heads the officer of the watch moved here and there.
Then I heard him move quickly. I knew what that meant. He was
making for the companion; and presently his voice was outside
30   my door.

"We are drawing in pretty fast, sir. Land looks rather close."

"Very well," I answered. "I am coming on deck directly."

I waited till he was gone out of the cuddy, then rose. My
double moved too. The time had come to exchange our last
whispers, for neither of us was ever to hear each other's natural voice.

"Look here!" I opened a drawer and took out three sovereigns.
"Take this, anyhow. I've got six and I'd give you the lot, only I
must keep a little money to buy some fruit and vegetables for the
crew from native boats as we go through Sunda Straits."

40   He shook his head.

"Take it," I urged him, whispering desperately. "No one can
tell what . . ."

He smiled and slapped meaningly the only pocket of the
sleeping jacket. It was not safe, certainly. But I produced a large old
silk handkerchief of mine, and tying the three pieces of gold in a

corner, pressed it on him. He was touched, I suppose, because he took it at last and tied it quickly round his waist under the jacket, on his bare skin.

Our eyes met; several seconds elapsed, till, our glances still mingled, I extended my hand and turned the lamp out. Then I passed through the cuddy, leaving the door of my room wide open. . . . "Steward!"

He was still lingering in the pantry in the greatness of his zeal, giving a rub-up to a plated cruet stand the last thing before going to bed. Being careful not to wake up the mate, whose room was opposite, I spoke in an undertone.

He looked round anxiously. "Sir!"

"Can you get me a little hot water from the galley?"

"I am afraid, sir, the galley fire's been out for some time now."

"Go and see."

He fled up the stairs.

"Now," I whispered loudly into the saloon—too loudly, perhaps, but I was afraid I couldn't make a sound. He was by my side in an instant—the double captain slipped past the stairs—through a tiny dark passage . . . a sliding door. We were in the sail-locker, scrambling on our knees over the sails. A sudden thought struck me. I saw myself wandering barefooted, bareheaded, the sun beating on my dark poll. I snatched off my floppy hat and tried hurriedly in the dark to ram it on my other self. He dodged and fended off silently. I wonder what he thought had come to me before he understood and suddenly desisted. Our hands met gropingly, lingered united in a steady, motionless clasp for a second. . . . No word was breathed by either of us when they separated.

I was standing quietly by the pantry door when the steward returned.

"Sorry, sir. Kettle barely warm. Shall I light the spirit-lamp?"

"Never mind."

I came out on deck slowly. It was now a matter of conscience to shave the land as close as possible—for now he must go overboard whenever the ship was put in stays. Must! There could be no going back for him. After a moment I walked over to leeward and my heart flew into my mouth at the nearness of the land on the bow. Under any other circumstances I would not have held on a minute longer. The second mate had followed me anxiously.

I looked on till I felt I could command my voice.

"She will weather," I said then in a quiet tone.

"Are you going to try that, sir?" he stammered out incredulously.

I took no notice of him and raised my tone just enough to be heard by the helmsman.

"Keep her good full."

"Good full, sir."

The wind fanned my cheek, the sails slept, the world was silent. The strain of watching the dark loom of the land grow bigger and denser was too much for me. I had to shut my eyes—because the ship must go closer. She must! The stillness was intolerable. Were we standing still?

When I opened my eyes the second view started my heart with a thump. The black southern hill of Koh-ring seemed to hang right over the ship like a towering fragment of the everlasting night.
On that enormous mass of blackness there was not a gleam to be seen, not a sound to be heard. It was gliding irresistibly towards us and yet seemed already within reach of the hand. I saw the vague figures of the watch grouped in the waist, gazing in awed silence.

"Are you going on, sir?" inquired an unsteady voice at my elbow. I ignored it. I had to go on.

"Keep her full. Don't check her way. That won't do now," I said warningly.

"I can't see the sails very well," the helmsman answered me, in strange, quavering tones.

Was she close enough? Already she was, I won't say in the shadow of the land, but in the very blackness of it, already swallowed up as it were, gone too close to be recalled, gone from me altogether.

"Give the mate a call," I said to the young man who stood at my elbow as still as death. "And turn all hands up."

My tone had a borrowed loudness reverberated from the height of the land. Several voices cried out together, "We are all on deck, sir."

Then stillness again, with the great shadow gliding closer, towering higher, without a light, without a sound. Such a hush had fallen on the ship that she might have been a bark of the dead floating in slowly under the very gate of Erebus.

"My God! Where are we?"

It was the mate moaning at my elbow. He was thunderstruck, and as it were deprived of the moral support of his whiskers. He clapped his hands and absolutely cried out, "Lost!"

"Be quiet," I said sternly.

He lowered his tone, but I saw the shadowy gesture of his despair. "What are we doing here?"

"Looking for the land wind."

He made as if to tear his hair, and addressed me recklessly.

"She will never get out. You have done it, sir. I knew it'd end in something like this. She will never weather, and you are too close now to stay. She'll drift ashore before she's round. O my God!"

I caught his arm as he was raising it to batter his poor devoted head, and shook it violently.

"She's ashore already," he wailed, trying to tear himself away.

"Is she? . . . Keep good full there!"

"Good full, sir," cried the helmsman in a frightened, thin, child-like voice.

I hadn't let go the mate's arm and went on shaking it. "Ready about, do you hear? You go forward"—shake—"and stop there"—shake—"and hold your noise"—shake—"and see these head-sheets properly over-hauled"—shake, shake—shake.

And all the time I dared not look towards the land lest my heart should fail me. I released my grip at last and he ran forward as if fleeing for dear life.

I wondered what my double there in the sail-locker thought of this commotion. He was able to hear everything—and perhaps he was able to understand why, on my conscience, it had to be thus close—no less. My first order "Hard alee!" re-echoed ominously under the towering shadow of Koh-ring as if I had shouted in a mountain gorge. And then I watched the land intently. In that smooth water and light wind it was impossible to feel the ship coming-to. No! I could not feel her. And my second self was making now ready to slip out and lower himself overboard. Perhaps he was gone already . . . ?

The great black mass brooding over our very mast-heads began to pivot away from the ship's side silently. And now I forgot the secret stranger ready to depart, and remembered only that I was a total stranger to the ship. I did not know her. Would she do it? How was she to be handled?

I swung the mainyard and waited helplessly. She was perhaps stopped, and her very fate hung in the balance, with the black mass of Koh-ring like the gate of the everlasting night towering over her taffrail. What would she do now? Had she way on her yet? I stepped to the side swiftly, and on the shadowy water I could see nothing except a faint phosphorescent flash revealing the glassy smoothness of the sleeping surface. It was impossible to tell—and I had not learned yet the feel of my ship. Was she moving? What I needed was something easily seen, a piece of paper, which I could throw over-board and watch. I had nothing on me. To run down for it I didn't dare. There was no time. All at once my strained, yearning stare distinguished a white object floating within a yard of the ship's side—white, on the black water. A phosphorescent flash passed under it. What was that thing? . . . I recognised my own floppy hat. It must have fallen off his head . . . and he didn't bother. Now I had what I wanted—the saving mark for my eyes. But I hardly thought of my other self, now gone from the ship, to be hidden for ever from all friendly faces, to be a fugitive and a vagabond on the earth, with no brand of the curse on his sane forehead to stay a slaying hand . . . too proud to explain.

And I watched the hat—the expression of my sudden pity for

his mere flesh. It had been meant to save his homeless head from
the dangers of the sun. And now—behold—it was saving the ship,
by serving me for a mark to help out the ignorance of my strangeness.
Ha! It was drifting forward, warning me just in time that the
ship had gathered sternway.

"Shift the helm," I said in a low voice to the seaman standing
still like a statue.

The man's eyes glistened wildly in the binnacle light as he jumped
round to the other side and spun round the wheel.

10   I walked to the break of the poop. On the overshadowed deck
all hands stood by the forebraces waiting for my order. The stars
ahead seemed to be gliding from right to left. And all was so still
in the world that I heard the quiet remark, "She's round," passed
in a tone of intense relief between two seamen.

"Let go and haul."

The foreyards ran round with a great noise, amidst cheery cries.
And now the frightful whiskers made themselves heard giving various
orders. Already the ship was drawing ahead. And I was alone with
her. Nothing! no one in the world should stand now between us,
20   throwing a shadow on the way of silent knowledge and mute affection;
the perfect communion of a seaman with his first command.

Walking to the taffrail, I was in time to make out, on the very
edge of a darkness thrown by a towering black mass like the very
gateway of Erebus—yes, I was in time to catch an evanescent glimpse
of my white hat left behind to mark the spot where the secret sharer
of my cabin and of my thoughts, as though he were my second self,
had lowered himself into the water to take his punishment: a free
man, a proud swimmer striking out for a new destiny.

ANALOGUES

ANALOGUES

A HELL-SHIP VOYAGE*
Basil Lubbock

We now come to the second period in the life of the *Cutty Sark.* . . . [142]

. . . In the spring of 1880 orders for the best Welsh steam coal to supply their fleet in Japanese waters were sent over to England by the American Navy Department.

The coal was wanted as soon as possible and big freights were offered in order to attract clipper ships, which would race out with it to Japan.

Uncertain as to what he would do with his cut down tea clipper, John Willis jumped gladly at the American offer, and thus we find the *Cutty Sark* leaving London in ballast on 6th May, 1880, bound to Wales in order to load steam coal for the American fleet in the Pacific.

Besides a new outfit of sails, spars and rigging, the *Cutty Sark* left London with a new set of apprentices, hastily collected from Willis's other ships, which happened to be at home.

Of these apprentices McCausland joined from the *Zenobia,* Sankey and Bill Barton from the *Fantasie*—better known as the old Steele-built clipper *Eliza Shaw*—Fullerton from the *Whiteadder,* and Stanton from Green's *Carlisle Castle,* whilst Parton and Kirby were first voyagers. With regard to the rest of the ship's company, jovial Captain Wallace remained in command.

The mate, though a Scotsman, was a regular bucko of "Down East" style—one of those hard-fibred, despotic characters which were more common in the virile days of sail than in these luxurious days of steam.[144]

The second mate was a rather colourless young Englishman, who was so short-sighted that Captain Wallace nearly always stood his watch with him. The third mate was an apprentice out of his time, who had failed to pass as second mate and had signed on as O.S. He lived in the half-deck.

The carpenter was one of those seamen, who, having fallen in

* Reprinted from Chapter V of *The Log of the "Cutty Sark"* by Basil Lubbock with permission of the publisher, Brown, Son & Ferguson, Ltd., Glasgow, Scotland. [The chapter covers pp. 142–192. Copy-text is the 1960 printing. Ed.]

love with a ship, look upon her in the light of a sweetheart and sign in her regularly voyage after voyage.

Chips had been in the *Cutty Sark* since her launch. He knew every timber and bolt and was a very privileged person, a favourite of "Old White Hat," a trusted adviser of Captain Wallace, and an oracle in the "Cutty's" half-deck.

The sailmaker was a big German, of that well-known type called "squareheads," who one and all answer to the name of "Dutchy."

Of the crew with which she left London we need say little. The short experience of Mr. Bucko Smith in the trip round to Wales was sufficient to send them and their bags flying over the rail directly the *Cutty Sark* reached the coal port of Penarth, where she arrived on 22nd May.

Captain Wallace found the usual difficulty in picking a crew at a Welsh coal port, his task being not rendered any easier by the sinister reputation of his mate. Finally he had to content himself with a very scratch lot of nationalities, consisting of 5 Englishmen, 3 Danes, 3 niggers (two of them steam-boat men) 2 Greeks and an Italian.

With cook and steward the *Cutty Sark* thus had her complement of 28 souls, one of the Englishmen serving as bosun.

Wallace sailed from Penarth on 4th June—a Friday, and at once a member of the crew began to prophesy the well-known consequences. This man was something of a character, a veritable sea croaker, a cross-grained, sour-tempered seaman of a type which used to flourish in sailing ship foc's'les. His conversation ran entirely in the minor key; he was a pessimist of pessimists: his yarns were all concerned with mutiny and murder, with shipwrecks and disaster, with foul weather and fearful diseases, whilst he was superstitious to the last degree.[145]

The man seemed to nurse a thousand wrongs within his hairy breast, to see death and destruction ever within an arm's length and to expect nothing else than hell and damnation for everyone within his ken. He was one of those hard-bitten sailors who required next to no sleep, and during the night watches below he would pace the deck muttering to himself for hour after hour. Naturally enough he was a prime seaman; there was no fear in his composition; he had brooded so upon horrors that nothing could daunt him, and no Liverpool packet-rat was ever tougher or more enduring.

The apprentices of the *Cutty Sark* were not long in finding a suitable nickname for this queer old man of the sea, whose prophecies of evil were soon to be so amply fulfilled. There was something so uncanny about him that the boys likened him to the Flying Dutchman, and he was soon known on board as Vanderdecken.

The first of his prophecies was almost instantly confirmed. The *Cutty Sark* was barely to sea on that fatal Friday before she was compelled to anchor in the Severn, whilst a wild sou-west gale shrieked up the Bristol Channel for three days of flying scud, raging seas and howling winds, which tested her ground tackle to the utmost.

The gale over, the pilot was dropped and departure taken from Lundy Island on 7th June. To the secret disgust of Vanderdecken, the *Cutty Sark* carried a strong fair wind to Cape Finisterre, then good N.E. trades gave her the course to the line. In the strength of the trades *Cutty Sark* fell in with *Titania,* which had left London on 3rd June. . . .

It would have been hard to find two more perfect ships of their size and type, and we may well imagine the wonderful picture[146] they must have made as they raced south, neck and neck, in that lovely trade weather. A morning came, however, when their courses differed and they gradually parted company, with the understanding that it was to be a race to Anjer.

Soon after this the *Cutty Sark* raised the Peak of Teneriffe, standing up like a black cone upon the horizon. This was the well-known mirage, for the Peak was over 150 miles away, and as the sun rose higher in the heavens the cone gradually disappeared.

The *Cutty Sark* made a splendid run to the line, but the usual work of shifting sail, as soon as the doldrums were reached, gave her bucko mate a splendid chance of working up his watch in proper "hellion" fashion.

His spite was chiefly vented upon the three darkies, especially one of them named John Francis, who was particularly incapable and clumsy. In shifting the mainsail this man managed to get his hand badly crushed in a buntline block. The pain roused his temper and he began to talk back at the mate, who was swearing at him from the deck with all the sting and concentrated venom in his composition.

Then the mate's watch began to show their sympathy for the nigger and very shortly the whole ship was in an uproar. By the time that the hands came down from bending the mainsail, matters had grown to such a pitch that Captain Wallace called his officers and apprentices aft and gave them arms. He then turned to the angry foremast crowd and boldly declaring that he meant to put a stop to the trouble once and for all, ordered Francis to apologise to the mate or else take a hiding from him.

The nigger, who saw red where the mate was concerned, flung off his coat in defiance. A ring was at once formed just forward of the poop. The nigger and the mate flung themselves upon each other with all the fury and lack of rules usual in sea fights, whilst the captain flourished his revolver and threatened to shoot the first man who attempted to interfere.

The two belligerents pounded away at each other for about a quarter of an hour without much result; then Captain Wallace stopped the fight and sent the hands forward with the caution that he would put the next man in irons whom he caught abusing his officers.[147]

This method of preserving discipline at least cleared the air; Captain Wallace had acted with decision, moreover, he was very popular with all hands: and henceforth, though the bucko mate was far from mending his ways and still vented his spite on the niggers, both watches worked keenly to make a record trip. . . .

This fight on the *Cutty Sark* reminds me of the famous battle between Captain Tom Bowling of the *Invercargill* and Brighton Bill. I give the story as it was given to me by one of the onlookers.

"Captain Bowling was a man of prodigious strength, and I have seen him take hold of a small anvil by the point and with a stiff arm raise it straight above his head. On one occasion, whilst I was with him, he had some trouble with a big A.B., known as 'Brighton Bill' after his home town.

"Bowling said something pretty sharp, and Bill retorted, 'It is only your coat that protects you.' At which Bowling said sharply:—'Come on to the quarter-deck at 4 bells (6 o'clock) and I will take my coat off.'

"We were in the south-east trades and the weather was fine, so at 4 bells all hands came aft to watch the fight. Both men stripped to the waist and they fought for two hours, but Bowling was just a bit better than the other man, so he was considered to have won. It was a Homeric combat such as is given few men the chance to witness, for both men were as hard as nails (though Bowling was a man well over 50 at the time) and both knew something about handling themselves.

"But ever after that no man dared say a word against Tom Bowling whilst Brighton Bill was about. I believe he afterwards sailed with Bowling as bosun."

It may be of interest to add that Captain Bowling was an old China clipper man; and when he retired from the sea had been 30 years in command of sailing ships out of 50 years afloat.

With the "old man" driving the ship and his bucko mate driving her crew, the *Cutty Sark* made a splendid run to the Cape meridian.

The first of really heavy easting weather occurred in 42° 30′ S., 23° 00′ E. when the wind began to come out of the sou'-west in[148] heavier and heavier squalls: then it gradually settled down to a blow of hurricane force, straight from the west. This was just the weather to bring out the daring and resourcefulness of Captain Wallace and show the *Cutty Sark* at her best.

The "old man" hung grimly on to his canvas until a particularly vicious squall tore his brand new fore and main topgallant sails from the boltrope; at the same moment the lower fore topsail sheet carried away and that sail went to tatters.

By this time a tremendous sea was running whose long hill-like ridges rolled up astern until it seemed that the "Cutty" must be pooped and swept out of existence. But in such a case the *Cutty Sark* was always game and running beautifully, lifting clear of each sea with a buoyancy which roused the enthusiasm of her crew.

Whilst she was in the trough her topsails fell into the mast, absolutely becalmed by the hissing crests of the great combers; then as she rose, the sails filled with a clap of thunder which shook the ship from stern to stem and threatened to tear the masts out of her.

The gale was about at its worst, when the men were sent aloft to bend a new lower fore topsail, which was swayed aloft to the tune of "Blow! Boys! Blow!" . . .[149]

. . . There is nothing like a chanty to put heart into men in bad weather, and up went the topsail in its stops, all ready for bending —but it was another matter to bend it.

For two hours the hands aloft fought to bend that sail, between gasps for breath, which was torn from their lungs by the storm fiend, they swore at the wind, they swore at each other in that mental irritation which is common at such moments.

Finger nails were torn in their effort to hold on to the bagging canvas. The sweat ran off their cheeks into the necks of their oilskins. The footrope swung and dipped as they braced themselves against the tilting yard, and strove to pass the rovings under the jackstay. The task seemed an impossibility, but that topsail had to be set in order to keep the *Cutty Sark* ahead of those monstrous chasing seas, and set it eventually was.

Whilst the battle raged aloft, one green sea did succeed in coming in over the stern and swept the length of the deck so that to the men on the yard there was nought to be seen but three masts sticking out of a maelstrom of boiling foam. Then, with deck ports clanging, the gallant little ship cleared herself and rushed headlong into the yawning hollow. Hardly was the topsail sheeted home before the gale settled down into a steady blow.

On the morning of the second day three test heaves of the log were taken, when the *Cutty Sark* seemed to be doing her best, and $17\frac{1}{2}$, 17 and $17\frac{1}{2}$ knots were recorded, whilst 16 knots were constantly on the log slate.

As usual the little clipper steered beautifully. Under foresail and fore lower topsail, the two main topsails and sometimes a main topgallant sail, the mizen lower topsail and two headsails (for safety in case of a broach-to), she almost steered herself, yet[150] it looked alarming enough to the man going aft to relieve the wheel. But in spite of the overtaking seas bumping under her stern as she rose on top of them, the *Cutty Sark* neither kicked nor yawed but piked along dead before it.

And during the whole of this strenuous time her mixed crew played up most gallantly, their only wish being to give the ship her chance and break the record.

At the first sign of a lull there came a call to stick out all three topgallant sails and out tumbled the watch below, gallantly indifferent to risk of life and limb or to the loss of their hard earned sleep.

Wallace, the sail carrier, had hung on to his topgallant sails to the last moment and he set them again at the very first opportunity: indeed no sooner had the storm spent its intensity than he sheeted home his royals.

The strongest part of the blow lasted for three days, and in those short days of easting the *Cutty Sark* ran 1050 miles—an average of 350 miles a day or $14\frac{1}{2}$ knots for 72 hours.

Captain Wallace was one of those skippers who took an interest in their apprentices. On Sundays it was his custom to ask a couple of them to dinner, and we may guess how the boys appreciated the treat.

Most captains believed in the hardening process, which they themselves had to undergo in their youth.

An apprentice in the *Lothair* under the stern Captain Orchard recounts that the only time his captain spoke to him during the whole voyage was to rebuke him for dropping ropeyarns on the sacred poop when he was serving the eyes of the ratlines in the mizen rigging.

Unfortunately for the boy, the captain had hardly finished speaking when down came another ropeyarn, which landed at the autocrat's feet, whereupon Orchard burst out with:—"Damn you, if you drop another ropeyarn on the poop I'll send you out of this altogether." After this threat we may be certain that the apprentice made sure of his ends going over the rail and not inboard.[151]

Two of Wallace's apprentices used to take sights regularly, and the captain was at pains to help them with their navigation.

The subject of navigation, indeed, suddenly assumed unusual importance, for, as the *Cutty Sark* neared the longitude of St. Paul's Island, the chronometers began to differ by five minutes in their rate, and Captain Wallace had no means of knowing which of the two was right. No ship was sighted: Tristan d'Acunha had been kept below the horizon and St. Paul's Island was given a wide berth.

The *Cutty Sark* continued to make good time, and it was soon necessary to haul up for Sunda Straits. The shift of helm caused the chief tragedy of this tragic voyage. It was the middle watch. The *Cutty Sark* was on the starboard tack, with a nice wholesail breeze from the south-east. The mate's watch was on deck, the troublesome nigger, John Francis, being on the look-out. At 3 a.m. Captain Wallace gave the orders to alter course from east to N.N.E. This meant squaring her in. Whilst the watch manned the foresheet, the mate sang out to the nigger on the foc's'le-head to let go the tack. But the order was not obeyed. Again the mate sang out. And again the look-out took not the least notice. This was more than the bucko could stand, and he went forward "on the jump," his mouth full of strong language and his heart full of rage.

Apparently the darkey met him with not only an insolent tongue but a raised capstan bar. There was a short sharp struggle, whilst the mate gained possession of the bar. Then it was the irate officer's turn, and without a moment's hesitation he brought it down on the man's head with such force that John Francis dropped senseless to the deck. It must have been a shrewd blow, for a black man's skull is notoriously hard, yet Francis never regained consciousness and died on the third day after the blow had been struck.

He was buried at sea, the captain reading the service. Though the nigger was far from being popular amongst his shipmates, the mate was still less popular. The ship suddenly became very silent. With gloomy faces and angry, bitter hearts the foremast crowd went about their work, in sullen silence; whilst the afterguard, sensing the atmosphere forward, were uneasy and full of foreboding.[152]

The mate retired to his cabin and was not seen again on deck for the rest of the passage, Captain Wallace taking his watch.

The *Cutty Sark* was now barely a week from Anjer, but, owing to the error in his chronometers, Captain Wallace dared not lay a direct course for Java Head, but, allowing a margin of about 80 miles, did not haul in for the land until he was in the latitude of the Straits.

A nice fresh sea breeze took the *Cutty Sark* in under the shadow of Krakatoa and then died away. And whilst she lay becalmed to leeward, her crew had the mortification of seeing their rival, the *Titania*, glide up the Straits before a nice little air of wind. Thus, through the error in her chronometers, the *Cutty Sark* went about a hundred miles out of her way and lost the race with *Titania* by 12 hours, both ships anchoring off Anjer on the same day.

The *Cutty Sark* had made a very good run out, being only

72 days from Penarth to Anjer, and 69 days from her departure from Lundy Island.

Whilst *Titania* continued her passage to Hongkong, where she arrived on 16th September, *Cutty Sark* had to wait for orders, for old Willis had not expected a run of this speed from his cut-down clipper, and Captain Wallace, though he thought that his destination would be Yokohama, found that there was no telegram awaiting him at Anjer confirming this.

This telegram did not arrive until 29th August.

Whilst the *Cutty Sark* lay off Anjer awaiting her belated orders, the mate took the opportunity of persuading his kind-hearted captain to help him to escape.

An American ship, the *Colorada*, had just arrived from Hamburg and lay at anchor ahead of the *Cutty Sark*. Captain Wallace found that the "old man" of the *Colorada* was quite ready to take the "Cutty's" bucko mate aboard, being only too glad to get hold of a man-handler of such reputation.

The next question was how to smuggle the mate aboard the *Colorada* without the knowledge of the "Cutty's" crowd; for it was known aft that the friends of the murdered nigger, headed by old Vanderdecken, had sworn that they would see the mate brought to book.[153]

They were hoodwinked in this fashion. Early one morning some native bumboats came alongside to starboard, whereupon the "old man" supplied the hands with some money, and both watches were soon busy bargaining over the side for packets of jaggery and bunches of small onions, for bananas and pineapples, for Java sparrows and screaming parrakeets.

Whilst this hullaballoo was going on, the mate, unnoticed by the excited men waging their brisk bargains with the gesticulating and screeching Malays, sneaked up on deck and quietly dropped into a sampan, or it may have been the *Colorada's* boat, which had cautiously dropped under the "Cutty's" port quarter. This escape of the *Cutty Sark's* mate has been a well-known yarn in ships' foc's'les for many years. Gradually it has been embroidered and enlarged upon until at last the celebrated Joseph Conrad was tempted to put it into one of his books.

But the version which stated that the mate swam off to the *Colorada* was an absurd one, for the Straits are infested with sharks and he would have had to swim against wind and current. The mate made the trip to the Down Easter in a boat. But he had hardly got safely away from the *Cutty Sark* and hidden aboard the *Colorada* before his escape was discovered.

It turned out that one of the men had noticed him with a

bundle in his hand, skulking about behind the deckhouse at 7.30 a.m., just after the bumboats had come alongside, and the foc's'le was not long in putting two and two together. Led by old Vanderdecken, they at once refused work, declaring that they would not turn to until the mate was found. In spite of his popularity, Captain Wallace was unable to pacify them, and he at last agreed to take some of the men ashore to see the authorities.

Men before the mast had small chance of getting fair play ashore in those days. The native police were certainly ordered to search all the ships lying off Anjer for the missing mate, but the crew of the *Cutty Sark* were not allowed to join in the search. There was a good deal of fuss, with, of course, no result.

The crew of the now notorious clipper were by no means satisfied with the steps taken by the authorities ashore—they knew they had been hoodwinked and so they still refused to turn to.[154]

The *Cutty Sark* had now been at Anjer a week, and at the psychological moment the belated orders arrived—she was to proceed to Yokohama.

It was now time to get underweigh, but not a member of the foc's'le would touch a capstan bar. Whereupon Wallace determined to up anchor and set sail as best he could with the aid of his devoted apprentices and petty officers; so the capstan was manned by the half-deck, carpenter, cook, steward and sailmaker.

The more determined of the crew immediately tried to interfere, but again Wallace acted with decision—the afterguard were given arms and the ringleaders of the crew, four in all, were captured and clapped in irons. At which the remainder of the crew retired sulkily to the foc's'le whilst six boys and four men set to work on the long weary job of weighing the anchor in that steamy, enervating heat.

The anchor was barely off the ground before a light draught of air gave the "Cutty" steerage way and carried her out of Anjer Roads into the Java Sea. It was the 5th September. Scarcely, however, was the *Cutty Sark* clear of the land before she ran into a clock calm which lasted on and off for three days. The ship now rang with old Vanderdecken's prophecies of disaster. He described the evils which would happen to the poor little *Cutty Sark* and all on board with such a wealth of detailed horror that some of the hands became really frightened. The whole ship's company felt tragedy in the air and it was not long in coming.

Captain Wallace had no sooner helped his mate to escape than he realised in what a predicament he had placed himself. He saw an official investigation looming ahead at Yokohama, in which there was little doubt but that he would be held responsible for the mate's escape, and the very best that he could expect was the suspension of his certificate. He had an old mother and a young wife dependent upon him, and the future for them as well as for himself looked black indeed.

The worry of it all so preyed upon the once jovial skipper that all hands began to pity his care-worn face. Ever since the escape of the mate he had been unable to sleep. Night and day he stood gazing out to sea or walked with bowed head up and down the poop in a misery which was plain to see.[155]

His friends in the half-deck watched him furtively with anxious eyes. There was no more singing in the dog watches—only the cease-less drone of that croaker, Vanderdecken, mingled with the lazy flapping of the listless, calm-ridden sails. The ship had lost all life. The calm aggravated the tension aboard. The sullen crew, still athirst for vengeance upon the missing mate, kept forward and allowed the half-deck to do what work was necessary. Discipline had grown lax under the influence of the captain's indifference to all around him, the steamy heat and the stagnant calm.

It was not a situation that could possibly last; something had to happen soon. One or two of the wisest recognised that the captain's mind and body could not stand the strain much longer. The reliable "Chips" stood watch with his skipper, ready to stand by his beloved ship and her unfortunate captain, but uncertain how to act in order to relieve the strain.

The scene was laid and the climax was at hand.

On the fourth day after leaving Anjer, the watch had just been called at 4 a.m., when the captain, who was standing at the break of the poop with the carpenter, turned to his faithful petty officer and asked if the second mate was on deck.

"Chips" replied that he was just coming up. Whereupon Captain Wallace left the carpenter and walked aft: called the helmsman's attention to the course; then deliberately stepped on to the taffrail and jumped overboard.

At the moment the *Cutty Sark* was sneaking along at about two knots before a faint draught of air. The man at the wheel quickly threw over two life-buoys and put the helm down. The crew, who had for so long refused work, flung themselves upon a boat, which had been used at Anjer and was still in the davits, and had it in the water in record time.

The sea was as calm as a mill-pond. The life-buoys were picked up, but no trace of the captain was ever found, though a number of sharks swimming furiously about gave only too clear an indication of his fate.

Thus passed a splendid seaman, a kind and capable shipmaster, and a man whose death was regretted by everyone aboard. The[156] crew took the death of their captain greatly to heart and blamed themselves bitterly for refusing duty. The half-deck lamented the loss of a true friend, whilst the *Cutty Sark* had been deprived of a skipper who understood her every mood and had proved that he knew how to get every ounce of speed out of her. Tragedies and misfortunes have a way of piling up. The *Cutty Sark* had sailed on a Friday, and old Vanderdecken's evil prophecies were fast beginning to mature; her run of bad luck had now fairly started, from henceforth there was to be no let up until the voyage was ended.

As soon as the boat was hoisted up and all hope of saving the captain abandoned, a consultation of all hands was held. The crew wanted the second mate to take the ship on to Yokohama, but that young man was quite unfit for such a responsibility; his navigation was very shaky, and his eyesight was so bad that he was compelled to ask Sankey, the star navigator amongst the apprentices, to help him in taking sights. There was evidently nothing for it but to head back for Anjer, and in that calm weather it took the *Cutty Sark* four days to regain the anchorage.

Nor were these four days without accident. When close to the Cap and Button Rocks and without a breath of wind, the *Cutty Sark* was caught in a strong tide-race, which swept her stern first round the north-west side of Thwarttheway Island.

The steep rocky sides of that well-known island rose sheer up from a great depth, and so close to the shore was the *Cutty Sark* taken by the current that her yards had to be braced up to avoid striking the towering cliffs. Luckily there were no out-lying reefs and the deep sea lead gave no bottom; but it was sufficiently alarming to make old Vanderdecken declare that the ship was bewitched. However, the island, so well named Thwarttheway, was cleared without mishap. A light breeze then sprang up and allowed the *Cutty Sark* to head in for the anchorage.

The inexperienced second mate next proceeded to anchor too far out and dropped his hook upon a shelving rock which terminated abruptly in deep water. The next day he was compelled to move the ship on to better holding ground nearer the land.

The *Cutty Sark* now had another week of idleness whilst cables passed to and fro between the incapable second mate and the[157] mystified John Willis, who had, of course, heard nothing of the killing of the nigger and the escape of the mate.

Whilst the second mate spent his days between the ship and the telegraph station, little work beyond wetting down the decks was done on board; but the lucky apprentices who manned the boat enjoyed many a stroll through the small native town and Dutch colony, which was so shortly afterwards to be wiped out by the appalling eruption of the extinct volcano of Krakatao. At first Willis, who was loath to forfeit such a good charter, wanted the second mate to proceed to Yokohama, but the man, if without grit, knew his own limitations and refused to undertake the responsibility. At last orders came out for the *Cutty Sark* to proceed to Singapore in charge of a Dutch pilot.

The next excitement was the working of the *Cutty Sark* through the narrow Banka Strait. The ship was put under "Calashee" watch, which meant that all hands stood by ready for a call to work ship, but no other work was done. The straits are narrow, not much wider than a large river in places; and what with tides and currents, rocks and shoals, calms and squalls and sudden shifts of wind, the ship had to be handled smartly. Nor did the bewitched clipper get through without one close call. With no wind and helpless in the grip of a strong current, the *Cutty Sark* drifted by some sunken rocks on which the surf was boiling.

For a few moments the hearts of all on board stood still, then, with her usual luck in extricating herself from almost certain disaster, the "Cutty" slid by the reef just clear of the broken water but so close to the jagged fangs which showed above the surf that the meanest thrower aboard could have tossed a biscuit on to them.

But for this scare the passage was a most enjoyable one. For the most part a gentle fair wind prevailed, which made it ideal sailing. Nor was the weather too warm, and amply clad in broad brimmed hats, rolled up dungaree pants and open throated shirts, the ship's company lounged about the decks as if on a yachting cruise. With the double tragedy but just beneath the horizon, the crew nevertheless were able to enjoy the trip with the usual sailor's shortness of memory for the unpleasant. A week of this idyllic[155] sailing brought the *Cutty Sark* into Singapore harbour, and on 18th September she once more dropped her anchor.

Singapore, already all agog with the *Jeddah* disaster and the dismasting of the *Bates Family*, received a still greater thrill when the cause of the famous *Cutty Sark's* first visit to the port began to get abroad. The story of the *Jeddah* has been immortalised in Joseph Conrad's great classic *Lord Jim*—it was a most disgraceful one, the captain and officers abandoning the ship in a panic and leaving over a thousand souls, native crew and pilgrims aboard a sinking ship, as they thought, to perish. The chief officer of the *Jeddah*[1] arrived at

---

[1] *Jeddah*, iron screw brig 993 tons net register, 1541 tons gross register, built by Denny of Dumbarton in 1872, owned by the Singapore Steamship Co.

Singapore on 15th September, and he plays the part of "Lord Jim" in Conrad's story.

The *Bates Family* disaster was more curious than disgraceful. She was a well-known Liverpool ship, notorious for her straight steamer stem, upon which the whole family of Bates was carved, forming a gigantic figure-head, which drew attention to her wherever she went. Being bound from Newport to Calcutta with coal, she was dismasted on 6th September in a very odd way. The iron jackstay on her foreyard chafed through the forestay, which suddenly carried away. At which the foremast fell back on the mainmast, the mainmast on the mizen, and the mizen in its turn upon the wheel, so that all three masts lay fore and aft along the deck like masts of a bottle ship before it is put into the bottle. On the deck everything was smashed up by the fall of the masts—boats, deck-houses, skylights, wheel and even rudder, whilst the bowsprit broke short off as well.

It is difficult to imagine a more complete smash up. On the following day the *British India* came along whereupon the captain of the *Bates Family* determined to abandon his ship, and taking the circumstances into consideration the Court acquitted him of all blame. The *British India* transferred the crew of the *Bates Family* to the *Copenhagen* on the 10th, which duly landed them at Algoa Bay, whilst the *British India* brought the news to Singapore.[2] [159]

The *Cutty Sark* was tied up to the Tanga Paka wharf, where a gang of Chinese coolies proceeded to unload the coals, which they shovelled into baskets and ran ashore, slung on bamboo poles.

An enquiry into the tragedy was now held, which resulted in the crew being given the option of their discharge. Only a few availed themselves to this concession, but chief amongst them was old Vanderdecken, who openly declared that henceforth his object in life would be to run down the mate and bring him to justice, for he was certain that the *Cutty Sark* would have no luck until the nigger killer was under lock and key.

Those remaining on board were far from sorry when they saw old Vanderdecken bundle over the rail, for they had begun to think that there was something uncanny about the queer old man and his prophecies, which had come true in such a tragic manner—in fact, many considered that he was the Jonah at the root of all the trouble.

Whether old Vanderdecken ran the mate to ground at San Franscisco or in a London pub does not very much matter, but the

---

2 *Bates Family*, iron ship (converted steamer) 2154 tons, built in Hull, 1859; owners E. Bates & Sons, Liverpool.

mate at any rate owed his arrest to being recognised by one of the crew, and was tried in London some two years later and sentenced to seven years imprisonment for manslaughter. . . .[160]*

---

* "A Hell-Ship Voyage" continues with a further account of the *Cutty Sark's* troubles—some of them bearing a remarkable likeness to details of Conrad's *The Shadow-Line*. [Ed.]

ARREST AND TRIAL OF SIDNEY SMITH
The Times

The Times, Wednesday, July 5, 1882. p. 6, col. d.

At the THAMES Police-court, JOHN ANDERSON [alias Sidney Smith], at present second mate of the ship Marianne Gottebohm [Ann Nottabohn in a later report], lying in the South-West India Dock, was charged before Mr. Lushington with feloniously killing and slaying John Francis by striking him on the head with a capstan-bar on the British ship Cuttysark while on the high seas. Inspector Wildey, of the Criminal Investigation Department, watched the case. John Somers, a young man, said he was a steward out of employment. He was a steward on the Cuttysark, which sailed from London on May 15, 1880, having on board the prisoner as chief officer, and John Francis as cook and steward. The night they were rounding the Cape of Good Hope the sailmaker ran into the witness's cabin and said the chief officer had knocked Francis down. There had been a little ill-feeling between the prisoner and Francis because he could not do his work as a seaman. On going forward the witness saw Francis being carried aft, and blood flowing from a wound on his head. The captain dressed the wound. On the following morning the prisoner said —"I have done for him; he will never lift the capstan-bar to me again." Francis died the same night, and was buried on the following day. In the beginning of September the ship was lying in the roads at Anjer. One night a boat was seen under the bows, and the prisoner disappeared from the ship. The second day after the ship left Anjer the captain committed suicide by jumping overboard into the sea. The ship was taken back to Anjer by the second mate, who telegraphed to the agents at Singapore. In answer to a question by the prisoner, the witness said he did not see how the affair happened. He was told of it. Mr. Lushington read an entry from the official log-book, which was to the effect that when the chief mate came on the poop Francis grossly insulted him, refused to obey orders, and on the chief officer going to expostulate with him, he made a blow at his head with a marline-spike. Anderson hit him on the head with a capstan-bar in self-defence. The captain said "This is awful work," and the mate said, "Well, what could I do, it was to be killed or to kill." Mr. Lushington remanded the prisoner for a week.

◆──◆

The Times, Friday, August 4, 1882. p. 4, col. 1.

CENTRAL CRIMINAL COURT, *August 3.*
(*Before* Mr. JUSTICE STEPHEN.)

John Anderson, 31, seaman [alias Sidney Smith], was indicted for the wilful murder of John Francis.

Mr. Poland and Mr. Montagu Williams prosecuted for the Treasury; Mr. Edward Clark, Q.C., and Mr. Besley appeared for the defence.

The accused, it appeared, was chief mate on board a tea clipper called the Cutty Sark, which sailed from the port of London in May, 1880. The deceased, who was a coloured man, shipped as an able seaman, and it was stated that he soon afterwards incurred the displeasure of the prisoner in consequence of his incompetency. About the 9th or 10th of August, 1880, the vessel had just rounded the Cape, and at a quarter to 9 o'clock the prisoner was in command of the watch. The night was dark and dirty, and the watch was occupied in hauling the sail round. The deceased not being competent to perform seaman's duty, had been placed on the forecastle on the look out. The watch on hauling the ropes found that the "fore lazy tack" was fastened, and the prisoner called out to the deceased to let the tack go. The deceased replied "Very well," or, according to the prisoner's version, "Go to the devil." Immediately afterwards the deceased let go the lazy tack, but instead of doing so as an able seaman would, he let the end go overboard. The prisoner said, "That ───── has done that out of spite." The deceased retorted, "Well, you told me to let it go," and the prisoner exclaimed "I will come on the forecastle and heave you overboard, you nigger." The deceased replied, "If you come up here I have got the capstan bar waiting for you." The prisoner then went on to the forecastle and was seen to raise the capstan bar, with which he struck the deceased on the head. The blow knocked the man over the forecastle on to the deck, and he never spoke again. The prisoner said to the watch, "Did you see that nigger lift the capstan bar to me," but the men replied that they did not. The prisoner said, "He will lift no more capstan bars to me, for I have knocked him down," and he

added, "I have knocked him down like a bullock; he never gave a kick."
The account given by the prisoner was that he did it in self-defence.
The captain of the vessel attended to the deceased, but he remained
insensible till the following day, when he expired from the injuries he
received, and was buried at sea. Before the arrival of the ship at Anjer
the accused, with the connivance of the captain, made his escape. The
vessel proceeded thence to Singapore, and during the passage the
captain committed suicide by jumping overboard, having previously
dropped into the sea the capstan bar used by the prisoner. At Singapore the matter was reported to a magistrate, who, in due course,
instituted an inquiry. The prisoner was arrested in London.

It was stated in cross-examination that the deceased man Francis
had on several occasions threatened the prisoner's life, and once he
sharpened his knife upon the grindstone for the purpose of carrying
his threat into execution.

Mr. EDWARD CLARKE, addressing his Lordship at the close of the
case, submitted that the evidence could not sustain the Court charging
the prisoner with murder.

Mr. JUSTICE STEPHEN concurred; and

Mr. CLARKE said that, in those circumstances, he could not resist
a verdict of manslaughter. The learned counsel addressed the Court
in mitigation of punishment, pointing out that the vessel had been
under-manned, and that at the time in question the accused had had
an important manœuvre to perform with respect to the sail. The
deceased behaved in an insolent and "lubberly" manner, and it was
absolutely necessary that the prisoner should assert his authority.

Numerous witnesses were then called on the part of the defence
to show that the prisoner bore an excellent character and was a man
whose disposition was humane and kindly.

The jury, by his Lordship's direction, then returned a verdict of
manslaughter against the accused.

Mr. JUSTICE STEPHEN, in passing sentence, told the prisoner he had
considered the case with anxious attention and with very great pain,
because the evidence which had been given showed that he was a
man of good character generally speaking and of humane disposition.
He was happy to be able to give full weight to the evidence given in
his favour. The deceased had certainly acted in a manner which was
calculated to make the prisoner very angry, but it must be clearly
understood that the taking of human life by brutal violence, whether
on sea or on land, whether the life be that of a black or a white man,
was a dreadful crime, and deserving of exemplary punishment. He
sentenced the prisoner to seven years' penal servitude.

THE CRITICS

THE JOURNEY WITHIN*
Albert J. Guerard

. . . "Heart of Darkness" is a slightly overembroidered exercise in Conrad's most elaborate style; "The Secret Sharer" and *The Shadow Line* perhaps his two great triumphs of a style plain and pure. . . . "A Smile of Fortune" and even the charming "Youth" may not belong with the best of Conrad. But "Heart of Darkness" and "The Secret Sharer" and *The Shadow Line* belong not only with that best. Historically speaking, they are among the first and best—one is tempted to say only—[14] symbolist masterpieces in English fiction. The sea voyages and the one great Congo journey are unmistakably journeys within, and journeys through a darkness.

The matter may come to seem dark indeed, so a brief forewarning is necessary. The term and concept of the *night journey,* borrowed from anthropology and now gaining some currency in criticism, will appear several times in the following pages. By it I refer to the archetypal myth dramatized in much great literature since the Book of Jonah: the story of an essentially solitary journey involving profound spiritual change in the voyager. In its classical form the journey is a descent into the earth, followed by a return to light. Sometimes the dream is literally an illuminating dream (as with Don Quixote's experience in the well); more often it is dramatized through an actual voyage and movement through space. A familiar variant concerns passage through a tunnel or other dark place; another describes descent to the depths of the sea. It is assumed that this myth, like any powerful and universal dream, has some other meaning than one of literal adventure, though this other meaning is often unintended. *We dream this dream because we are the people we are; because our conscious and unconscious lives alike have certain psychic needs.* The nature of the vision may vary; so too may vary the nature of the change and rebirth experienced.

---

* Reprinted by permission of the publishers from Albert J. Guerard, *Conrad the Novelist,* Cambridge, Mass.: Harvard University Press, Copyright, 1958, by the President and Fellows of Harvard College, pp. 14–33. [See the Bibliography at the end of this volume for earlier criticism by Albert J. Guerard —criticism similar in point of view to this selection, and frequently referred to by other critics. Ed.]

But very often the dream appears to be about the introspective process itself: about a risky descent into the preconscious or even unconscious; about a restorative return to the primitive sources of being and an advance through temporary regression. Psychologists have their different geographies of the unconscious, they too using or creating myths and symbolic figures to suggest unseen realities. Not all would agree that the male shadow, female anima, and occult mandala have as definite an existence as Jung implies, and not all would agree with him that integration of the personality is impossible without a full descent into the unconscious. But nearly all would agree that an unconscious exists.

It therefore should go without saying that a powerful successful[15] dreaming of the night journey is itself likely to be unconscious to some extent; the dreamer may have no clear awareness of the nature of his dream. I suspect the myth of the night journey is unusually conscious in "The Secret Sharer," slightly less conscious in "Heart of Darkness," still less conscious in *The Shadow Line*. Psychologically speaking, "Youth" offers no real night journey at all.

The subtleties and symbolisms of "The Secret Sharer," *The Shadow Line,* and *The Nigger of the "Narcissus,"* and all the controversies over their meaning, tempt us to forget that these are also stories of actual voyages, important to their author as voyages. The navigational maneuvers were literally matters of life and death, not merely symbolic vehicles. Conrad wanted us to see and know these ships and their crews, vanishing before the rush of time. "My task which I am trying to achieve is, by the power of the written word, to make you hear, to make you feel—it is, before all, to make you *see*." And the intensity of the mature Conrad's response to his youthful captains— the fact that he could still become so involved in their trials and initiations—may lead us to forget how far he had left them behind, at least in time and flesh. But it is starkly there and should not be overlooked or minimized, the great break in his life: the turn to the sedentary convict labor of converting "nervous force into phrases"[1] after twenty years of adventure and practical work on the stubborn seas. Thus the least interesting of the autobiographical short novels, "Youth" (1898), may be the closest to the author's ordinary waking experience in its nostalgic backward glance. It exists first of all as the feat of memory Conrad claimed it to be: a literal and vivid rendering of his voyage in the doomed *Palestine*. And it dramatizes the most

---

[1] "... for me writing—*the only possible writing*—is just simply the conversion of nervous force into phrases" (letter to H. G. Wells, November 30, 1903, *Life and Letters*, I, 321).

obvious personality conflict (youthful seaman—landlocked meditator)
in such simple terms that there seems to be no conflict at all.

There is, rather, a total separation and twenty years' gulf in time
between the second mate's ignorant "youth" (the eagerness with which
he courts danger, his vanity and youthful[16] illusion of omnipotence,
his discovery of romance in disaster, his blindness to the old captain's
tragedy) and the narrator's disenchanted maturity. In *Lord Jim* Marlow is proxy for the intellectual, probing, moralistic side of a divided
self, yet is intimately involved with a side both romantic and vulnerable. In "Youth" the division is the ordinary one imposed by time upon
ordinary men; Marlow looks back on the still untested twenty-year-old
with some affection and no little irony. But that earlier self is truly
dead. It can be evoked only by the feat of memory, and does not involve him morally. In *The Mirror of the Sea*, under the title "Initiation," Conrad recalls his own loss of romantic illusion concerning the
sea. He was elated by the chance to head a lifesaving crew, then
shocked into an awareness of reality by the haggard appearance of the
survivors.[2] In "Youth," no such important change occurs. The reason
for the story's serenity, almost unique in Conrad's work, is thus simple
enough: it is the only personal story in which the would-be initiate
learns nothing, being still too young to learn. The brilliant nautical
detail of "Youth," the thinness of its psycho-moral content, the clear
but slightly mannered style, the recurring sentimentality of Marlow
("Pass the bottle!")—these suggest what Conrad's work would have been
like, had it not involved important conflicts and anxieties. The tem-
peramental condition of his greater books is that the conflicts are still
very alive and real. They must still be struggled with and lived through
and appeased.

"You fellows know there are those voyages that seem ordered for
the illustration of life, that might stand for a symbol of existence." So
Marlow forewarns his hearers at the outset of "Youth." Yet the story
requires no interpreting. It seems more than any other of Conrad's to
invite a simple enjoyment of its surface charm. The physical rendering
of the *Judea's* misadventures is always vivid; the absurd ship becomes
heroic, as the absurd often does. And the pages on her death escape the
story's cloying mannerism of breathless parallel clauses. The fine
visualization is supported by rhythms exactly suited to the action:[17]

Half an hour passed. Suddenly there was a frightful racket, rattle,
clanking of chains, hiss of water, and millions of sparks flew up into the
shivering column of smoke that stood leaning slightly above the ship.
The cat-heads had burned away, and the two red-hot anchors had gone

---

[2] See *The Mirror of the Sea*, pp. 141, 142, 148.

to the bottom, tearing out after them two hundred fathom of red-hot
chain. The ship trembled, the mass of flame swayed as if ready to collapse,
and the fore top-gallant-mast fell. It darted down like an arrow of fire,
shot under, and instantly leaping up within an oar's length of the boats,
floated quietly, very black on the luminous sea.[3]

Such a passage usefully reminds us, at the outset, that although
psychological process was a major concern for Conrad the writer, so
too was the remembered visible world.

There are certain moments in our lives, or clusters of experience,
to which the unappeased imagination returns again and again, en-
dowing them with significances no one could have seen at the time.
Conrad's first voyage on the *Otago* in 1888, in command of a ship for
the first time, with the events and months surrounding that voyage,
clearly represents such a core of experience, to be valued and revalued
by art. The long-delayed then extremely difficult trip from Bangkok to
Singapore with a cholera- and dysentery-weakened crew was as severe a
test as any insecure man could ask for. The trip took three weeks. But
in retrospect, and as the imagination kept returning to it, that trip
became the culminating episode in a whole period of emotional crisis.
It would ultimately evoke, in addition to certain important pages of
Lord Jim and a large share of the novelette "Falk," two of Conrad's
most personal short novels: "The Secret Sharer" and *The Shadow Line*.
It is interesting to observe Conrad move, over the years, toward a more
and more personal account of that voyage. In the "Falk" of 1901 only a
few paragraphs[4] refer directly to the sickness of the crew and to the
narrator-captain's ignorance of his ship. Much of the rest is anecdote.
But *The Shadow Line* of 1917, if we are to believe Conrad, is in part
straight autobiographical record. And its preoccupations are certainly
subjective.[18]

The material facts, to be sure, are not very important. The
spiritual ones are. Jean-Aubry says of this period that physically and
morally Conrad "was passing through one of those transformations
which are common enough in the lives of men, but differ in each case
according to temperament and imagination and in being either restrained or explosive."[5] The comment may seem abnormally vague, but
such crises are always exceedingly hard to define. An injury on the
Highland Forest in the summer of 1887 was followed by "inexplicable
periods of powerlessness, sudden accesses of mysterious pain,"[6] and

3 *Youth*, p. 32.
4 See especially "Falk," *Typhoon*, pp. 188–189.
5 *Life and Letters*, I, 100.
6 *The Mirror of the Sea*, pp. 54–55.

some weeks in a Singapore hospital. Conrad then served four and a half months as second mate on the *Vidar,* and made the Malayan voyages that were to supply him with so much material for his early work. On January 5, 1888, he suddenly gave up this berth which he would long afterward remember with pleasure. But fourteen days later he was given, as unexpectedly, the command of the *Otago.* (Lord Jim goes through a telescoped version of these experiences: a disabling accident and period of demoralizing ease in a hospital, at the end of which he suddenly gives up the idea of going home and takes a berth as chief mate of the *Patna.* The *Patna* is, like the *Vidar,* owned by an Arab, and hence free from the severe discipline of the home service.)[7] Perhaps Conrad was tired of the *Vidar's* monotonous round of island voyages, as Jean-Aubry suggests. Or perhaps he feared and resisted that demoralization by an easy billet which he would later dream for Lord Jim. There is another and doubtless more remote possibility: that he was already obeying the writer's instinct to separate himself from material the unconscious has recognized as destined to be "used." But any more exact awareness of Conrad's fears and preoccupations must come from our reading of the stories themselves.[8] [19]

We shall see, presently, how Conrad's imagination associated two famous crimes—the abandonment of the *Jeddah* by its officers and the killing of a rebellious member of the crew on the famous *Cutty Sark*—with this first testing voyage. The gravest issue at crucial moments in *Lord Jim* and throughout "The Secret Sharer" is what attitude to take toward one's brother or "double" who has committed a crime. In the diffuse and otherwise uninteresting "Falk," Conrad seems to be groping toward this central subject and conflict. And in so doing he associates a third major crime of the sea—cannibalism on a drifting ship, murder in order to survive—with his own period of immobilization at Bangkok while preparing for that first voyage. The new captain's problem is to

---

7 *Lord Jim,* pp. 11–14.

8 Conrad was twenty-nine to thirty-one during the period in question. But a highly subjective work of art necessarily reflects, even more, the time when it was written. Conrad wrote "The Secret Sharer" in November 1909 (at the age of fifty-one) at Hythe, where he found his house an "odious" hole; 1908 had been a bad year, during which he feared a breakdown (Jean-Aubry, *Life and Letters,* II, 5). And 1909 too. *The Shadow Line* was begun in 1914, immediately after the Conrads had escaped from Poland and the Continent, and was finished amid wartime anxieties, in March 1915, according to Jean-Aubry (*ibid.,* 8, 164). Conrad's Author's Note says that it "was written in the last three months of the year 1916. Of all the subjects of which a writer of tales is more or less conscious within himself this is the only one I found it possible to attempt at the time." It is not unreasonable to connect the visit to Poland with this renewed preoccupation with his first command. Only major and solid success, as a seaman or as a writer, could silence the accusing Polish voices of his sixteenth year.

get his ship out of the river, but Falk, who has the only tugboat on the river, refuses to take him. He regards Falk as his enemy, and for some pages the story promises to deal with or at least express neurotic feelings of gratuitous persecution. But in fact the persecution is real and is not gratuitous. A misunderstanding over a girl is presently cleared up; and, in order to get his ship taken down the river, the captain agrees to help Falk win her.

Thus far the story has touched upon but failed to develop the materials of *The Shadow Line*. The land has not yet become, symbolically, a paralysis of the spirit, and the menace of unreason has not yet become a conscious subject in its own right. But meanwhile—with the suspect bargain and with the act of commitment to a man not really known, and who in fact turns out to have committed a crime—we are entering another familiar area of Conradian discourse. Do circumstances excuse? The story, upon exposing Falk's crime, asks this familiar Marlovian question, to which Conrad's[20] answers are usually hesitant if not equivocal. And the narrator remains loyal to the guilty man who refuses to commit suicide because he had committed a "marginal" crime, to *the man who wants to go on living*—as Marlow will remain loyal to Lord Jim, and the narrator of "The Secret Sharer" to Leggatt; as Captain Wallace of the *Cutty Sark* was loyal to his mate who had killed a man.

These then—as we look at "Falk" and momentarily look ahead to the two other short novels and to *Lord Jim*—are some of the feelings and real or imagined situations associated with Conrad's first voyage as captain: an untested man who does not have the feel of his ship and who has made insufficient or improper preparations for his first voyage, and who is so belabored by bad luck that he is driven close to paranoid unreason; an immobilized ship that cannot get started on its voyage or cannot reach the winds of the open sea, and that presently passes through an intense preternatural darkness and over a sea containing submerged hazards; and, of course, a man who either bargains with a criminal or actually identifies with him as brother and double. And the crimes themselves: the crimes of courageous or well-meaning men (except in *The Shadow Line*), yet each one a breach of trust.

So much for the "core of experience" and cluster of recurrent dreams. We may now look at the fictions themselves, though not in the order they were written.

"On my right hand there were lines of fishing-stakes resembling a mysterious system of half-submerged bamboo fences, incomprehensible in its division of the domain of tropical fishes..." The strange first paragraph of "The Secret Sharer," with its dream landscape of ill-defined boundaries between land, air and sea, prepares us for this most frankly psychological of Conrad's shorter works. Even at a quite explicit level it is the story of a personality test: "I wondered how far I should turn out faithful to that ideal conception of one's own personality every man sets up for himself secretly." The narrator-captain is insecure at the start; he looks forward to leaving "the unrest of the land."[21] The story moves from his sense of being stranger to his ship, and to himself, to a final mature confidence and integration: "And I was alone with her. Nothing! no one in the world should stand now between us, throwing a shadow on the way of silent knowledge and mute affection, the perfect communion of a seaman with his first command." This is the end of the experience. But he must give up, almost at its beginning, his illusion of the sea's great security and "untempted life." For the temptation appears on the very next page in the guise of Leggatt, fugitive from the *Sephora* because he had killed a member of his crew. Whatever test occurs, or whatever change in the narrator's personality, must be due to his relationship with Leggatt. For that relationship is the whole story.

He knows that the test must be faced in solitude: "far from all human eyes, with only sky and sea for spectators and for judges." Hence, in marked defiance of custom, he takes the anchor-watch himself, sending the other officers and men below. The direct result of this departure from routine is that the rope side-ladder is left hanging: the ladder up which Leggatt will climb moments later. The captain sees at the bottom of the ladder, when he tries to haul it up, a "headless corpse," "ghastly, silvery, fishlike." There is no way of knowing whether Conrad here intended the sea from which Leggatt climbs as a symbol of the unconscious, or whether he intended a reflexive reference to his opening sentence. What the scene does insist upon is that the captain is *responsible* for the dangling ladder and for Leggatt's coming. He has in a sense summoned Leggatt, who later remarks that it was "as if you had expected me." Even before the fugitive has a chance to reveal his crime, a "mysterious communication was established" between the two. The captain fetches a sleeping-suit, which is just the right size, and on the next page refers to Leggatt as his "double" for the first of many times.[9] "It was,[22] in the night, as though I had been faced by my own reflection in the depths of a sombre and immense mirror." He at once leaps to the most charitable interpretation of Leggatt's crime. He suggests it was due to a fit of temper.

---

[9] The excellent motion picture based on the story handles the "double" situation with great tact by making Leggatt a slightly coarser, more brutal version of the captain. At one point it underlines the theme of sympathetic identification as Conrad does not: by having the narrator reënact in dream Leggatt's crime.

It would be improper to forget, while preoccupied with the psychological symbolism, that Leggatt is substantial flesh and blood. The story dramatizes a human relationship and individual moral bond at variance with the moral bond to the community implicit in laws and maritime tradition. The narrator at once makes his decision to hide and protect the fugitive and at no time remotely considers betraying him. Leggatt must be hidden from the captain's own crew. And he must be kept hidden from the captain of the *Sephora* (with his fidelity to the law) on the following day:

To the law. His obscure tenacity on that point had in it something incomprehensible and a little awful; something, as it were, mystical, quite apart from his anxiety that he should not be suspected of "countenancing any doings of that sort." Seven-and-thirty virtuous years at sea, of which over twenty of immaculate command, and the last fifteen in the *Sephora*, seemed to have laid him under some pitiless obligation.[10]

We do not need to go to the biography and letters to discover Conrad's respect for "immaculate command" and "pitiless obligation," or for such a traditional figure; it is implicit in much of his fiction. The narrator's sympathy, however, is wholly for the criminal Leggatt.

The reader too incorrigibly sympathizes with Leggatt. But it is well to recall that Leggatt appears to be a rather questionable seaman: a man who had got his post because his "people had some interest" with the owners, who was disliked by the men, who "wasn't exactly the sort for the chief mate of a ship like the *Sephora*." His crime was, like most crimes in Conrad, a marginal one. His order and his actions had saved the ship in a crisis; the same "strung-up force" had within the same hour fixed the foresail and killed a man. But still more essential (from an officer's point of view) is his contempt for law, his feeling that innocence and guilt are[23] private matters. "But you don't see me coming back to explain such things to an old fellow in a wig and twelve respectable tradesmen, do you? What can they know whether I am guilty or not—or of *what* I am guilty, either?" It is entirely wrong to suppose, as some readers do, that Conrad unequivocally *approves* the captain's decision to harbor Leggatt. The reasons for the narrator's act are defined as "psychological (not moral)." Who knows what Conrad the responsible master-mariner might not have done, had he so connived in a fugitive's escape? The excellent captain of the *Cutty Sark* committed suicide four days after letting Leggatt's prototype go free.

This then is the situation in its purely human and material terms —a situation Conrad will dramatize again and again: the act of sympathetic identification with a suspect or outlaw figure, and the ensuing conflict between loyalty to the individual and loyalty to the com-

10 "The Secret Sharer," *'Twixt Land and Sea*, p. 20.

munity. It is, at our first response, a dramatic outward relationship.
But as double Leggatt is also very inwardly a secret self. He provokes a
crippling division of the narrator's personality, and one that interferes
with his seamanship. On the first night the captain intends to pin
together the curtains across the bed in which Leggatt is lying. But he
cannot. He is too tired, in "a peculiarly intimate way." He feels less
"torn in two" when he is with Leggatt in the cabin, but this naturally
involves neglect of his duties. As for other times—"I was constantly
watching myself, my secret self, as dependent on my actions as my own
personality, sleeping in that bed, behind that door which faced me as I
sat at the head of the table." He loses all "unconscious alertness," his
relations with the other officers become more strained, and in the navigational crisis of Koh-ring he realizes that he does not know how to
handle his ship. He has been seriously disoriented, and even begins to
doubt Leggatt's bodily existence. "I think I had come creeping quietly
as near insanity as any man who has not actually gone over the border."
The whispering communion of the narrator and his double—of the
seaman-self and some darker, more interior, and outlaw self—must have
been necessary[24] and rewarding, since the story ends as positively as it
does. But it is obvious to both men that the arrangement cannot be
permanent. Nor would it do for Leggatt *to come back to life* in his own
guise.

The narrator therefore takes his ship close to the land, so that
Leggatt can escape and swim to the island of Koh-ring. But he takes
the ship much closer to that reefed shore than necessary. He is evidently compelled to take an extreme risk in payment for his experience. "It was now a matter of conscience to shave the land as close as
possible ... perhaps he [Leggatt] was able to understand why, on my
conscience, it had to be thus close—no less." Before they separate he
gives Leggatt three pieces of gold and forces his hat on him, to protect
him from the tropic sun. And this act of "sudden pity for his mere
flesh" saves the ship. At the critical moment when the captain must
know whether the ship is moving, in that darkness as of the gateway of
Erebus, he sees his hat, a saving mark, floating on the water. Now he
can give the order to shift the helm; the ship at last moves ahead and
is saved. The final sentence refers to Leggatt: "the secret sharer of my
cabin and of my thoughts, as though he were my second self, had
lowered himself into the water to take his punishment: a free man, a
proud swimmer striking out for a new destiny." Leggatt is perhaps a
free man in several senses, but not least in the sense that he has escaped
the narrator's symbolizing projection. He has indeed become "mere
flesh," is no longer a "double." And the hat floating on the black water
now defines a necessary separateness.

"The Secret Sharer" is at once so closeknit in texture and so large in suggestion as to discourage interpretation. We know that in Jungian psychology a hat, in dreams, represents the personality, which can be transferred symbolically to another. But what are we to make of this hat floating on the night sea—that a wished transference of personality has luckily failed? In psychological terms the positive end of the introspective experience is incorporation not separation and split. But such an end would have required Leggatt to remain on board indefinitely, an absurdity in dramatic if not psychological[25] terms. The truer significance of the ending would seem to lie in a desperate hope that both sides of the self might live on and go free, neither one destroyed. In Jungian terms, again, integration of personality cannot occur until the unconscious has been known, trafficked with, and in some sense liberated. And we do feel this to be the general burden of the story, whatever the logic or illogic of the ending. The outlaw has had his innings, yet the captain has emerged a stronger man.

In any event, general deductions are more rewarding than dogmatic paraphrase. What can we say in very general terms? First, I think, that the story reflects insecurity and a consequent compulsion to test the self; or, a willingness to engage in the "heroism of self-analysis." In broad terms "The Secret Sharer" concerns the classic night journey and willed descent into the unconscious. But even broader terms may be as true: that Conrad apparently detected in himself a division (possibly damaging, possibly saving) into a respectable traditional rational seaman-self and a more interior outlaw-self that repudiated law and tradition; and again, a division into a seaman-self operating from "unconscious alertness" and an introspective, brooding-self of solitary off-duty hours. In *Dejection: An Ode* Coleridge would doubtless have liked to prove that the introspective "abstruse researches" had not crippled his faculty for feeling. But he couldn't. Does not the positive ending of "The Secret Sharer" seek to prove that the self-analytic, introspective bent (reflected on every page of the story itself) has *not* crippled the seaman and active human being? The great danger of introspection is neurotic immobilization, and this is still another area "The Secret Sharer" touches upon. But Conrad deals with it more directly in *The Shadow Line*.

It might be objected that such an interpretation pays scant attention to the "work of art." On the contrary, the art of "The Secret Sharer" consists in its having conveyed so much human material so briefly and with such absolute authenticity. Its triumph is to have made one uninterrupted human relationship and story render so much: the suspenseful and[26] sympathetic plight of Leggatt, the insecure narrator's resolution of his conflict, the deep human communion between the two men, the profound human experience (incorporating all the preceding) of the introspective night journey. We can say after the fact that a story attempting so much would be likely to split apart into its several themes. What holds it together? Partly, I think, a rigid economy and willed art of omission. The narrator, aside from his insistence that Leggatt is his "double," almost never adopts the language of psychological abstraction. He wisely makes no attempt to convey the hysterical immediacy of near-insanity (as Marlow in "Heart of Darkness" does); he avoids, as wisely, reporting the conversations of the two men at length. But most of all the story is saved and held by the narrator's grave, quiet, brooding voice, by the meditative seriousness of his tones. That voice commits us, from the beginning, to the interior resonance of the story. The point of view is not, as it happens, Conrad's usual one when employing the first person. His normal manner is to employ a retrospective first person, free to move where he wishes in time, and therefore free to foreshadow his conclusion. "The Secret Sharer," which carries us consecutively from the beginning of the experience to its end, is Conrad's most successful experiment by far with the method of nonretrospective first-person narration. The nominal narrative past is, actually, a harrowing present which the reader too must explore and survive.

(We may note, parenthetically, the way in which Conrad associates a famous crime with his first voyage as a captain—two crimes to be exact —and from the association derives this most subjective of his stories. And the story of the *Cutty Sark* suggests one of the reasons why *Lord Jim* and "The Secret Sharer"—in their marginal crimes, sympathetic identifications, and introspective concerns—belong to the same fictional and moral worlds.

The incidents on which the two stories were based—the abandonment of the *Jeddah*, the killing of a rebellious member of the crew on the famous *Cutty Sark*—both occurred in the summer of 1880. The chapter "A Hell Ship Voyage" in[27] Basil Lubbock's *The Log of the "Cutty Sark"*[11] provides certain details on the prototype of Leggatt, a "bucko mate" named Sidney Smith. He had vented his spite on three Negroes and especially on the incapable John Francis. When Francis refused to obey an order and the mate rushed upon him, the Negro raised a capstan bar. Smith wrested it away and struck the Negro with it, who on the third day afterward died. The mate persuaded "his kindhearted captain" to let him escape, and at Anjer he was passed secretly to the American ship *Colorado*. Apparently only the crew of the *Cutty Sark*, though disliking both Francis and the mate, wanted to see justice done. The near-mutiny on board the *Narcissus* shows this pattern. Some years later Smith was apprehended, tried for murder on the high seas, and sentenced to seven years' hard labor.

---

11 Boston, 1924.

Conrad's use of this material in "The Secret Sharer" and elsewhere suggests how an imagination both moral and sympathetic transforms a raw reality:

1. The character of Leggatt is made less brutal than that of Smith, but his crime has as much or as little justification.

2. The lawless act of sympathy was committed by the captain of the *Cutty Sark*—though he too, like the captain of the *Sephora*, had a fine reputation to uphold. He apparently regretted his act, for on the fourth day after leaving Anjer he committed suicide in a manner that reminds us of Brierly's suicide in *Lord Jim*. He called the helmsman's attention to the course, then jumped overboard. The apparent motive for Brierly's suicide was his sympathetic identification with Jim; though an assessor at the trial, he had wanted Jim to run away. Captain Wallace of the *Cutty Sark* thus enacted in real life one of the essential Conradian dramas: the torment of the conscientious man who has been guilty of a lawless sympathy, and of following an individual ethic in conflict with the "ethic of state."

3. The captain of the *Colorado* received Smith, according to Lubbock, because he was "only too glad to get hold of a manhandler of such reputation." Thus the narrator of "The Secret Sharer" combines both the sympathy of the *Cutty*[28] *Sark's* captain and the formal receiving role of the *Colorado's*. Lubbock's book suggests, incidentally, that life on board the sailing-ships of that time could be at once more brutal and less disciplined than Conrad's novels and autobiographies indicate. At one time, earlier in the voyage, Francis and the mate had fought for fifteen minutes before being stopped by the captain.

4. However inhumane, Smith had "plenty of grit." He emerged from prison with his certificates gone but slowly worked his way up to command of an Atlantic tanker, and died in 1922, at the age of seventy-three. Did Conrad know what happened to Smith after the trial and imprisonment? In any event his sympathy must have been stirred, as it was with Lord Jim, by the spectacle of the man who wanted to go on living. One wonders, too, whether Sidney Smith read "The Secret Sharer" before he died?

The *Cutty Sark's* trials were far from over, and some of them may have suggested other scenes to Conrad. The ship worked its way back to Anjer after the captain's suicide, encountering such difficulties that a seaman given to gloomy prophecies claimed she was bewitched, and would have no luck until the murderous mate was under lock and key —which reminds us of Mr. Burns in *The Shadow Line* and of Singleton in *The Nigger of the "Narcissus."* Some of the crew felt that the prophet himself was "the Jonah at the root of all the trouble." When the *Cutty Sark* reached Singapore on September 18, it was to find the city "already all agog with the *Jeddah* disaster" which lies behind *Lord Jim.*)

According to the Author's Note, *The Shadow Line* concerns "the change from youth, care-free and fervent, to the more self-conscious and more poignant period of maturer life." The story itself speaks at first of the region of "early youth" that must be left behind; two pages later of "the green sickness of late youth." But the ennui described by the narrator in the first two chapters often seems closer to the *démon de midi* experienced by so many men in early middle age: a "rebellious discontent" and "obscure feeling of life being a waste[29] of days"; a "spiritual drowsiness" and "feeling of life-emptiness"; generally, a directionless longing for change. One might refer again to those "inexplicable periods of powerlessness" after an accident and the subsequent stay in a hospital. But I prefer a general but strong subjective impression: *The Shadow Line* is, in part, about the living through and throwing off of an immobilizing neurotic depression. If we are to hazard any guesses at all (looking forward to Conrad's many immobilized heroes and apathetic underlings) we must hazard this one: that he radically feared paralysis of will and spiritual dryness, the "calme plat, grand miroir/ De mon désespoir."[12] How much of this anxiety goes back to remembered periods of fitful apathy and how much reflects contemporary difficulties as a writer (the *stérilité des écrivains nerveux*) is impossible to say. But the preoccupation with immobilization, together with the various explicit statements that action alone can save us, is one of the important Conrad recurrences.

The Shadow Line, while written in part in the pure unpretentious prose of "The Secret Sharer," is distinctly less perfect. It gets underway very slowly and uncertainly. To make the two stories truly analogous we need only cut out the first two chapters of *The Shadow Line*: need only begin with the two untested narrator-captains on board for the first time, communing with themselves. Conrad apparently conceived of *The Shadow Line* as dealing with the passage from ignorant and untested confidence through a major trial to the very different confidence of mature self-command. So conceived the story ought logically to have reflected, in its first pages, a naïve and buoyant confidence. What it really presents is a neurotic immobilization onshore, for which the opportunity of a first command is expected to provide a cure. But the dead calm of the Gulf of Siam simply mirrors in intensified form the same "moral dissolution" to be lived through, faced out, survived. The narrator comes closer to the phase he is leaving, much closer to

_____
12 These lines from Baudelaire furnish the epigraph to *The Shadow Line* and an important clue to its meaning.

the narrator of "The Secret Sharer," and doubtless much closer to Conrad himself, when he speaks of that "strange sense of insecurity in my past. I always suspected that I might be no good." Again I[30] think we are very close to Conrad himself whenever the story makes a distinction between a seaman-self and a self more introspective and vulnerable. "The seaman's instinct alone survived in my moral dissolution." The conclusion is simply that of "The Secret Sharer": we cannot be good seamen, alone with our ships, until we have faced out, recognized, and subdued those selves which interfere with seamanship (i.e., action). We cannot achieve wholesome integration of the personality until we have made the archetypal journey into self.

The night journey (as in "The Secret Sharer") is described in symbolic terms. The narrator-captain relies on panaceas, as the inexperienced do. "My education was far from being finished, though I didn't know it." He assumes that mere movement from land to sea will solve all his troubles (including the fevers of his men), but ship and men are "snared in the river . . . as if in some poisonous trap." Later, the panacea is quinine. But his dead predecessor had sold the quinine and stuffed the bottles with a useless powder. The deranged chief mate attributes their material difficulties and even the strange calms of the Gulf to the malevolent spirit of the captain, buried in its depths. And at the very crisis of the story, immediately before the healing rain falls and the saving wind blows, the narrator-captain momentarily shares his superstitious fancy. Mr. Burns insists that the spirit of the dead, like Coleridge's Polar Spirit, controls their navigation. Is this the narrator's extreme peril of the soul: that he should come to believe these atavistic fantasies? The great experience of the story is not the saving rain and wind but the intense dead calm, the preternatural stillness of the air and preternatural blackness of the critical night, "the closing in of a menace from all sides." Critical night: the facing of a crisis and final saving break through the "creeping paralysis of a hopeless outlook." Like the Ancient Mariner, the narrator must surmount despair as well as apathy. And he too must live with his "sense of guilt," materially attached to his seaman's failure to verify the quinine. The end suggests that one must live with it, the sense of guilt, but also face it out. "A[31] man should stand up to his bad luck, to his mistakes, to his conscience, and all that sort of thing."

The drama of integration in "The Secret Sharer" is classically, and neatly, conveyed through the mechanism of the double. We shall see more than once that Conrad, like Dostoevsky, finds this the best way to dramatize the schisms of the spirit: to objectify in a physical outsider a side of the self we sympathize with yet condemn. In "The Secret Sharer" the process is quite explicit. In *The Shadow Line* it exists as a

subtle and possibly unintended nuance, and the division of the soul is
into three not two. The sick Mr. Burns in his irrational fears, and con-
fined through most of the voyage to his cabin, recalls the primitive
Nigger of the *Narcissus*. He comes on deck only at the blackest moment
of the decisive night; the narrator stumbles over him and momentarily
takes him for the ghost of the dead captain. The rational Ransome,
fearful of his weak heart yet of a saving extrovert temperament, represents an almost opposite force. At the end of the voyage both Mr. Burns
and Ransome leave the ship, and the narrator is alone with it. He no
longer needs either.

Published between the diffuse and often sentimental *Victory* and
the minor, radically imperfect *Arrow of Gold, The Shadow Line* is
Conrad's final important achievement as an artist. It represents his last
and largely successful effort to make a minutely rendered material
world serve symbolic ends: the real and the symbolic in perilous balance, neither toppling or violating the other. And it is the last work
to offer few peripheral entertainments. Once again the narrating voice
is authentic and moving. The unpretentious "spoken" prose is capable
of evoking, richly, the daylight calms and the menacing black of the
night. But the first two chapters are seriously defective, perhaps because
they are so dependent on literal recall: of the material difficulties involved in getting the *Otago* underway, of a period of undefined anxiety.
The irritability of the narrator at last becomes irritating to the reader.

In these chapters the author is groping toward discovery of his
subject. Did he ever wholly discover it? Even the later[32] chapters
suffer from uncertainty. The novel is in no important sense that tribute
to a crew Conrad wanted it in part to be: a record of sailors "worthy
of my undying regard." And the narrator's sense of guilt is not attached, as it was in "The Secret Sharer," to a significant human action.
It is instead a state of being—which may be true enough to life but is
unrewarding for fiction. Uncertainty, too, clouds the crisis, and if there
are many novels weakened because the novelist has too clear a con-
ceptual view of his theme, there are others that suffer because he does
not see that theme clearly enough. Briefly, *The Shadow Line* professes
to deal with a physical experience so trying that it tempts the narrator
to share Mr. Burns's paranoid unreason;[13] or, again, to deal with the
passage from youth to maturity. But at its best the novel dramatizes
rather the experience of immobilizing depression. Such a subject is
humanly important, for all the dangers Matthew Arnold saw in it. But

---

13 Various readers have detected resemblances to *The Ancient Mariner*. The
climax should be compared with that of Yvor Winters' great and little-known
short story "The Brink of Darkness," available in Alan Swallow's anthology of
psychological fiction, *Anchor in the Sea*.

perhaps only a rich environing fantasy, as in Kafka, or a frame of environing action, as here with a sea voyage, can save it for fiction.[14] [33]

14 We can understand Conrad's exasperation because some readers took *The Shadow Line* to be a story of the supernatural, or because Sidney Colvin hesitated to review it because he was unacquainted with the Gulf of Siam. Between the two positions a reader might argue this one: If *The Shadow Line* is faithfully based on an actual voyage delayed by sickness and by unusual calms on the Gulf of Siam, *why should it be regarded as being about anything more than that?* The answer is given by the narrator's tone of voice, and by his insistent preoccupation with his own states of mind.

LEGATE OF THE IDEAL*
Daniel Curley

The role of Leggatt in "The Secret Sharer" is commonly agreed to be that of double or second self to the captain. With this there seems little possibility of disagreement. Not so readily acceptable, however, is the almost equally widespread opinion that the self represented must be the captain's lower, darker, more evil self—that Leggatt is, in Guerard's words, "criminally impulsive."

It is quite true, as Guerard goes on to say, that ". . . every great work of art operates on multiple levels of meaning and suasion . . . and . . . may have something particular to say to every new reader."[1] But it is also true that a work of art cannot be made to say everything. In "The Secret Sharer" three sorts of evidence seem specifically to exclude the interpretation of Leggatt as "criminally impulsive." First is Conrad's own statement; second is the pattern of changes Conrad made in adapting his material from the actual voyage of the *Cutty Sark;* third is the evidence of the story itself.

In a letter to John Galsworthy, dated Monday, 1913, Conrad says: "Dearest Jack . . . I can't tell you what pleasure you have given me by what you say of the 'Secret Sharer,'—and especially the swimmer. I haven't seen many notices,—three or four in all; but in one of them he is called a murderous ruffian,—or something of the sort. Who are those fellows who write in the Press? Where do they come from? I was simply knocked over,—for indeed I meant him to be what you have at once seen he was. And as you have seen, I feel altogether comforted and rewarded for the trouble he has given me in the doing of him, for it wasn't an easy task. It was extremely difficult to keep him true to type, first as modified to some extent by the sea life and further as affected by the situation."[2]

In order to understand this completely, we would need to have the Galsworthy letter Conrad is agreeing with, but even without the letter we can be sure that Conrad intended above all else that Leggatt should

---

* This is the first publication of Mr. Curley's article. [Ed.]

[1] Albert J. Guerard, Introduction to the Signet edition of *The Heart of Darkness and The Secret Sharer* (New York, 1950), pp. 8–9.

[2] G. Jean-Aubry, *Joseph Conrad: Life and Letters* (New York, 1927), I, 143.

not be a murderous ruffian. Beyond that it seems safe to accept the evidence of the story itself for an indication of the type to which Conrad intended Leggatt to be true; that is, he is presented as the son of a parson with all that implies. In addition, he is a graduate of the training ship *Conway*. A gentleman, son of a gentleman, educated and trained to the best traditions of the sea, he is as far as possible from being a murderous ruffian, although he is involved in a violent death. Even the captain of the *Sephora*, who may be considered a hostile witness, says, "He looked very smart, very gentlemanly, and all that."

It is true that authors are not always to be trusted in their comments on their own work. In this case Conrad might have felt that the story would sooner or later speak for itself and that solidarity in friendship was more important than correcting a misinterpretation of the text. Therefore, if there were no more solid evidence than the letter, Conrad's own attitude might be discounted—although the letter does seem to go far beyond the needs of friendship and to be indeed the bitter cry of a baffled author.

The same objection of inconclusiveness can also be raised to Conrad's reference to the story in the Preface to *The Shorter Tales* some ten years later. "The second story deals with what may be called the '*esprit de corps*,' the deep fellowship of two young seamen meeting for the first time."[3] But here again the author, although not indicating the exact nature of the fellowship, seems specifically to exclude the possibility that it is a fellowship of violence or evil.

The second sort of evidence can also be interpreted in different ways. This evidence relates to the changes Conrad made in converting the historical material of the *Cutty Sark* into the fictional material of "The Secret Sharer." The most likely objection to a study of these changes is that Conrad was simply rearranging things to make a better story. However, it can be demonstrated that Conrad in shaping his material made changes of a consistent pattern intended to produce not just any better story but a very specific better story—a story, furthermore, that can properly be understood only in terms of the answer to a very specific question: Why does the hellion mate of the *Cutty Sark* become the gentleman of the *Sephora*, a man who is by birth, education, and his own acts to be known as "one of us"?

Concerning the actual mate of the *Cutty Sark* we know little, and even that little is contradictory. The evidence at his trial lays stress on his "good character" and "humane disposition";[4] whereas, Basil Lubbock's account, drawn from the log of the *Cutty Sark* itself, presents

---

3 Joseph Conrad, Preface to *The Shorter Tales of Joseph Conrad* (New York, 1924), p. xi.

4 *Times*, August 4, 1882, p. 4, col. f.

him as a regular bucko mate in the best Yankee tradition.[5] Human nature and the courts being what they are, perhaps we should give less weight to the character testimony of defense witnesses than to the account of a journalist who might at worst tend to heighten the dramatic elements of his material. In neither case, however, is there the least suggestion that the mate is a gentleman or in the least bit educated beyond the requirements of his position. He is certainly a violent and hard-bitten man in both versions. He is, in fact, exactly the man to be referred to as a "murderous ruffian" and "criminally impulsive," but he is not Leggatt.

In shaping this material to the end he desired, Conrad was faced with two really difficult problems. He had to find a way of separating his protagonist's legal and moral responsibilities, and he had to invent for Leggatt an action that would be a crime in form but not a crime in fact.

The simplest way to adapt the story of the *Cutty Sark* would have been to transfer the entire action to the new captain's ship. As a new captain he was totally unfamiliar with his officers. The mate with the terrible whiskers could easily have been the bucko mate. Events would then take their course. A man would be killed, and the captain would have to act in a morally responsible manner. But what would be the captain's responsibility in this case?

Taking into consideration Conrad's rigid concept of sea morality, there can be little doubt that he would have felt the captain to be under the same kind of obligation as Captain Vere in *Billy Budd* to honor the conditions under which he held command of his ship and to let the law take its course. This is, in fact, the very pattern followed by the captain of the *Sephora,* and he is held in contempt by the narrator and depicted as a man afraid to act. On the other hand, the actual captain of the *Cutty Sark* did act: he helped the mate escape but with fatal consequences to himself.

If, then, these two captains can be taken to represent the possibilities of the situation, there is no way in which Conrad could guide his young man safely through a trial to a new destiny. On the one hand, he would have to refuse responsibility like the captain of the *Sephora* and live on "densely distressed," or, on the other hand, he would have to accept responsibility like the captain of the *Cutty Sark* and forfeit his career and his very life. The problem is actually insoluble. The captain must slight his legal responsibility to the ship or his moral responsibility to his subordinate. This may be a decision that an estab-

---

[5] Basil Lubbock, *The Log of the "Cutty Sark"* (Glasgow, 1960), p. 153 *et passim* [p. 46 above].

lished man—Captain Vere—can make, but it is not the kind of decision to be demanded of a young man in an initiation-ritual story.

Clearly, therefore, it would not do to give the young captain command of a ship like the *Cutty Sark;* but the story of the *Cutty Sark* itself suggests another possibility, and that is to have the mate of the *Cutty Sark* escape to the young captain's ship. Now the captain is freed from any legal responsibility for the death and can apply himself solely to the moral aspects of the affair.

Even as the story is finally constituted, the young captain's problem is not an easy one. It takes its most obvious form in regard to his handling the ship. He must bring the ship close enough to shore to allow Leggatt to escape safely, and he must stay far enough away from shore to keep from wrecking the ship. He could stay so far from shore that the ship was absolutely safe and leave Leggatt to drown—an obvious betrayal of Leggatt and of himself because Leggatt is, of course, himself—or he could give Leggatt absolute safety and wreck the ship—a betrayal of the crew, the owners, and himself because as he himself says, "... all my future, the only future for which I was fit, would perhaps go irretrievably to pieces in any mishap to my first command." But in the end he proves himself able to judge nicely in balancing against each other the dual risks of responsibility to self and responsibility to society, and he has good luck. Leggatt was as good a judge, but his luck was bad.

For both Leggatt and the captain, this concept of luck enters at the crucial moment and plays a decisive role. In one case the luck is bad and in the other it is good. The wave and the hat are the marks of the luck. They are verses from "the chapter of accidents which counts for so much in the book of success." There is a clear implication that the captain's good luck is the indirect result of his own spontaneous sympathy for Leggatt in giving him the hat, but there is no suggestion that good luck of necessity follows right action. In fact, Leggatt's case clearly shows the contrary; so it is proper only to say that right action may result in a happy outcome. However, more important than the outcome is the knowledge of one's own right action and the strength such knowledge gives for facing the outcome, whatever it may be. Ultimately it can be said that the captain and Leggatt do not represent two possibilities of character but two possibilities of outcome, both of which are met with pride and confidence.

This, then, is the meaning of the changes in the mate's character. Each change is made to increase the identification between him and the captain and to establish unmistakably the nature of that "deep fellowship" and that "*esprit de corps*" of which Conrad speaks in the Preface already quoted. No such changes would have been necessary, however, if Conrad had intended the fellowship to be based on a secret bond of criminal impulsiveness. The bucko mate of the *Cutty Sark*, just as he was, would have served admirably for this purpose; but instead of using the mate as he was, Conrad carefully removed from his character all the elements that could have supported the interpretation Guerard and others have forced on the story. The result of the changes is precisely that it is not the mate of the *Cutty Sark* but Leggatt that the captain recognizes as an extension of himself, and it is not merely a possible extension but an actual extension. The very closeness of the identification indicates that Conrad was after something other than a recognition of possibility, because he proceeds quite differently when he is presenting a character who is being led to penetrate the darkness of his own heart. A case in point is that of Captain Brierly in *Lord Jim,* who apparently has nothing whatever in common with the disastrous Jim but who, because of an insight into possibility, is driven to commit suicide in a manner strikingly reminiscent of the suicide of the captain of the *Cutty Sark.*

In defining the situation within which his young captain must act, Conrad has eliminated the possibility of any automatically imposed correct solution. The captain must create out of the tradition of his life and profession an individual moral solution to meet the totally unexpected situation, and he must do it in the face of the counter moral pressure of his own crew and of the captain of the *Sephora*. It would be easy for him to act in a way that would win him social approval, to make a choice that would be universally acknowledged moral, but it requires a fully developed moral being to make a choice that he alone knows to be moral and that everyone else believes to be criminal or mad.

These observations apply equally to Leggatt. His steadiness throughout the story is the result of the moral strength he has already won by the choice he has already made, and the circumstances of Leggatt's choice involve the second major change in the *Cutty Sark* material. The change that has made the mate into Leggatt has also made the original form of death impossible to his new character. The story demands, however, that there still be something which looks like a murder; that Leggatt be made to appear to do something his character will not allow.

It must not be supposed that the choice Leggatt makes is the choice of violence; for his choice, like the captain's, is a choice of responsibility. Further, it is a choice made under trying circumstances when the natural source of responsibility, in the captain of the *Sephora,* has totally failed. Leggatt is in effect in command of the ship, thereby underlining Conrad's parallel of two morally responsible individuals. The death is merely a by-product of the choice and affects neither its correctness nor its effectiveness: "It was all very simple. The same strung-up force which had given twenty-four men a chance, at least, for their lives, had, in a sort of recoil, crushed an unworthy mutinous existence." Within the story itself Leggatt twice renounces violence as a way out. He refuses to attempt to break out of his cabin on the *Sephora*: "...I did not mean to get into a confounded scrimmage. Somebody else might have got killed—for I would not have broken out only to get chucked back, and I did not want any more of that work." Later he says, "Do you see me being hauled back, stark naked, off one of these little islands by the scruff of the neck and fighting like a wild beast? Somebody would have got killed for certain, and I did not want any of that."

If there is anybody in the story who recognizes violence as a possibility in himself it is Leggatt, not the captain; but Leggatt specifically renounces violence when only his personal freedom or his life is at stake. He labels it "fighting like a wild beast," and in the second instance the omission of *more* seems to indicate that he makes a clear distinction between what happened when he saved the ship and what might happen in a struggle to save himself. He has clearly stated his choice: "I meant to swim until I sank." He has clearly justified the captain's repeated comment, "He was sane."

Leggatt's resolutions are not those of a "criminally impulsive" man, nor do they fit with the one action that is charged against him. Again it is desirable to look at the *Cutty Sark* material to see the original action out of which Leggatt's action grew. In both the version in the *Times* and the version in Lubbock, the sailor is brained with a capstan bar, a device rather more potent than a baseball bat. It really makes little difference whether the sailor got first cracks or not, the mate's blow was not the act of a humane and gentle man, and the mate did not have the excuse of being under undue strain, for the maneuver was a simple change of tack in a "nice wholesail breeze."[6]

In "The Secret Sharer" the death takes place under quite different circumstances, and the scene purely from a dramatic point of view is a great improvement with its terrific weather, its sailor half crazed with funk, and its awful sea. But the total effect of the scene is to commit Leggatt to an action that he cannot control and that the reader cannot easily evaluate. Some of the difficulties of evaluation are suggested by the conduct of the judge who tried the much more clear-cut case of the mate of the *Cutty Sark*. In the first place, the judge allowed the reduction of the charge from murder to manslaughter. He also gave full weight to testimony of good character and to the fact that the mate had an important maneuver to perform and needed to assert his authority.[7]

---

6 Lubbock, p. 152 [p. 45 above].
7 *Times*.

He accepted all these points in arriving at a sentence, for indeed there can be no standard by which they are not relevant.

If we consider, then, the infinitely greater complexity of Leggatt's case and the fact that Leggatt's skill and courage had just succeeded in setting the sail that saved the ship, it is small wonder that the young captain concluded that "it was all very simple." But in a sense Conrad has made it even simpler than that, because Leggatt in asserting his authority had no intention of harming the man. He just wanted him out of the way, so he felled him like an ox. Certainly under the circumstances the action was not only not wrong but actually the correct thing to do and of no more significance than throwing a glass of water in the face of a screaming child. However, when the sailor came at him again, Leggatt was forced to adopt stronger measures and began to throttle him into submission. When the wave broke over the ship, Leggatt's reflex led him to hold fast to anything. Unfortunately he happened to have hold of a man's throat. Here, then, is the murder in form that is not a murder in fact. Leggatt's own remark, "It's clear I meant business," is not at all an expression of guilt, because the business that he meant was far from the business that resulted.

By this adaptation of the *Cutty Sark* material Conrad has removed the death from the area of the young captain's legal responsibility, and he has made Leggatt the victim of circumstances. He has so contrived things that the captain's decision must be made in purely moral terms, and he has so changed the character of the mate that Leggatt cannot be considered a "murderous ruffian" but must on the contrary be held to be what the story itself clearly suggests him to be: the ideal conception of himself that the captain has set up for himself secretly.

This signpost in the story represents the third kind of evidence about Leggatt and points the way to an interpretation that bars any conception of Leggatt as lower nature. Indeed, so clear is the sign that one would feel officious in calling attention to it if it had not been so persistently ignored by commentators on the story.

The basic error, however, is not in equating Leggatt with the captain's instinctive self but in equating *instinctive* with *evil*. Conrad himself explicitly includes instinctive action among the necessary virtues of the ideal seaman: "There are to a seaman certain words, gestures, that should in given conditions come as naturally, as instinctively as the winking of a menaced eye. A certain order should spring on to his lips without thinking; a certain sign should get itself made, so to speak, without reflection." The captain's newness in command has resulted in a self-consciousness that cripples his power of instinctive action. Leggatt is a manifestation of this instinctive nature, isolated and useless in the cabin, and it is only when Leggatt slips back into the sea that the instinctive nature of the captain slips into its proper place as part of an integrated personality. At that point the captain has, like Leggatt, passed his test and gained a right to the confidence Leggatt has displayed throughout the story.

The story is clearly an initiation-ritual story. The new captain, "untried as yet by a position of the fullest responsibility," is "at the starting point of a long journey," which is to be the "appointed task" of his existence. The story must undertake to provide him with a test of his fitness to enter upon this existence, and it must also provide him with a standard by which he can measure his success in coping with his test. That he passes his test is unequivocally indicated at the end of the story, but the standard by which he is to be judged is entirely unstated if Leggatt is assumed to represent anything other than an ideal conception.

The nature of the test has already been considered in detail. It is a unique test that cannot be passed by any except a fully aware moral being. Further, the test is so devised as to take place before no witnesses or, to be more exact, "with only the sky and sea for spectators and for judges." Material help—the tug—disappears back into the land, and spiritual help—the pagoda—is left behind. The only standard by which the captain can now be judged is an entirely personal one, his own, and it is his own as made manifest in Leggatt. His success in meeting the challenge is represented in its most obvious form when he is told that he has understood "from first to last."

What the captain has understood is, of course, Leggatt's position, but he has done a good deal more than understand in a passive way. He has demonstrated his understanding by a pattern of conduct which in its quick action and stubborn self-control closely parallels Leggatt's own conduct and which can only spring, as is said of Leggatt, from "that something unyielding in his character which was carrying him through so finely." Specifically, the captain is carried through by that ideal conception of himself made manifest in Leggatt, who is "one of us" by birth and training and by his own acts. Leggatt's qualification for this role, in addition to his background, is precisely his confidence as a man who knows he has already passed his test. From the moment he appears, it is this confidence that most impresses the young captain. This is how he hopes he can act when his own time comes, and it is against this that we can measure his success and the validity of his claim to be considered a free man and a proud swimmer.

❖ ❖

CONRAD'S TWO STORIES OF INITIATION*
Carl Benson

It has become fashionable in some circles to say that Conrad's prefaces and autobiographical utterances are to some extent over-simplifications and therefore misleading. And, of course, brief essayistic statements of overtly moral intent cannot adequately suggest the inter-play of emotional struggles, ideals, and human depravity so richly and variously presented in the conflicts of Conrad's fictional world. Indeed, there may lurk beneath the conscious artifice of fiction subconscious psychic depths, hinted at in such symbols as may reasonably be ex-ploited in terms of Jungian archetypes. I do not for a moment doubt the validity and plausibility of such approaches to Conrad.

Here, however, I am concerned with the conscious intent of Con-rad, in so far as it may be discovered or inferred, in the writing of his twin stories of initiation into maturity and its demands—"The Secret Sharer" and The Shadow Line. It is not, I think, remarkable that a reader who turns to the short novel after the long story should ask: For what reason, or reasons, did Conrad decide to handle the same problem (initiation), same ship, same crew, same captain twice? Is not The Shadow Line in a sense a peculiarly significant rewriting, done because Conrad realized that the initiation of the captain of "The Secret Sharer" was humanly abortive—and this despite the last phrase, more applicable to the captain than to Leggatt, about "a free man, striking out for a new destiny"? Or to put it another way, is it not possible to view the initiation of The Shadow Line as the communal counterpart to that of "The Secret Sharer"? The latter, written five years earlier,[1] has as its central moral problem the conquering of the

---

* Reprinted with permission of the author and the Modern Language Association from PMLA, LXIX (March 1954), 46–56.

[1] In Nov. 1909. See G. Jean-Aubry, Joseph Conrad: Life and Letters (New York, 1927, II, 5. There is some doubt about just when Conrad completed The Shadow Line. In one letter he says, "I was writing that thing in Dec., 1914, and Jan. to March, 1915" ibid., p. 182). In another letter he says he finished it in Jan. 1915 (p. 193). But he dates the last page of the MS. (which the committee in charge of rare books in Yale Univ. Library has kindly permitted me to see in microfilm) "Dec. 15, 1915." Conrad's writing of the month and the year is quite legible, though the "15" is obscure. This may be the date on which he completed final revisions, in plenty of time for first publication in The English Review, Sept. 1916 to March 1917.

feeling of personal insufficiency and the fears attendant upon insecurity within the self of the captain. *The Shadow Line,* on the other hand, although it also shows the commanding officer overcoming his secret fear of being "no good," has as its moral core the redemption of the captain through his realization that no man, not even one upon whom dynastic rule has been conferred, is truly *self*-sustaining, that the[46] lot of the one is ineluctably involved with that of the many. This is the lesson the young captain of *The Shadow Line* has to learn, and when he has learned it he is no longer young. In other words, whereas the captain of "The Secret Sharer" has ended "striking out for a new destiny," the captain of *The Shadow Line* has reached the destination of the common human lot. To put it thus baldly may seem to be indulging in sentimental commonplace, but Conrad's grasp of moral reality is rarely sentimental though, abstracted thus, it may appear commonplace. Moreover, such a summary statement is not fair to Conrad, for he is at great pains to document the captain's initiation with specific dramatic incidents so contrived as to put increasing stress on the captain.

In any event, an appraisal of the two stories, alike in basic situation, but very different in the posing and the answering of central moral questions, may have some literary significance, since by means of such an appraisal we come to terms with Conrad's attitude towards his chief fictional problems.[2]

In a sense the true action of both stories opens with a presentation of the psychic state of the captain as he assumes his first command. (I shall return to the significance of the difference in the openings.) At the outset the two rejoice, and for the same reasons, at having chosen the life of the sea. Pacing the deck of his vessel (before the coming of Leggatt) the captain of "The Secret Sharer" says, "suddenly I rejoiced in the great security of the sea as compared with the unrest of the land,

---

[2] It seems to me that what I shall say of the attitude and of the central problems constitutes an elaborate footnote supporting the Conrad criticism of Robert Penn Warren and Morton D. Zabel. Warren says, Introd. to the 1951 Modern Library edition of *Nostromo,* "The characteristic story for Conrad becomes the relation of man to the human communion" (p. xvii), and suggests, "The central process that engaged Conrad is the process of the earned redemption" (p. xix). He says of *The Shadow Line* specifically, "It is through the realization of this community that man cures himself of 'that feeling of life emptiness' which has afflicted the young hero of *The Shadow Line* before he came to his great test" (p. xvii). Zabel, Introd. to the New Directions *Under Western Eyes,* quotes Conrad on "unavoidable solidarity . . . the solidarity in mysterious origin, in toil, in joy, in hope, in uncertain fate, which binds men to each other and all mankind to the visible earth," and then says of Conrad, "The solidarity he so insistently invoked, exemplified as much by his personal courage as by the art he practised against appalling obstacles of doubt and insecurity, offered little but this grim consolation to his skepticism; but this much it did offer, and on that principle of trust and sincerity he staked his faith" (pp. xxxiv–xxxv).

in my choice of that untempted life presenting no disquieting problems, invested with an elementary moral beauty by the absolute
straightforwardness of its appeal and by the singleness of its purpose"
(p. 6).[3] As the captain of *The Shadow Line* awaits the coming of the
first mate, he stares at himself[47] in the mirror, feeling little, he says,
except "some sympathy for this latest representative of what for all
intents and purposes was a dynasty; continuous not in blood indeed,
but in its experience, in its training, in its conception of duty, and in
the blessed simplicity of its traditional point of view on life" (p. 53).

In both stories Conrad insists at the beginning on the isolation inherent in command. The sailors of "The Secret Sharer" are of limited
moral significance: "They had simply to be equal to their tasks; but I
wondered how far I should turn out faithful to that ideal conception of
one's own personality every man sets up for himself secretly" (p. 5).
And the captain of *The Shadow Line:* "In that community I stood
like a king in his country, in a class all by myself. I mean an hereditary
king, not a mere elected head of a state. I was brought there to rule by
an agency as remote from the people and as inscrutable almost to them
as the Grace of God" (p. 62).

Thus the captain in both instances begins with a black-white oversimplification of the duties inherent in moral being. Perhaps it is an
oversimplification justified in terms of these stories by the given facts:
since it is a first command, the captain, inexperienced in his job, may
reasonably have thought he saw in his previous commanding officers
manifestations of such aloof responsibility. But the point is that at the
end of "The Secret Sharer" the captain is little nearer to a realization
of his communal duties than he was at the outset.[4] It is only in a
limited, egocentric way that he has measured up to the ideal image he
"has set up for himself secretly." He has conquered his feeling of insecurity, and he has demonstrated to the crew that he is firmly in command of the vessel. Certainly the establishment of authority is necessary. But it should be said, too, that (from the point of view of the

---

[3] Page references throughout are to the 1926 Canterbury edition of the
Complete Works. "The Secret Sharer" is in *'Twixt Land and Sea* (pp. 91–143).
[But references to "The Secret Sharer" have been regularized to the present
volume. Ed.]

[4] At the end of the story the captain rejoices: "And I was *alone* with her.
Nothing! no one in the world should stand now between us, throwing a shadow
on the way of silent knowledge and mute affection, the perfect communion of a
seaman with his first command" (my italics). To anticipate, I do not feel that
the captain of *The Shadow Line* could have said "alone" in such a context at
the end of his voyage, though he might have at the beginning. And I shall argue
that "material conditions" throw such shadows that for the Conrad of *The Shadow
Line* the concept of "perfect communion" would seem immature and illusionary.

crew) he has demonstrated the power of authority in a needlessly fear-inspiring way, by taking the ship far too close to the rocky coast.

For it cannot be said that Leggatt needed such a risk; he can swim two miles, as we have already been told. For a time the captain seems to forget this: "It was now a matter of conscience to shave the land as close as possible—for now he must go overboard whenever the ship was put in[48] stays" (p. 33). But the true reason for the dangerous course is insisted on when the captain suggests that Leggatt would be able "to understand why, on my conscience, it had to be thus close—no less." Why? I am not sure that an easy answer is possible, but I think what Conrad intends us to understand, here and through-out the story, is that Leggatt is the captain's double, his other self, not, as Guerard suggests,[5] the Captain's lower, potentially criminal self (whose nature must be lived through in order to be lived down), but rather his opposite, a being of outwardly somewhat similar ap-pearance, but inwardly very different, for Leggatt possesses the traits the captain most lacks. For example, he has demonstrated his bravery under intense pressure by setting the sail that saved the *Sephora* when his captain was incapacitated by funk. Again, in the face of fear transformed into mutinous insubordination on the part of a worthless seaman, he has throttled, though unintentionally, the guilty man. So the vessel has to be taken very close to the doom of the rocks in order for the captain to prove to himself that he has conquered his fear and has measured up to the model of assured courage he has set for himself. Leggatt will understand, for, confronted by his own terrible test, he has behaved bravely and has emerged so calmly confident of the justness of his motives (which Conrad in other stories would question sharply) that he is willing to bear in the eyes of society the "brand of Cain." It is, of course, the stupidly conscientious captain of the *Sephora* and not our captain (or Conrad) who regards the accidental killing of a mutinous sailor as murder.[6]

5 Albert Guerard, Jr., *Joseph Conrad* (New York, 1947), pp. 37 ff., and Introd. to the Signet edition of *Heart of Darkness* and *The Secret Sharer*, pp. 8-9. In the latter Guerard says, "The two men [Marlow and the narrator of "The Secret Sharer"] ... must recognize their own potential criminality and test their own resources, *must travel through Kurtz and Leggatt*, before they will be capable of manhood ... manhood and 'moral survival.' The two novels alike exploit the ancient myth or archetypal experience of the 'night journey,' of a provisional descent into the primitive and unconscious sources of being" (p. 9). I dislike to find myself in disagreement with so able and penetrating a critic of Conrad as Guerard, and I feel that he has made an acceptable and rewarding reading of *Heart of Darkness*, but the reading does not seem to me applicable to "The Secret Sharer." As Guerard indicates, "The Secret Sharer" is a troublesome story, and "various interpretations are possible" (*Joseph Conrad*, p. 40 n.).

6 See the letter to Galsworthy, *Life and Letters*, II, 143-144: "I can't tell you

"The Secret Sharer," in short, is not a story of full initiation into mature responsibilities; it is the beginning of the initiation, but it does not[49] portray, as does the later novel, the passage from egocentric youth to human solidarity. And this is precisely the intent of *The Shadow Line*. In it we see immediately the difference in communal orientation. Instead of beginning abruptly with the assumption of the new command, it opens with the captain-narrator giving up his job as first mate on a steamship, offering no better reason for the action, inexplicable even to himself, than to say that he was in that treacherous period between youth and maturity he calls "the shadow line." But Conrad has given to this character a capacity for a great social awareness. Although he is youthfully determined to have his own way, contemptuous of older heads, and harsh in his estimates of others,[7] he is troubled by his belief that his action will appear foolish to others; and it is because he is so troubled that he is quick to resent adverse judgment.

The means of achieving the end of the story—of moving the young captain from his irresponsibility at the opening to his tolerant respect for others at the end—is to subject the captain to a prolonged test. The novel is formed around the elaboration of the terms of the test and the responses of the captain. His responses are cumulative in effect, and they finally add up to a hard-won compassion.

The terms of the test need more delineation. I have already indicated the contempt with which the narrator treats Captain Giles, the old "initiated" one, who also seems to serve as a father image; and I have called attention to the hero's belief in the "blessed simplicity" of the life of the sea and his vision of himself as one in a dynastic line. As if to accentuate the rigors of the tests to come later, Conrad has stressed the dream-like unreality that surrounds the young captain before he takes over his new ship. For example, the obtaining of the command was "beyond my imaginings, outside all reasonable expectations." The captain was possessed by a "feeling

---

what pleasure you have given me by what you say of the 'Secret Sharer,'—and especially the swimmer. I haven't seen many notices—three or four in all; but in one of them he is called a murderous ruffian,—or something of the sort. Who are those fellows who write in the Press? Where do they come from?" I have not been able to find the Galsworthy letter to which this is a reply.

7 Of the Steward of the Officers' Home in Singapore, e.g., he says, "He doesn't seem very fit to live" (p. 39). There is an interesting parallel in "The Secret Sharer," where Leggatt speaks of the man he killed as one of the "miserable devils that have no business to live at all" (p. 9). The parallel phrasing actually lights up the difference between the two stories, for in *The Shadow Line* Captain Giles, who is the model of compassionate maturity against whom the captain measures himself, replies, "As to that, it may be said of a good many," and by the end of the story the young captain possesses a similar tolerance.

of wonder—as if I had been specially destined for that ship I did not know, by some power higher than the prosaic agencies of the commercial world" (p. 36). At one point he says, "I was very much like people in fairy tales. Nothing ever astonishes them" (p. 40). He is so lost in the dream brought on by the unearned command that he first sees his ship "disengaged from the material conditions of her being. The shore to which she was moored was as if it did[50] not exist" (p. 50). These evasive, somewhat escapist dreams are shattered when the test submits him to an enforced consideration of the power of material conditions.

The first shock the captain receives comes when Burns, his first mate, tells him of the behavior of his predecessor. Dynastic rule should carry with it dynastic obligation and responsibility, but the hero learns that the former captain has been absolutely unfaithful to the trust implied by command and has shamelessly and wantonly betrayed the owners, the ship, and the crew. This knowledge intensifies the captain's loneliness; trustworthiness, he sees, does not necessarily accompany command. "I was oppressed by my lonely responsibilities," he says (p. 75), and he refers to the "endless vigilance of my lonely task" (p. 76).

Convinced that fresh sea air will cure his feverish crew, he has unwisely and against the doctor's advice taken his ship out of its anchorage and into the open sea; but despite this risk, entailing his dependence on the seamen, his feeling of lonely separation has not given way to the companionship of shared dangers. It takes a combination of cumulating and terrible circumstances to divorce him from his idea of the captain as a representative of dynastic rule.

In the first place, the crew continues to be ill. No sooner does the fever leave one man weak and unfit for duty than it descends upon another. Finally only the captain himself and the cook, Ransome, are left untouched. The sea is maddeningly calm, so that, in effect, the captain has only a nominal command, and he curses the island of Koh-ring (which also appears in "The Secret Sharer") for it is the last thing he sees at night, the first thing he sees in the morning. Since both mates are sick, the captain is on duty at all times and restful sleep is impossible. Physical and mechanical troubles are not all the captain must endure; Burns persists in believing that his late commanding officer is in some mysterious and occult way casting a spell on the ship. Though the captain is rational enough to take no stock in this hallucination, it nevertheless affects his courage. Finally the captain discovers that the supply of quinine, upon which he has put his trust, has been misappropriated, probably sold by his predecessor; and he blames first the doctor and then himself for not having made a complete inspection of the supply of drugs:

But, as a matter of fact, it was hardly fair to blame the doctor. The fittings were in order and the medicine chest is an officially arranged affair. There was nothing really to arouse his slightest suspicion. The person I could never forgive was myself. Nothing should ever be taken for granted. The seed of everlasting remorse was sown in my breast.

"I feel that it's all my fault," I exclaimed, "mine and nobody else's." (p. 95)

The sowing of the seed of remorse may be equated with the awakening[51] of the captain's humanity. When he tells the crew of the lack of quinine, they are silent: "I would have held them justified in tearing me limb from limb. The silence which followed upon my words was almost harder to bear than the angriest uproar. . . . They had kept silent simply because they thought they were not called upon to say anything" (p. 96). The sailors who have been before little more than human machines for operating the ship are now viewed as objects worthy the profoundest sympathy; the captain says, "Every time I had to raise my voice it was with a pang of remorse and pity" (p. 98). The hero, now conscious steadily of what he considers his own dereliction, wonders at the lack of complaint among the sailors: "I expected to meet reproachful glances. There were none. The expression of suffering in their eyes was indeed hard enough to bear. But that they couldn't help. For the rest, I ask myself whether it was the temper of their souls or the sympathy of their imagination that made them so wonderful, so worthy of my undying regard" (p. 100).

Accompanying this realization of the patient yet glorious worth of the seamen is the captain's new self-appraisal. In a diary that he keeps during this time of stress, he shows that while the men are spiritually equipped for their duties, though sick, he, though sound, is rendered almost powerless through fear: "What appals me most of all is that I shrink from going on deck to face it. It's due to the ship, it's due to the men who are there on deck—some of them, ready to put out the last remnants of their strength at a word from me. And I am shrinking from it. From the mere vision. My first command. Now I understand that strange sense of insecurity in my past. I always suspected that I might be no good. And here is proof positive, I am shirking it, I am no good" (p. 107).

And now, having sunk to the lowest possible level of self-esteem through perceiving his failure of courage, and having begun the spiritual ascent by the acknowledgement of that cowardice, which must be faced before it is defeated, the captain is prepared (and the story is ready) for the resolution. The resolution is accomplished by the captain's acceptance of his role in the human society, a society forever characterized by evils and weaknesses as well as by ideals. Indeed, in Conrad's world spiritual strength is conditioned by and can grow only from the acknowledgement of the pervasiveness of human frailty and evil. Or, as Conrad has put it in an essay: "We are children of the earth. It may be that the noblest tradition is but the offspring of material conditions, of the hard necessities besetting men's precarious lives. But once it has been born it becomes a spirit. Nothing can extinguish its force then. Clouds of greedy selfishness, the subtle dialectics of revolt and fear, may obscure it for a[52] time, but in very truth it remains an immortal ruler invested with the power of honour and shame."[8]

The spiritual and psychic recovery of the narrator is handled in symbolic terms, the symbolism of baptism. Just as he completes the entry in his diary, Ransome comes to tell him he should be on deck, for a storm is gathering. The hovering poise of the shrouding and almost tangible darkness is masterfully suggested, as is the feeling of tense expectancy. Suddenly the rain falls, as if in recognition of the contrite heart, the confession, and the new life of the captain; and the rain is followed by steady breezes which bring him and his crew to the haven of their kind. It is a haven populated by imperfect beings, by such beings as make ideals which ignore the "material conditions" ultimately impossible; but it is in a world worthy of struggle, a struggle which, because of the inequality of the human materials, must be unceasing.

The last part of the voyage to Singapore is marked by the captain's respect and concerned affection for his crew, by his understanding that they and he are linked in a little world of necessarily joint enterprise. When the captain reaches Singapore, he meets Captain Giles and tells him what he has learned. There is no inclination now to sneer at the stuffiness and seeming obtuseness of Giles. And when Giles hears of his decision to complete his voyage as soon as possible, he understands that the young captain will "stand up to his bad luck, to his mistakes, to his conscience and all that sort of thing," and he tells the captain, "You'll do" (p. 132).

It has been inconvenient to introduce the subject into the preceding summary, but there is in The Shadow Line a figure analogous to Leggatt of "The Secret Sharer." The double in the later work is Ransome, who is employed significantly to emphasize the opposition of a sick heart, or soul, in a sound body and a sound soul in a sick body. During the exigencies of the voyage Ransome manifests a weak heart in physical fact but a strong heart figuratively, whereas with the captain the situation is reversed; and it is Ransome's willingness to give of his strength that chiefly excites the admiration of the captain for his crew, and makes him see what is "due to" the seamen.

---

8 "Well Done" in Notes on Life and Letters, p. 183.

The importance of the character is especially evident at the conclusion of the novel, when, with the dangerous demands of the voyage over, Ransome gives way to the fear he has been fighting and asks to be "sent ashore and paid off" (p. 128), and confesses, "I am in a blue funk about my heart, sir" (p. 133). And it is indicative of the complete victory of the captain's humanity that he can[53] understand and sympathize with this funk (only recently overcome in himself): "I listened to him going up the companion stairs cautiously, step by step, in mortal fear of starting into sudden anger our common enemy it was his hard fate to carry consciously within his faithful breast" (p. 133). In this case it is the captain and not the double who has triumphed unequivocally; and the humanity of the triumph is attested by the sympathy for the failure of Ransome—a failure that has sprung from the "material conditions" the captain has learned to reckon with.[9]

That Conrad may have felt somewhat dissatisfied with the incomplete initiation of "The Secret Sharer" is suggested not only by the composition of *The Shadow Line,* but also by certain facts of his life and writing career. In the first place, the passage of the hero of "The Secret Sharer" from insecurity and fear to a rather simple and unqualified assurance at the end is certainly atypical. One has only to remember the brooding, searching genius that created such powerful and detailed studies of man's struggle to find and define himself in social terms as *Nostromo* and *Under Western Eyes* (so brilliantly discussed by Warren and Zabel) to see that the conditioned victory of *The Shadow Line* is more in keeping with Conrad's mature judgment than is the overly simple, unilateral triumph of "The Secret Sharer." "All a man can betray is his conscience," says Razumov, when he is trying to avoid commitment to his community; but he spends the rest of his life learning that conscience is rooted in, and so defined by, the community, though his recognition comes too late for any except a spiritual atonement. Incidentally, "The Secret Sharer" was written in 1909, in the midst of Conrad's agonized labor on *Under Western Eyes* (1908–10) and may have been written as a relief from that ordeal.

"The Secret Sharer" is atypical in another way, too. It was written very swiftly. Mrs. Conrad singles it out: "I can remember only one story that was completed even before I saw it, typed within the space of a week and posted to the publisher. . . . *The Secret Sharer.* I remember bitterly reproaching my husband for not having ever

---

9 A letter to Sir Sidney Colvin calls especial attention to the importance of Ransome: "My last scene with Ransome is only indicated. There are things, moments, that are not to be tossed to the public's incomprehension, for journalists to gloat over" (*Life and Letters,* II, 182).

spoken of this episode before he wrote the story. He gave a hoot of delight, and then as soon as he recovered from his unusual outburst of mirth ... explained: 'my dear, it is pure fiction'."[10] *The Shadow Line* is anything but pure fiction; Conrad, indeed, considered it authentic spiritual autobiography: "The whole thing is exact autobiography. The very speeches are (I won't[54] say authentic—they are that absolutely), I believe, verbally accurate. ... I'll only say that experience is transposed into spiritual terms—in art a perfectly legitimate thing to do, as long as one preserves the exact truth enshrined therein."[11] Conrad, as many letters indicate, was worried over the reception of *The Shadow Line*. He proposed to dedicate the book to his son Borys and felt that it might not be thought worthy. It was written while Borys was serving in the British army; and it is not unreasonable that Conrad, an affectionate father, should at such a time be peculiarly concerned with the theme of solidarity. Indeed, the dedication "To Borys and all others" is pointed up by a statement in the preface: "Nobody can doubt that before the supreme trial of a whole generation I had an acute consciousness of the minute and insignificant character of my own obscure experience" (p. viii).

I do not intend to belittle the artistic achievement of "The Secret Sharer." It certainly has compression, an exciting narrative thrust, and a symbolic richness. And it catches at least a part of Conrad's major theme: there must be *self*-awareness before one can discover how much that self is limited and shaped by the community. It is also extremely interesting to the student of Conrad as perhaps the sharpest presentation of a sort of aristocratic withdrawal or aloofness which beset Conrad the man, and which Conrad the man-become-writer had to conquer by conscious and tortuous explorations in imaginative sympathy, in such works as *Lord Jim, Nostromo, Under Western Eyes,* and *The Shadow Line.*

The Shadow Line is a small canvas on which Conrad has painted a single figure surrounded by a group of associates who, though carefully drawn, are chiefly interesting as they are used in the articulation of the chief portrait. As a consequence of this focus, it lacks the richness of some of his other novels—*Lord Jim, Victory, Heart of Darkness,* and especially *Nostromo* and *Under Western Eyes*—which record more truly and fully the interplay of forces of good and evil, of ideals and material facts, in that unending and whirling clash which is the life of man. If we assume that Conrad is at his best when he realizes dramatically the fullness of this struggle, when he commits

---

10 Jessie Conrad, *Joseph Conrad and His Circle* (New York, 1935), p. 77.
11 *Life and Letters,* II, 182–183. See also pp. 181, 184–185, 195, and the "Author's Note" to *The Shadow Line.*

his theme to forces completely objectified in the characters of his fiction, we may see that *The Shadow Line* is properly regarded as a minor work; that is, the aim itself is minor, though the theme is not. Reinforcing such a judgment is the fact that the experiences, as I have already indicated, were extremely close to Conrad, and he chose to handle them autobiographically, so that we miss the objectification that Conrad at his very best achieves through the use, say, of a mediating Marlow or an old English teacher.[55]

Even so, it is a sort of précis treatment of the whole of his theme, and it is typical of Conrad's attitude towards central issues in his work, as "The Secret Sharer" is not. In view of the striking similarities in the two, even to the inclusion of a more objective double in *The Shadow Line,* it seems reasonable to suggest that the later book is, aside from being a good short novel in its own right, Conrad's critical judgment of the earlier story. In it the dark and narrow inwardness of "The Secret Sharer" is counterpointed by the deliberate outwardness of human responsibility. At the end of the story the captain has learned that the proudest self must come to terms with the material conditions of earth and men, and he has understood that true courage may be modulated by resignation. I do not speak of a resignation which means a retreat from a spiritual or physical battle, but such a resignation as Conrad defined in his well-known preface to *A Personal Record.* "Resignation," he says, "is not indifference" (p. xvii). And later: "The sight of human affairs deserves admiration and pity. They are worthy of respect, too. And he is not insensible who pays them the undemonstrative tribute of a sigh which is not a sob, and of a smile which is not a grin. Resignation, not mystic, not detached, but resignation open-eyed, conscious, and informed by love, is the only one of our feelings for which it is impossible to become a sham" (p. xxi).[56]

CONRAD AND "THE SECRET SHARER"*†
R. W. Stallman

I

The nearer a work approaches art, Conrad declared, "the more it acquires a symbolic character. . . . All the great creations of literature have been symbolic, and in that way have gained in complexity, in power, in depth and in beauty." (*Life and Letters*, by G. Jean-Aubry. II, 205.) It is a mistake to assume that Conrad subscribed to the theory of Realism, the illusion that literature is copyistic of reality. And yet if you take the author at his professed intention, which in his Author's Notes appears to be no more than to render faithfully the facts of the visible world unadorned by conscious invention, you tend to be bound to this misconception. No wonder that his readers failed to see what his books were about, or that his critics persistently pigeon-holed him under that infernal classification—Realist! Privately he protested (as in his letter to Richard Curle, II, 316), but publicly he helped to make that label stick. His conception of the art of the novel must be pieced together from the scattered dicta of his letters and from hints directly or allegorically imbedded in his imaginative works—as in the "Heart of Darkness" where Marlow, that master craftsman, talks in cunning analogies. In the prefaces the professed trade secrets are seldom the key ones, but in the tales Conrad frequently reveals[275] them. We know when Marlow says "I am not disclosing any trade secrets" that Conrad in these key words is actually opening up the door. Even if you take his artistic credo from the letters, you are apt to misconstrue his intent as artist. In making the pronouncement that "All the great creations of literature have been symbolic," Conrad was alluding to *Victory*—which is to say that *Victory* is a symbolic work. And yet in this same letter (written to Barrett H. Clark) he goes on to profess that *Victory* is a very simple book: ". . .

---

* From "Conrad and 'The Secret Sharer,'" *Accent*, IX (Spring 1949), 131–143. [Stallman's note.]

† Reprinted with permission from R. W. Stallman, "Conrad and 'The Secret Sharer,'" from *The Art of Joseph Conrad*, ed. R. W. Stallman. East Lansing: Michigan State University Press, 1960, pp. 275–288. [See the Bibliography at the end of this volume for earlier criticism by R. W. Stallman—criticism similar in point of view to this selection, and frequently referred to by other critics. Ed.]

and indeed I must say that I did not wrap it up in very mysterious processes of art .... and I don't think there is a critic in England or France who was in any doubt about it." Now this is nothing less than a strategic feint to conceal the secret intentions of *Victory,* and it is characteristic of that cunning strategy by which he everywhere conceals what his books are really about. His books are never so obvious as he would have his readers believe. Their artistic secrets eluded all his contemporary critics, and these included his closest literary friends. His unwary and imperceptive critics assumed that Conrad in his prefaces was continually striving to make clear the motives by which he was impelled, that here in his public commentaries on his craft he was making intimate disclosures about his literary aims and the bases upon which his books rest—and all this solely in order to help his readers to comprehend them. The claim of his prefaces that his public has understood his books is belied by the complaint of his letters: "I have not been very well understood. I have been called a writer of the sea, of the tropics, a descriptive writer, a romantic writer—and also a realist."

The fact is that Conrad's theory of the novel is no other than the modern canon that every work of art is symbolic. Every great novel has a symbolic meaning, imparts a significance which transcends mere plot or fable. Symbolism, it has been aptly said, does not deny Realism; it extends it. Realism in art has to do with technique. Realism attaches to methods of presenting points of view, methods of psychological insights, devices of chronology, of grouping and perspective. It is in such technical matters of grouping and perspective that the "realism" of Conrad's books consists. "It is in my scheming for effects," he told Richard Curle, "wherein almost all my 'art' consists. This, I suspect, has been the difficulty the critics have felt in classifying it as romantic or realistic." (II, 317.) Of course, a work which is realistic in method, as Robert Louis Stevenson once pointed out, may yet be hollow at its core. But the fact remains that if a work attains an illusion of achieved reality it attains it through technique —or not at all.

Because a novel is a product of language, a novel depends for its very life upon the word. What we term the characters of a novel are nothing more that the author's verbal arrangements. Being composed of words, they function (as Bonamy Dobrée puts it) as the part-symbols out of which the whole symbol is constructed. Conrad's credo —"Give me the right word and the right accent and I will move the world"—transposes into "Give me the right symbol and the right rendering and I will make a world." For Conrad, "the *whole* of the truth lies in the presentation;[276] therefore the expression should be studied in the interest of veracity. This is the only morality of *art* apart from *subject*." (I, 280.) The criterion of absolute correspondence between the characters, events and effects of art with those of reality constitutes, I think, a critical fallacy. Realism taken as plastic or graphic verisimilitude, critically considered, is plainly irrelevant. Truth in art consists not in the artist's fidelity to the observed facts of the actual world; it consists, rather, in the artist's fidelity to the felt truth of his vision. And it is *there* that the honor of the writer lies— in his fidelity to his image-making conception. Truth in art lies in the faithful formulation of patterned images. On his conscience, the artist must create his vision with the utmost fidelity to what Conrad called "the image of truth abiding in facts . . . ." Images are true and their rendering is true when they create a potential scheme of relationships to the other images, so that the meaning each part elicits and the effect they produce keep scrupulously true to the conceiving purpose of the whole which controls them. Fidelity is the crux of Conrad's artistic code as well as of his moral code. And fidelity is also the theme upon which almost all his imaginative works pivot.

Mere Realism—the exact and lifelike registration of the observed facts of actual experience—Conrad himself scoffed at. "You just stop short of being absolutely real," he wrote Arnold Bennett, "because you are faithful to your dogmas of realism. Now realism in art will never approach reality." And he goes on to say, "And your art, your gift, should be put to the service of a larger and freer faith." Every artist is at bottom a Realist whose aim is to evoke an impression of "life as it actually is," but his work approaches art only insofar as his images of reality take upon themselves the dimension of symbols. Surely every artist is first of all an Impressionist whose aim is to make his readers feel and see as he himself saw and felt, but what distinguishes his work as art is not his achievement in mere pictorial intention. Marlow in "Heart of Darkness" makes us see and feel the overpowering sinister atmosphere of the wilderness as Conrad himself saw and felt it, so that (to quote F. R. Leavis) "the details and circumstances of the voyage to and up the Congo are present to us as if we were making the journey ourselves." True, but we do not make that journey solely for the sake of the evoked atmosphere. That is not everything. There is a great deal more. Some secret intention controls Conrad's realistic and pictorial particulars, by which the atmosphere gets itself engendered; but what Marlow must make us perceive is this controlling subsurface purpose. The river of our journey through that impenetrable jungle of unspeakable secrets ascends significantly and symbolically towards Kurtz—towards the theme.

II

Everything in "The Secret Sharer" is charged with symbolic purpose. It is this symbolic part of the business that eludes the reader, if not the moral and psychological intention, since these meanings which attach to[277] the narrative or surface level are less likely to be missed. On a first reading it appears perhaps as simply a spectacular story about a young, newly appointed sea-captain who risks his ship and his career in order to rescue a refugee who happens to bear a striking resemblance to himself. He is a fugitive from the legal consequences of an act of manslaughter; he has killed a man in a desperate scrape, but he is "no homicidal ruffian." The captain, recognizing their connection in thoughts and impressions, identifies the stranger with himself, guesses his guilt and shares his conscience. He hides him in his cabin and takes extraordinary pains to conceal him from the crew. He risks everything for the sake of this stranger. To help him reach land so that he can begin a new life, the captain takes his ship as close into land as possible, and, while the swimmer makes for shore, he watches in terror the approaching mass of land shadows which threaten to engulf the ship. What saves him is the warning marker left by the swimmer ("the saving mark for my eyes"). It is the captain's own hat, by which he can tell that the ship has gathered sternway. The ship is saved, and the captain at last is fitted for his task. He has established perfect communion with his ship. As he catches a last glimpse of his hat, the captain senses again that mysterious identity with the secret sharer of his cabin and of his thoughts. He describes him as though he were describing himself: "a free man, a proud swimmer striking out for a new destiny."

Conrad's most characteristic works are stories of action: *Nostromo, The Secret Agent, Victory, Suspense*. In "The Secret Sharer" the external action consists almost solely in the drama of the ship in the moment of the captain's crisis. Action and plot are subsidiary to the analysis and exhibition of a psychological process. This psychological or internal action, from which the external drama is projected, prepares for its counterpart and at the climactic moment coincides with it. The whole story may be defined as a prolonged analysis of a series of tensions anticipating one culminating moment, the moment of the captain's crisis and triumph. The story is charged, however, not only with suspense and impending crisis but also with meaning. Like Henry James, his acknowledged master, Conrad is an intensely conscious craftsman. Again like Henry James, Conrad in his prefaces and Author's Notes lets us in on his aims as a writer. With Conrad, however, the accounts of the sources of his tales and the disclosures

about his literary aims are highly deceptive, often deliberately misleading.

The prefaces of Conrad stand in striking contrast to the prefaces
of Henry James. For whereas Henry James is everywhere telling us
what his "exquisite scheme" is, Conrad is continually telling us that
he has no scheme at all. "You must realize," he admonished Norman
Douglas, "the inconceivable stupidity of the common reader—the
man who forks out the half crown." The problem was to win over the
common reader, and how could he win over the common reader if, as
Conrad put it, he gave him all the bones? "It might destroy their
curiosity for the dish." As a matter of fact Conrad felt much the
same as Arnold Bennett felt about the public[278] comprehension. The
public comprehension, Bennett observed, is limited severely because
"Only other creative artists can understand a creative artist." Which
is to say that every artist has his secret intentions. Conrad not only
concealed his secret intentions but even disguised them by planting
his Author's Notes with bogus trade secrets about his literary aims
and false clues as to what his books are really about. Conrad's readers
need only D. H. Lawrence to tip them off—"Never trust the artist.
Trust the tale." As Albert Guerard points out, for the author to
describe only the source of "The Secret Sharer," to profess that the
story is the account of a real incident which occurred on such and such
a ship (the *Cutty Sark,* specifically), is to provide the reader with a
false clue. The real fact is that Conrad has contrived his story with a
secret intention. We can get at it only through the story itself. We
can work it out, to start with, by questioning certain central motives
—the facts basic to the why and the wherefore of what happens in the
story.

Even the reader who reads only for "the story" is likely to ask some
of the questions, the key ones being these: (1) Why does the captain
undertake the risk to his ship for this particular stranger, a risk which
he would not impose upon her for any other? (2) Why must he take the
ship as close into land as possible?

If we, as Conrad's readers, happen to think in the manner of
the chief mate ("He was of a painstaking turn of mind. As he used
to say, he 'liked to account to himself' for practically everything that
came in his way . . ."), we certainly will try to evolve a theory about
the captain and his secret sharer. But to do so, in emulation of the
chief mate we had better "take all things into earnest consideration."
We had better answer our question first of all at the narrative or
literal level. It's a fact that what the youthful sea captain does for
this fugitive, whose mishap was not entirely of his own making, is
what any other young sea captain might do, out of common decency,
in order to save a decent young chap. He feels impelled to do this

out of a moral necessity, his relationship to the fugitive being that of
host to guest. But why does he make this commitment?—why for the
sake of this particular stranger? Well, the fact that the captain bears
an uncanny resemblance to him—Leggatt's similarity not only in
appearance and age but in background and experience and in situation
—provides us one answer. (It's this sense of identity that prompts the
remark: "I saw it all going on as though I were myself inside that
other sleeping-suit.") Besides, the captain recognizes not alone this
physical identity but also a psychic one. "He appealed to me as if our
experiences had been as identical as our clothes." Each feels that he
is "the only stranger on board," and each feels that he has, as it were,
"something to swim for." Each stranger is isolated and wholly alone,
pitted against the world and being tested by it. What impelled Leggatt
to swim out to the ship was his lonesomeness ("I wanted to be seen,
to talk with somebody, before I went on"), and the same impulse
motivates the captain and prompts him to greet the newcomer so
hospitably.[279] Hospitality, welcome, and self-recognition are stressed
from the start. "A mysterious communication was established already
between us two—in the face of that silent, darkened tropical sea." Later
in thinking back to this moment Leggatt confides: "It's a great satisfaction to have got somebody to understand. You seem to have been
there on purpose." The same confession could have come from the
captain. Each stranger feels the same urgency to communicate with
somebody in order to unburden his plight.

It is this mutual, sympathetic understanding of what the other's
plight means to him that bolsters and morally fortifies their spiritual
being, Leggatt's no less than the captain's. "And then you speaking to
me so quietly—as if you had expected me—made me hold on a little
longer." Leggatt's "calm and resolute" voice induces in the captain a
corresponding state of self-possession. Through Leggatt that initial
mood of calm and resolute self-confidence with which the captain
begins and ends his arduous enterprise is gradually reinstated. Leggatt, as we later get to know him, is bold and enterprising, proud and
stubborn, determined in moral fiber. While the captain's remark
"You must be a good swimmer" has reference to the fact that the
nearest land is as far distant as the land at the very bottom of the
sea, there is also an implied ethical judgment in these words of
encouragement and appraisal. To be "a good swimmer" is to be "a
strong soul." What the captain marvels at in his double is "that
something unyielding in his character which was carrying him
through so finely." The overconfident soul of the swimmer stands in
contrast to the self-questioning, Hamletlike soul of the newly appointed captain. He observes about the fugitive that there was nothing
sickly in his eyes or in his expression, and, with this telling reflection

about himself, he notices that "he was not a bit like me, really; yet, as we stood leaning over my bed-place, whispering side by side, with our dark heads together and our backs to the door, anybody bold enough to open it stealthily would have been treated to the uncanny sight of a double captain busy talking in whispers with his other self." When Leggatt happens to rest a hand "on the end of the skylight to steady himself with, and all that did not stir a limb," the captain simultaneously rests a hand too on the end of the skylight. When on a later occasion the captain made a move "my double moved too." As "the double captain" is about to slip from the ship into the sea, the captain, struck by a sudden thought, snatches his hat and rams it "on my other self." He visualizes Leggatt's plight as his own: "I saw myself," he says, "wandering barefooted, bareheaded, the sun beating on my dark poll." Again and again "[W]e, the two strangers in the ship, faced each other in identical attitudes." And in identical clothes. It is the captain's secret self that is "exactly the same" as the fugitive, who, dressed in "the ghostly gray of my sleeping suit" (the garb of the unconscious life), must always remain concealed from the eyes of the world.

    In terms of the ethical allegory, Leggatt is the embodiment of the[280] captain's moral consciousness. His appearance answers the captain's question—"I wondered how far I should turn out faithful to that ideal conception of one's own personality every man sets up for himself secretly." In darkness he first appears, mysteriously "as if he had risen from the bottom of the sea," and "the sea-lightning played about his limbs at every stir; and he appeared in it ghastly, silvery, fish-like." At the first sight of him "a faint flash of phosphorescent light, which seemed to issue suddenly from the naked body of a man, flickered in the sleeping water with the elusive, silent play of summer lightning in a night sky." And at the last sight of him, when the secret sharer is making for the shore of Koh-ring (an unknown island), there issues from the discarded hat the same mysterious light: "White on the black water. A phosphorescent flash passed under it." It's all very mysterious. Leggatt's emerging in a sudden glow from "the sleeping water" seems very much like the flash of an idea emerging from the depths of the subconscious mind. "It was, in the night, as though I had been faced by my own reflection in the depths of a somber and immense mirror." That dark glassy sea mirrors the captain's *alter ego*. In terms of the psychological allegory, Leggatt represents that world which lies below the surface of our conscious lives. Just before he makes his appearance the riding-light in the fore-rigging burns, so the captain imagines, "with a clear, untroubled, as if symbolic, flame, confident and bright in the mysterious shades of the night." These moral qualities, though the captain attributes them to the riding-light, belong with equal and very suggestive appropriateness to the captain's as yet undisclosed second self. The captain's subconscious mind has anticipated, in the fiction of the symbolic flame, the idea of a second self—the appearance, that is, of someone untroubled, unyielding, self-confident. (The captain is just the opposite, being of a mind troubled and filled with self-doubt.) The symbolic flame materializes in human form. Leggatt bodies forth the very commonplace upon which the whole story is built: no man is alone in the world, for he is always with himself. Leggatt, this other self, becomes the psychological embodiment of the reality, the destiny, the ideal of selfhood which the captain must measure up to. He provides him the utmost test.

All this, in sum, answers our first question: Why is it that the captain risks his ship for this particular stranger? The initial matter-of-fact answer prepared us for, or rather teased us into making, the allegorical one. In answering the first question we have anticipated the answer to the second: Why is it that the captain must take his ship as close into shore as possible? To begin with a fact, the ship, as the story opens, is anchored inside the islands at the mouth of the river Meinam and is lying cleared for sea. (Her location and voyage can be traced on a map.) She is in dead calm and waits for "the slightest sign of any sort of wind." "There was not a sound in her—and around us nothing moved, nothing lived, not a canoe on the water, not a bird in the air, not a cloud in the sky." At last there's enough wind to get under way with, and then for four days[281] she works down "the east side of the Gulf of Siam, tack for tack, in light winds and smooth water...." When the wind comes and the ship first moves to his own independent word—precisely at this point it is that the captain begins to come to terms with his ship. At midnight of the fourth day out she is put round on the other tack to stand in for shore, and still at the following noon she has had no change of course. The captain has by now attained enough self-confidence to dare this risky maneuver—"to stand right in. Quite in—as far as I can take her." His excuse for the order to the mate is that the ship isn't doing well in the middle of the gulf, and at the mate's terrified protests he retorts: "Well—if there are any regular land breezes at all on this coast one must get close inshore to find them, mustn't one?" And this is why, *literally* why, he must shave the land as close as possible.

It is not solely in order to shorten Leggatt's stretch to shore. For Leggatt, that expert swimmer, is capable of making it from almost two miles out. (From the islet to the ship, he figured, "That last spell must have been over a mile.") It's not a test of Leggatt. It's a test of the captain. "The youngest man on board (barring the second mate), and untried as yet by a position of the fullest responsibility. . . ." He is "the only stranger on board . . . a stranger to the ship; and if all the truth must be told, I was somewhat of a stranger to myself." For four days the ship has had a captain who has not been "completely and wholly with her. Part of me was absent." Though she has had "two captains to plan her course for her," nevertheless she is still, so to speak, a ship without a captain. The time has come for the irresolute commander to command—to prove to the crew, to the world, and to himself that he is fitted for his task. It is time that he put to trial that secret conception of his ideal self, to reckon, in sum, with that destiny which from the start he has anticipated with such intensity. For four days the ship has had very little wind in her sails. Instead of waiting for the wind to come to him he determines now to go after it. It's *his* conscience that is on trial ("on my conscience, it had to be thus close—no less"). It's not a test of the crew—"They had simply to be equal to their tasks; but I wondered how far I should turn out faithful to that ideal conception of one's own personality every man sets up for himself secretly." "All a man can betray is his conscience," Conrad wrote in *Under Western Eyes*. The captain does not betray, even though the entire world seemed leagued against him. Everything—"the elements, the men were against us—everything was against us in our secret partnership; time itself—for this could not go on forever." And "It was now a matter of conscience to shave the land as close as possible—for now he must go overboard whenever the ship was put in stays. Must! There could be no going back for him." Nor for the captain: "I had to go on." Not to let Leggatt strike out for land would be "a sort of cowardice"; it is cowardice not to face up to one's destiny. Like Leggatt, who has "something un- yielding in his character," the captain is tenaciously determined not to compromise his soul. There are limits to self-knowledge, how- ever,[282] and beyond this dividing mark of self-knowledge no man dare go. We are told that "all the time the dual working of my mind distracted me almost to the point of insanity." "On that enormous mass of blackness there was not a gleam to be seen, not a sound to be heard." The black hill of Koh-ring hangs right over the ship "like a towering fragment of the everlasting night," and such a hush falls upon her "that she might have been a bark of the dead floating in slowly under the very gate of Erebus." It is the ship, but it is also the captain's soul, that is almost swallowed up beyond recall. "I think I had come creeping quietly as near insanity as any man who has not actually gone over the border." "My God! Where are we?" cries the terrified mate. "Lost!" The captain has Leggatt to fortify him, where- as the terrified mate hasn't even "the moral support of his whiskers." The transferred moral quality of Leggatt has infused itself into the captain's soul and it is this transaction—symbolized in the spot of white hat—that saves him. (The hat is Conrad's symbol for his theme of fidelity.) It is by virtue of his fidelity to that ideal of selfhood that the captain triumphs, and at that decisive moment of his destiny when he measures up to it a new existence begins for him—a spiritually unified one. It begins for him when the cabin is emptied and Leggatt, the secret sharer of his cabin and of his thoughts, has been deposited into that once dark and mysterious but now sunlit sea.

III

"We cannot escape from ourselves," Conrad has said, and more than once, both in his novels and in his Author's Notes. We cannot escape from ourselves, from our past, from our memories. It is in this sense that "the creator can only express himself in his creation," wherefore "every novel contains an element of autobiography."—*A Personal Record.* Once, in writing *The Secret Agent,* Conrad "had to fight hard to keep at arm's length the memories . . . lest they should rush in and overwhelm each page of the story. . . ." Memories molded Conrad's art. All his imaginative work is founded on personal reminiscences of actual incidents and people encountered during his twenty years of active sea life. But, though all of his writing draws upon personal contacts with reality, the experience in every one of his stories "is but the canvas of the attempted picture." Of all his narratives less than a half dozen can be claimed as "autobiographies." The "Heart of Darkness" is taken straight from life, but even this, the most directly autobiographical of all his stories, represents experience pushed beyond the actual facts of the event. There is this personal basis for Conrad's art, but his art is nevertheless impersonal. "The more perfect the artist," T. S. Eliot has declared, "the more completely separate in him will be the man who suffers and the mind which creates." Conrad is that artist. "The Secret Sharer" provides us the perfect instance of a work of art which is at once personative and yet a wholly depersonalized and anonymous creation.

It is said that this story was written in order to resolve a personal[283] crisis; writing it served Conrad as a neurotic safety valve. But whatever that crisis was which motivated him to the act of creation, it is nevertheless by no means identical with the imagined one confronting the sea captain. The private plight of the author has been objectified in a dramatic framework of meaning that is impersonal and universalized. The story is autobiographical only in a spiritual sense. The captain's problem, however, can be read as an allegory of Conrad's problem, for the situation between the captain and his secret sharer corresponds to the situation between the artist and his creative act. Read thus, "The Secret Sharer" is a double allegory. It is an allegory of man's moral conscience and of man's aesthetic or artistic conscience. "The artist," wrote Flaubert in one of his letters, "ought to be in his work like God in Creation, invisible and all powerful; let him be felt everywhere but not seen." Conrad's story allegorizes the plight of Conrad as artist. His problem is to come to terms with his story, even as the captain's problem is to get on terms with his ship. "My strangeness, which had made me sleepless, had prompted that unconventional arrangement, as if I had expected in those solitary hours of the night to get on terms with the ship of which I knew nothing, manned by men of whom I knew very little more."

The artist in his act of creation is of necessity estranged from normal everyday life. "In this breathless pause at the threshold of a long passage we seemed to be measuring our fitness for a long and arduous enterprise, the appointed task of both our existences to be carried out, far from all human eyes, with only sky and sea for spectators and for judges." Isolated with his vision, he begins in self-doubt his newly appointed task. Everything seems to threaten perfect communion with his vision. Being faced by "the breath of unknown powers that shape our destinies" (as the young captain in *The Shadow Line* says) he anticipates the possibility of failure. Sky and sea and "all that multitude of celestial bodies staring down at one"—the entire world seems hostile to the creator in his creative enterprise. Everything—"the elements, the men were against us—everything was against us in our secret partnership; time itself—for this could not go on forever." As the captain must establish communion with his ship, so the artist must establish perfect communion with the things created, and command over them. The artist, Conrad admits in his Note to *The Nigger of the "Narcissus,"* "the artist descends within himself, and in that lonely region of stress and strife ... finds the terms of his appeal."[1]

---

[1] In *A Personal Record* (pp. 98–99), describing the terrible strain put upon him during the formidable period of creating *Nostromo*, Conrad speaks of his plight in the same terms as the sea-captain in "The Secret Sharer." "The Secret Sharer" dramatizes this experience:

"All I know is that, for twenty months, neglecting the common joys of life that fall to the lot of the humblest on this earth, I had, like the prophet of old, 'wrestled with the Lord' for my creation, *for the headlands of the coast, for the darkness of the Placid Gulf* ..., and for the breath of life that had to be blown into the shapes of men and women.... These are, perhaps, strong words, but it is difficult to characterize otherwise the intimacy and the strain of a creative effort in which mind and will and conscience are engaged to the full, hour after hour, day after day, *away from the world*, and to the exclusion of all that makes life really lovable and gentle—*something for which a material parallel can only be found in the everlasting sombre stress of the westward passage*

The artist in the act of creation tests his integrity, even as the sea captain tests his in the dangerous act of maneuvering the ship. The problem of the artist—indeed the problem which every man confronts —is resolved, no less than the captain's, by the trial he imposes upon his secret self. It is his creative conscience that he must not betray. No man of uncommon moral quality can escape this test of selfhood. That "The Secret Sharer" comes round is by virtue of the creator's fidelity to his vision. He has measured up to that ideal of artistic integrity, that ideal conception of one's aesthetic conscience, which every artist sets up for[284] himself secretly. She weathers the crisis, the crisis which every creator risks. She comes round, she succeeds! Nothing can stand between them after that. "Nothing: no one in the world should stand now between us, throwing a shadow on the way of silent knowledge and mute affection, the perfect communion of a seaman [or of an artist] with his first command." He has mastered "the feel of my ship," and now, like that other invisible stranger, he is at last "a free man, a proud swimmer striking out for a new destiny."

(1949)

Note

I have left my reading of "The Secret Sharer" essentially as originally published (1949). Since then another critic argues that Leggatt is not the captain's ideal; he is a failure. "If Leggatt has failed, as he so plainly has, can stand as 'the psychological embodiment of the reality, the destiny, the ideal selfhood which the captain must measure up to'? Literally, Leggatt is strong and firm because, having failed, he has no expectations." I find no evidence, however, that Leggatt is without expectations, without hope. In what sense is Leggatt a failure?

He is a success in saving the *Sephora,* and he is a success in escaping the law and transcending its hollow forms of authority, dehumanizing and abstract codes personified by Captain Archbold. And Leggatt is a success too in saving the captain-narrator, by serving

round Cape Horn. *For that too is the wrestling of men with the might of their Creator, in a great isolation from the world, without the amenities and consolations of life, a lonely struggle under a sense of overmatched littleness, for no reward that could be adequate, but for the mere winning of a longitude. . . ."* (Italics mine.)

Again, in his preface to *The Secret Agent* he speaks of "the mass of oppressive doubts that haunt so persistently every attempt at creative work." *Conrad's Prefaces,* ed. Edward Garnett, p. 110.

[New note by Stallman. Ed.:] In discussing the composition of *The Rover* Conrad put it this way: "I wanted the deck cleared before going below. As to leaving any loose ends hanging over the side, I couldn't bear the thought of it."

him as model in being simultaneously his double and his opposite ("he was not a bit like me, really"). At every point in his defeated career Leggatt is courageous, resolute, confident, resourceful, bold and enterprising, proud and unyielding. I call this the condition of success, and so does Conrad. Leggatt has spirit and tenacity, whereas Captain Archbold is characterized solely by his "spiritless tenacity." It is the vexed captain-narrator who doubts success and expects only the worst: "And as to the chapter of accidents which counts for so much in the book of success, I could only hope that it was closed. For what favorable accident could be expected?" The captain-narrator gains certitude through Leggatt, "a strong soul" inspiring him with the undaunted spirit of youth. "Something to swim for" sums up his determination, his expectations amidst black waters and hopeless prospects of being salvaged.

Leggatt makes his appearance immediately after the captain has broken protocol, immediately after notifying the second-mate of "my unheard-of caprice to take a five hours' anchor-watch on myself." The parallel to the captain's breaking of the rules is Leggatt's unlawful deed aboard the *Sephora*. It is an irrational act that the captain commits in taking Leggatt aboard and concealing him in his cabin, an act of immaturity or inexperienced judgment; Leggatt's case again provides the parallel. The *Sephora* affair stands as the metaphor of the captain's plight.

Conrad's way of affirming a thing is always by affirming also its opposite. No Conrad hero attains an unmitigated success. The example is[285] Lord Jim, or the captain of "The Secret Sharer." It's always success-failure, or failure-success, the one measured by the other. So too for Leggatt: "The same strung-up force which had given twenty-four men a chance, at least, for their lives, had, in a sort of recoil, crushed an unworthy mutinous existence." The only flat failure is Captain Archbold. He epitomizes man's subjugation to legalized conventions; he represents the external law, Leggatt the internal. The storm that threatened the *Sephora* and the lives of her crew—"it was a sea gone mad! I suppose the end of the world will be something like that"—causes the crack-up of fixed authority and of the code he represents. In spite of his having served thirty-seven years at sea (twenty of them spent in "immaculate command"), at the crisis Captain Archbold loses his nerve and whimpers in terror while the helpless ship runs for her life. Leggatt, acting without authority, saves the ship by setting the foresail, but meanwhile he has had to do away with an insolent shipmate who obstructed his rescue of the *Sephora*. Captain Archbold regarded Leggatt as unfit to serve as chief mate of the *Sephora*, yet he himself at the crisis is unfit to command. So the captain-narrator, similarly, doubts whether he is fit to command, whereas Leggatt, having learned through failure, succeeds in remaining confident and in self-control, unnerved by his plight. The captain is instructed by his example, by the example of his other and opposite self. Leggatt murdered a shipmate in a moment of loss of self-control; so the parson's son becomes by circumstances a murderer and thus, as judged by the external law, a failure. But his failure is matched by his success. He restores order to the irrational crew and the uncontrolled ship—at the expense of committing an irrational act in a fit of temper. He had no choice: "Do you think that if I had not been pretty fierce with them I should have got the men to do anything?"

The man he murdered in a fit of temper was one of those "Miserable devils that have no business to live at all. He wouldn't do his duty and wouldn't let anybody else do theirs." He had to silence him in order to save ship and crew. It is at this point in the narrative that the captain, recognizing that "my double there was no homicidal ruffian," remarks: "He appealed to me *as if our experiences* had been as identical as our clothes." What this tells us is that the captain recognizes a kinship between himself and Leggatt not only in physical appearance, in age, in background (they are both Conway graduates), and in situation, but also in what each has experienced. What the young captain has experienced we do not know, but he has experienced enough of life to enable him to recognize the potentiality in himself for committing an irrational and possibly even a criminal act and to sympathise therefore with Leggatt's plight.[2] "I saw it all going on as though I were myself inside that other sleeping-suit." It is the recognition of the capacity for guilt from which no man dares to presume himself exempt. He recognizes in Leggatt, apart from his unlawful act, not his weakness but his strength, physically and spiritually. Unlike the captain, there is "nothing sickly in his eyes or in[286] his expression." He seems "invulnerable." Unlike the captain, Leggatt has the cool-headed capacity for analyzing his past experience, the situation from which he has successfully escaped; the capacity for thinking *as* "a stubborn if not a steadfast operation; something of which I should have been perfectly incapable." The captain's "troubled incertitude" draws strength from Leggatt's invulnerability, his moral courage. Though both are dressed in sleeping-suits, the

---

[2] Guerard makes the same point in his excellent introduction to the Signet edition of *"Heart of Darkness"* and *"The Secret Sharer"* (1950): "What does this unreflective and immediate sympathy for a 'double' mean but sympathy for one's second, irrational self? The captain hides and protects Leggatt because he vaguely realizes—for the first time in his life—that he too might have stumbled into such a crime." "The two novels alike exploit the ancient myth or archetypal experience of the 'night journey' of a provisional descent into the primitive and unconscious sources of being."

garb of the unconscious life (as M. C. Bradbrook was first to point out), the difference is that the captain is committed to the outer and conscious life of the ship and crew, whereas his other self, because guilty, must remain concealed from the eyes of the world. Ironically, Leggatt concerns himself with the outer world, as in his asking at the very start of his encounter with the captain what the time is; whereas the captain, reflecting inwardly at the start, dismisses his officers and takes over their deck-duty and thereby prevents "the anchor-watch being formally set and things properly attended to. I asked myself whether it was wise ever to interfere with the established routine of duties even from the kindest of motives." It is through his inadequacy and negligence, his not keeping to the established routine and external code, that he meets the outcast Leggatt. At that moment of their meeting the captain is a failure, and Leggatt (in one sense) a success.

The characteristic of Conrad's work is the opposition of conflict between the inner and outer standards, between the standards of conscience and those of external codes, conventions and laws. Lord Jim, crucified by legalized convention, vindicates himself by creating Patusan, a world of his own making (as it were), Patusan being symbolic of the inner world untouched—until Brown arrives—by the outer world of convention. In *Nostromo* neither the external world nor the internal one is exempt from corruption; Nostromo, representing the romantic self-deluded idealist, betrays his "incorrigible" integrity. In *Victory*, Heyst is destroyed by the external world, by Gentleman Jones, the exponent of its corruption and evil; ironically, he is nevertheless saved by having committed himself to the necessity of participating in life, through Lena. In "Heart of Darkness" the corrupted Kurtz is "incorruptible," and though a moral sham he is nevertheless saved by Marlow because he earned redemption of his inner darkness by disclosing its truth; "It was an affirmation, a moral victory paid for by innumerable defeats, by abominable terrors, by abominable satisfactions. But it was a victory! That is why I have remained loyal to Kurtz to the last." In *The Nigger of the "Narcissus"* the ideal— Jim Wait—is exposed as a sham. In "The Secret Sharer," to the contrary, the values lie in the weighted scale of the inner world, and it is similarly so in *Lord Jim,* "Heart of Darkness," and *Under Western Eyes.*

Leggatt does not consider himself a failure, any more so tha Lord Jim. He judges himself (like Lord Jim) by his own interna code: Not Guilty. "What can they know whether I am guilty or not —or of *what* I am guilty, either? That's my affair." To the retributive laws of society he refuses to submit because he considers himself subject only to the laws of conscience.[287] He's no more a murdering brute than the captain. Whereas at the start the captain's ideal of selfhood is a simple and naïve conception, at the end it has undergone a radical change through the captain's experiencing Leggatt's destiny *as if* his own, through his experiencing the reality of his other self, through his recognition of their bond of guilt. That Leggatt has committed a criminal act (that "brand of Cain" business) signified the dark potentialities within us all. It is in this double sense that Leggatt stands as the psychological embodiment of the captain's conscience. His double consciousness embraces predicaments of the internal and the external code. "Do you see me before a judge and jury on that charge?" Leggatt asks him. The captain shares Leggatt's convictions that the inner standard is what man must rightly be judged by, that the final appeal is to that ideal of selfhood which every man secretly sets up for himself. The ideal is conscience, and that is what Leggatt represents. It's the same for Kurtz and Razumov and Nostromo. In Conrad all is ambiguous and contradictory; nothing is absolute; nothing is but what is not. The critic who pigeon-holes Conrad's heroes as "failures" oversimplifies by half-truths.   (1959)[288]

CONRAD AND THE TERMS OF MODERN CRITICISM*
Marvin Mudrick

The critical achievements of our time—those achievements which extend and redefine the canon of enduring criticism—made breathing room for themselves by clearing out the exhausted categories of Victorian ethicalism, ninetyish purple-patchery, and Bloomsbury impressionizing. The job may have been done impolitely; but it had to be done. The literary criticism of the past thirty years has succeeded, whatever its manners, in turning the reader's attention from gossip to analysis; from the critic to the author; from the author's laundry bills to his choice of techniques; from the work as a reflection or evasion of life and the world to the work as a made object discontinuous with, but analogous to, life and the world.

Every fresh criticism is a reëmphasis of neglected facts: principles, details, relations. Once, however, the critic has persuaded himself of the acceptability of his work, once he has become respectable, he is likely to forget, and by his authority to compel others to forget, that what he has rescued may not be all there is; that indeed any critical reëmphasis, having subordinated minor ideas and disposed of dead ones, may in its turn strain and expand into an overemphasis that will seem as grotesque to our successors as, say, Rymer's "correctness" (when applied to Shakespeare, for example) seems to us.

One fact that our own self-confident age of criticism has justly reëmphasized is the awareness, the trained skill, of the artist: we are assured that he is a conscious craftsman, expertly familiar with his materials, competent—above all—to select and relate them into calculated effects. Now this truism has never been wholly rejected (though in the nineteenth century especially, even here and there in the twentieth, it has been held in contempt as a mechanic's notion of art); and, qualifying it discreetly at need, mindful of its strength against the not merely popular notions of art as a kind of lunacy or at best as an irresponsible outburst, we may be gratified by the virtual unanimity with which it is being reaffirmed. Yet if it is useful it is also, in certain constricted overconfident uses that have been made of it, dangerous; and these uses, moreover, seem to possess

* Reprinted by permission from *The Hudson Review*, Vol. VII, No. 3 (Autumn 1954), pp. 419-426. Copyright 1954 by The Hudson Review, Inc.

an irresistible appeal for critics who have uncritically adopted the
terminology of modern criticism.

How does the critic set about discovering and evaluating the
effects that the writer is aiming at? The piety at present undetachable
from such terms as myth, tone, image, metaphor, symbol testifies to
an accomplished revolution, of terminology at least: in the criticism
of lyric and dramatic poetry, this assumption of power has been un-
challenged for over two decades; in the[419] criticism of fiction, the
enforced succession has been more reluctant, doubtless because of the
relative unwieldiness of fiction, but there too the terms are already
sanctified. We have agreed, then, to assume that these terms name and
direct, if not ways of seeing, at least ways of consciously and usefully
classifying, the effects that the writer—more or less consciously, pre-
meditatedly, even overtly—is aiming at, and that are in the end a
single effect: to project by detail and pattern what seems an epitome
of some aspect of the human condition; an analogue of life as difficult
as life and yet with a final convincing coherence that life itself is
too large and perhaps too planless to offer to our understanding.

Still, it turns out that the terms, whatever their relevance and
propriety in the abstract, may in practice become—like any other
fashionable and striking critical term—conjuring words, hobby-horses,
excuses for inadequate observation, vindications of imperfect judgment, or even muses inspiring the kind of criticism which is a nar-
cissistic little poem of its own. Contemporary examinations of image
and metaphor are abundant and of an unprecedented thoroughness;
but liable to prefer, by implication, the spectacular (and therefore
readily discussable) to the unobtrusively exact: Donne's figures, for
example, have been analyzed in scores of excellent or merely self-
congratulatory critiques,[1] while Chaucer's rest serenely intact in the
amniotic fluid of scholarship. Tone is another term that seems to
have had careful treatment and illustration; yet our first impression
fades before the fact: it is not so much tone as a single species of tone
—irony—that has been isolated with any care, and even irony has
been examined for the most part in its showier manifestations—again,
representatively, Donne's, not Chaucer's. As for myth and symbol, each
has furnished its adherents with a career: the mythicist seems usually
content to certify a work by documenting its faithfulness to Jung, the
symbol-monger dotes on large, repetitive images heavy with a sense of
fatality and futility; but neither is very strenuous at demonstrating, in

---

[1] Mr. Eliot, it may be provocative to note at this point, has characterized the
Donne of the sermons—those much admired, highly figured "prose-poems"—as
the Billy Sunday of English divines ("Lancelot Andrewes", *Selected Essays*, Har-
court, Brace, New York, 1950, p. 302).

the text itself, the relevance and propriety of his pet idea to the author's effects (or failures) of substantiality, and total design.

Having frequently cheapened the valuable terms they have helped make current, many of our critics, especially the literal-minded second generation of modern criticism, have proceeded to cheapen the crucially valid notion of the artist as craftsman. Mistaking their own emphasis for the entire work, they have tended to find the author's fulfillment not in a totally designed structure whose simplest and most conventional appearance is an aspect, and conditions every other aspect, of its being, but in a disingenuous treasure of hints and clues, shrewdly buried by the author beneath the misleading or[420] innocuous surface, to be as shrewdly dug up and displayed by the critic in proof of his own matching adeptness: nose to nose, critic confronts writer and, astonished, discovers himself.

The best writer is, then, the writer most prolific in modish clues of myth, metaphor, symbol, *etc.* throughout his eventless and uncharactered story. The outmoded terms recede into harmless disuse: plot gives way to myth; character and incident are neither elaborated nor confirmed, they are replaced, or at least submerged, by metaphor and symbol; and, emancipated from the perplexities of a transparent style and a frighteningly recognizable world (consider Herbert Read's bewildered rejection of Jane Austen[2]), the critic turns gratefully to those writers who seem to have anticipated what he is looking for.

One of the chosen is Conrad—"not . . . a man who merely tells a tale," says Morton Dauwen Zabel, "but . . . a poet in fiction"[3]; "a philosophical novelist," says Robert Penn Warren, "willing to go naked into the pit, again and again, to make the same old struggle for his truth"[4]—and Conrad is an especially instructive example because admiration of his meretricious effects tends to divert attention from his genuine gifts: he is, when he declines to unclothe himself for the purpose Mr. Warren prescribes, a first-rate story-teller—perhaps the best in English since Smollett—and a master of solidly accurate descriptive prose (of which the storm episode in *The Nigger of the Narcissus* is only one of many superb instances). There is, nevertheless, in Conrad a persistent self-dramatizing and sentimentalizing impulse, at the root of his well publicized "aristocratic aloofness": he will without scruple betray his entertaining narrative and his rather unsubtly contrasted characters at the appeal of any portentous image or generalization or symbolic gesture, often wholly impertinent, and liable, if not in fact calculated, to forestall criticism by flattering the up-to-date

---

2 *English Prose Style*, London, 1932.
3 Editor's Introduction, *The Portable Conrad*, Viking, New York, 1950, p. 45.
4 Conrad, *Nostromo*, Modern Library, New York, 1951, xxxviii.

reader that he is in touch with subterranean truths far more profound than any mere representation of character and relationship. Over-powered, the narrative becomes a contrived exemplum, and the char-acters bogus-heroic gestures or dispensable emblems, of the author's foggy self-sustaining metaphysic.[5]

Victory is one of Conrad's typical failures of this sort. . . .[421]

. . . The Conradian contrivance and bathos are clear enough, however, and more briefly examinable, in two of his most celebrated pieces of short fiction: "The Secret Sharer" and "Amy Foster". . . .[422]

. . . "The Secret Sharer" promises more than "Amy Foster": it is, at least in outline, a genuine story, not—like the latter—an embroi-dered anecdote; its suspense is inherent, not imposed by pauses during which the narrator lights his pipe, scratches behind his left ear, or glumly contemplates the mysterious, fateful, tragic, inscrutable, in-comprehensible Infinite; it is grounded in the details of life at sea—Conrad's only element, in spite of his angry disclaimers—and it occurs during a decisive moment of that life.

But it has other qualities as well. Summing up post-Jungian critical opinion of one of the "half dozen greatest short novels in the English language", Albert Guérard, Jr. points out that it "exploit[s] the ancient myth or archetypal experience of the 'night journey', of a provisional descent into the primitive and unconscious sources of being"; what we find, if by his advice we reread it as carefully as he has done, is that "the purely adventurous story of rescue and escape has become a psychological and symbolic story of self-exploration, self-recognition, and self-mastery. We find that Leggatt, however real his physical presence, is also the captain's ghostly 'double' or twin. What does this unreflective and immediate sympathy for a 'double' mean but sympathy for one's second, irrational self?"[6] *etc.*

What indeed? Who could fail to predict every item of the depth-psychology paraphernalia that will tidily turn up? And who could possibly miss, on the most inattentive first reading, Conrad's over-simplified, imposed mythical structure, symbol to character in the

<hr/>

5 F. R. Leavis has called attention to Conrad's efforts, particularly in *Heart of Darkness*, "to impose . . . a 'significance' that is merely an emotional insistence on the presence of what he can't produce" ("Joseph Conrad: Minor Works and *Nostromo*", in *Critiques and Essays on Modern Fiction* 1920–1951, sel. John W. Aldridge, Ronald Press, New York, 1952, p. 111); and he offers his own unimpeachable examples. But, valuing Conrad very highly indeed, Dr. Leavis regards the defect as a minor one, not as the chronic and radical defect it may appear to others; and his own critical purposes give him no occasion to explain why several respected critics of our time have paintakingly explicated this compulsory "significance", why they have been quite taken in by what should be plainly visible as the butcher's thumb on the scales.

6 Conrad, *Heart of Darkness* and *The Secret Sharer*, Signet, New York, 1950, p. 10.

crudest one-to-one relationship, nailed into the flesh of the narrative in almost every sentence? Mr. Guérard thinks that we may be unaware of Leggatt's function as the captain-narrator's "ghostly 'double' ". Here are some phrases of the captain's, taken at random[424] from the story, describing Leggatt: "like my double", "My sleeping suit was just right for his size", "as though I had been faced by my own reflection in the depths of a somber and immense mirror", "murmured my double" (all these on a single page); "as though I were myself inside that other sleeping suit"; "My double"; "we, the two strangers in the ship, faced each other in identical attitudes"; "he must have looked exactly as I used to look in that bed"; "I felt dual more than ever"; "the dual working of my mind"; "I was constantly watching myself, my secret self"; "Anybody would have taken him for me"; "we two bent our dark heads"; "my second self"; "I had a back view of my very own self"; "My double". Noteworthy also is the emphasis on popular-priced psychoanalytic terms like "secret", "depths", "inside", "back view", "dark", "sleeping suit", "bed", by means of which Conrad—not only anticipating psychoanalysis but showing how to vulgarize it—makes his "myth" clear: perhaps destructively clear, for by the time we have given our energy to relating such coarse, obvious, and superabundant clues at the neatly systematic clinical level proper to them—the interest of myth reduced to the interest of the murder "mystery"—we have lost interest and faith in the narrative itself. If "The Secret Sharer" proves that Conrad is one of the many artist-precursors of depth psychology (we need only turn to the vigorous substantial particulars of Dostoievsky to see how such a precursor can be also, and primarily, an artist), what Conrad offers us here is not even a convincing case history: the captain-patient is too conscious of the symbols—or rather symptoms—that the artist-doctor would like him to exhibit. Conrad might have done better, clinically as well as artistically, if he had been describable by his critical partisans not as a poet in fiction, but as a man who merely tells a tale.

A writer is not responsible for the defects of his admirers, but it is perhaps some sort of judgment on Conrad that he has inspired so much criticism which must be filed under the phony-poetic, and of which the following effusion is representative: " 'The Secret Sharer' is a double allegory. It is an allegory of man's moral conscience, and it is an allegory of man's esthetic conscience. The form of 'The Secret Sharer', to diagram it, is the form of the capital letter L—the very form of the captain's room. (It is hinted at, again, in the initial letter of Leggatt's name.) One part of the letter L diagrams the allegory of the captain's divided soul, man in moral isolation and spiritual disunity. The other part of the letter represents the allegory of the artist's split soul ('the man who suffers and the mind which creates').

The captain stands at the angle of the two isolations and the two searches for selfhood. 'Such was my scheme,' says the captain, 'for keeping my second self invisible.' "[7] On all of[[425]] which C. H. Rickword, anticipating this deluge by twenty years, made the most charitable comment: "... the judgment of 'values' arrived at through a consideration of the symbolic aspect of character is unreliable because of the danger, almost the certainty, that attention will be diverted from the symbol to what it may be guessed to symbolize, which, if the artist is incompetent and the critic hospitable and sympathetic, will be much. It is for no other reason than that Conrad's heroes have been discerned by many earnest people to stand for something really tremendous in the matter of soul, that that writer has been so overestimated."[8]

The mythic and symbolic approach to Conrad is an example, and a representative one, of recent practice in the criticism of fiction. The problem attending this approach is also representative, beyond any single author: it is not that our fashionable (yet useful, indeed indispensable) critical terms compel an overvaluing of Conrad, but that in their claim to systematized usefulness, in their specious completeness, above all in their snowballing authority with critics understandably anxious to substitute categories for an active and disciplined taste, they may get in the way of our seeing any author except as a more or less skilful manipulator of disparate, thrillingly suggestive words.

We can, in fact, profitably stop here at words, and not go on to examine those word-patterns we have, at least till recently, agreed to call characters and events. Henry James once remarked on that "odd law by which the minimum of valid suggestion always serves the man [and, we may add, the *reader*] of imagination better than the maximum". Mr. Zabel, in his appreciation of Conrad, recalls it to us in passing; but it is a law that modern criticism—of Conrad and others —would do well, not casually to recollect, but, in justice to its unfashionable relevance, conscientiously to apply.[[426]]

---

[7] R. W. Stallman, "Life, Art, and 'The Secret Sharer' ", in *Forms of Modern Fiction*, ed. William Van O'Connor, Minneapolis, 1948, p. 241. For an even riper instance of the critic as preening phony-poet, the reader is directed in Mr. Stallman's essay to the three paragraphs beginning "Art is an aquarium" (pp. 234–6).

[8] "A Note on Fiction", in *Forms of Modern Fiction*, p. 296.

CONRAD'S BIOGRAPHY AND "THE SECRET SHARER"*
Jocelyn Baines

By the end of 1908 the Conrads had had enough of Someries and decided definitely to move back to Kent. They had found a cottage in Aldington, of which they were to have half, and seem to have made the move early in March.[1] But the change did not improve Conrad's health, and he was in and out of bed for the first seven months of the year.[2] Thus he seems to have seen scarcely any of his friends, and went to London only once, in order to see Galsworthy's play, *Strife,* in March.[3] But Conrad had one visit that had important repercussions on his work; it was from a Captain Marris who lived in Penang and was married to a Malayan girl. He described the visit to Pinker:

> It was like the raising of a lot of dead—dead to me, because most of them live out there and even read my books and wonder who [the] devil has been around taking notes. My visitor told me that Joshua Lingard made the guess: 'It must have been the fellow who was mate in the *Vidar* with Craig'. That's me right enough. And the best of it is that all these men of 22 years ago feel kindly to the Chronicler of their lives and adventures. They shall have some more of the stories they like. [Monday (October 1909), *LL.*, II, 103]

Conrad kept his word. This visit no doubt stirred his memory and prompted him to write the three stories set, broadly speaking, in the[354] Indian Ocean: 'The Secret Sharer', 'A Smile of Fortune', and 'Freya of the Seven Isles'. They were published together as *'Twixt Land and Sea; Tales* and dedicated to Captain Marris.

Conrad wrote 'The Secret Sharer' some time during the end of November and early December[4]—exceptionally quick for him. It is undoubtedly one of his best short stories, but certain critics, notably

* Reprinted with permission from *Joseph Conrad, a Critical Biography*, by Jocelyn Baines. Published by Weidenfeld & Nicolson, London, 1960, pp. 354–359, and McGraw-Hill Book Co., Inc., New York. Copyright, 1960, by Jocelyn Baines. [Title mine. Ed.]

1 Cf. Letter to Davray from Aldington of 10 March 1909, *Lettres Françaises*, 97.

2 Letter to Gibbon, 19 December 1909 (Berg Collection).

3 Letter to Galsworthy, 29 March 1909, *LL.*, II, 96.

4 Letter to Galsworthy, 14 December 1909, to Gibbon, 19 December 1909 (Berg Collection) and to Pinker, Wednesday.

Albert Guerard and Douglas Hewitt, have claimed for it a position
as a key story in Conrad's work and attributed to it a significance
which I do not believe that it can hold. It is intensely dramatic but,
on the psychological and moral level, rather slight.

The story is based on an incident which happened on board the
Cutty Sark in 1880.[5] The *Cutty Sark* had put in to Singapore on 18
September, three days after the chief officer of the *Jeddah* (the *Patna*
in *Lord Jim*) had arrived there.[6] In Conrad's adaptation of the *Cutty
Sark* incident, Leggatt, the mate of the *Sephora*, kills a disobedient
member of the crew during a storm and is put under arrest by his
captain. But he escapes and swims to another ship of which the
narrator of the story is captain. The captain is a young, comparatively
inexperienced man who has just been given his first command—
here Conrad seems to draw on his own experiences on the *Otago*—'a
stranger to the ship' and 'somewhat of a stranger to myself'.[7] He
had taken the anchor watch himself and thus spots Leggatt in the
water, clinging to a rope ladder; without calling anyone, for 'a
mysterious communication was established already between us two',[8]
he lets Leggatt come on board and fetches some clothes for him.

In a moment he had concealed his damp body in a sleeping-suit of the
same grey-stripe pattern as the one I was wearing and followed me like
my double on the poop.[9]

When the captain has heard Leggatt's story he decides that he
must hide him in his cabin. He does this at great risk and strain to
himself and at the cost of becoming somewhat estranged from the
rest of the crew because of the precautionary antics he has to go
through to prevent Leggatt being discovered.

After some eventful days which include a visit from the captain
of the *Sephora* he is able to come in close to shore and allow Leggatt
to escape.[355]

Constantly throughout the story it is emphasised that the young
captain regards Leggatt as his double, and in a letter to Pinker
Conrad suggested for titles of the story 'The Second Self', 'The
Secret Self', 'The Other Self'[10] (these three phrases, without the

5 *'Twixt Land and Sea*, xvi. For an account of the incident see Basil Lubbock,.
The Log of the 'Cutty Sark', third edition, Glasgow, 1928, pp. 183–202 and 410–12.
[See above, pp. 39–52. Ed.]
6 *Singapore Daily Times*, 18 September 1880. Another ship in Singapore was.
the *Bates Family* which had been totally dismasted and had the whole deck smashed
up. She may have been Conrad's model for the *Apse Family* in 'The Brute'.
7 'The Secret Sharer', *'Twixt Land and Sea*, 4.
8 *Ibid.*, 8.
9 *Ibid.*, 8–9.
10 Undated (December 1909).

definite article of course, occur in the text); he also suggested 'The Secret Sharer', but wondered whether it might not be too enigmatic. The point of this, apart from heightening the dramatic effect, and the point of the story, is to suggest that the fates of these two men were interchangeable, that it was quite possible for an ordinary, decent, conscientious person to kill someone or to commit some action which would make him 'a fugitive and vagabond on the earth.'[11] Thus Leggatt takes his place alongside Jim and Razumov. There is no suggestion of a transcendental relationship between Leggatt and the captain or of the 'double' being a psychological manifestation of an aspect of the original as there is in Poe's vulgar, trashy 'Richard [William] Wilson' or Dostoevsky's obscure nightmare, 'The Double'.

But that is the way in which Guerard interprets the story. For him the 'hero' is the young captain: 'The real moral dilemma is *his*, not Leggatt's'.[12] He, and Marlow in 'Heart of Darkness', 'must recognise their own potential criminality and test their own resources, must travel through Kurtz and Leggatt, before they will be capable of manhood . . . and moral survival'.[13] The story will bear this interpretation, as long as it is realised that such was no part of the author's conscious intention. However, Guerard goes on to assert that Leggatt is not merely an 'other self', he is a 'lower self', 'the embodiment of a more instinctive, more primitive, less rational self'.[14] I believe that this misses the whole point. Leggatt is not a symbol of the unconscious but a man on precisely the same level as the young captain; their selves are interchangeable (the epithet 'secret' might imply the opposite but its context and the whole tone of the story show that the word was intended in its literal sense: Leggatt was 'secret' because he had to be kept secret or hidden). Guerard's interpretation makes nonsense of the last sentence of the story, in which Leggatt departs, 'a free man, a proud swimmer striking out for a new destiny'. This is no way for a symbol of the unconscious to behave; Guerard's answer is that Leggatt is both a symbol and a 'man of flesh and blood'.[15] He continues: 'By seeing his own dilemmas[356] and difficulties in Leggatt, the captain has turned this man into symbol and spirit. . . . But at the end, emerging from his self-examination, the captain can see Leggatt as a separate and real human

11 'Twixt Land and Sea, 35.

12 Introduction, p. 10, to Heart of Darkness and The Secret Sharer, Signet Books, 1950.

13 Ibid., 9.

14 Ibid., 10. Curiously, R. W. Stallman (Accent, IX, 1949, pp. 131-44), one of the alchemical critics, has decided that Leggatt is a manifestation of the captain's superior self.

15 Ibid., 11.

being'.[16] But there is no indication in the story, explicit or implicit, that the captain sees any of his dilemma or difficulties in Leggatt or that he performs any self-examination. Nor is there any 'moral dilemma'.

Guerard's interpretation is based partly on what I believe is a mistaken assessment of the narrator's, or Conrad's, attitude to Leggatt's action. He claims that for Conrad, 'a crime on shipboard . . . was simply and irrevocably a crime'.[17] But there is no suggestion that Conrad or the captain-narrator condemns Leggatt's action; quite the contrary. At the start the captain says that he knew Leggatt was 'no homicidal ruffian';[18] and when the foolish mate comments on the event as 'A very horrible affair. . . . Beats all these tales about murders in Yankee ships', the captain snaps back: 'I don't think it beats them. I don't think it resembles them in the least'.[19] His own opinion is summed up: 'It was all very simple. The same strung-up force which had given twenty-four men a chance, at least, for their lives, had, in a sort of recoil, crushed an unworthy mutinous existence'.[20]

In this connexion it is interesting to see that Conrad softened the crime, if it can be called a crime, which took place on the Cutty Sark and also softened the character of the mate. The mate of the Cutty Sark was apparently a despotic character with a sinister reputation.[21] An order which he gave to an incompetent negro named John Francis was twice disobeyed, and when he went forward to deal with Francis the insubordinate seaman attacked him with a capstan bar; after a struggle the mate got hold of the bar and brought it down on Francis's head so heavily that he never regained consciousness and died three days later. Nonetheless the captain of the Cutty Sark, who was by no means a hard man, is supposed to have said that it served Francis right, and he helped the mate to escape from the law. When the mate was eventually captured and tried, he was acquitted of murder and the judge, 'with great pain', sentenced him to seven years for manslaughter.[22]

Leggatt was, however, clearly an exemplary sailor, and his provocation was greater; it was in the middle of a storm when the fate of the ship was at stake and the captain had lost his nerve. Leggatt was in the process of performing an action, which probably saved the[357]

16 Ibid., 12.
17 Ibid., 10.
18 'The Secret Sharer', 'Twixt Land and Sea, 10.
19 'Twixt Land and Sea, 23.
20 Ibid., 24.
21 Basil Lubbock, The Log of the 'Cutty Sark', 182–3. [See pp. 41 and 45, above. Ed.]
22 Basil Lubbock, ibid., 410–1. [See p. 55, above. Ed.]

ship, when one of the sailors was insubordinate; Leggatt 'felled him like an ox. He up and at me. We closed just as an awful sea made for the ship. All hands saw it coming and took to the rigging, but I had him by the throat, and went on shaking him like a rat, the men above us yelling, "Look out! look out!" Then a crash as if the sky had fallen on my head.'[23] Although Leggatt says, 'It's clear that I meant business, because I was holding him by the throat still when they picked us up,'[24] his action was far less deliberate than that of the mate of the *Cutty Sark*.

The object of this digression is to show that Conrad had no wish to condemn Leggatt but considered him an honourable man who had done something that other honourable men might equally well have done under similar circumstances. He was in fact 'simply knocked over' when a reviewer described Leggatt as 'a murderous ruffian',[25] and certainly had no intention that he should be a symbol of the dark impulses of human nature.

Although his interpretation is not so extreme, Hewitt also regards Leggatt as a symbol, 'an embodiment of his [the captain's] original feeling of being a "stranger" to himself, of that fear that there are parts of himself which he has not yet brought into the light of day', and this 'strangeness' is finally exorcised with the departure of Leggatt.[26] But this is again reading a meaning into the story which the text neither explicitly nor implicitly warrants; and despite the young captain's initial feeling of 'strangeness', the passage at the end where he says 'Nothing! no one in the world should stand now between us, throwing a shadow on the way of silent knowledge and mute affection, the perfect communion of a seaman with his first command'[27] can be countered by a similar passage, before Leggatt turns up, where the captain is alone in 'quiet communion' with the ship, his 'hand resting lightly on my ship's rail as if on the shoulder of a trusted friend'.[28]

▷   Although I do not believe that Conrad intended 'The Secret Sharer' to be interpreted symbolically, it is easy to discover an unconscious symbolism which has no direct literary relevance but is important psychologically and autobiographically. Conrad had just left off writing his reminiscences for the *English Review*, in which he had been particularly concerned to justify his action in leaving Poland

23 'The Secret Sharer', *'Twixt Land and Sea*, 10.
24 *Loc. cit.*
25 Monday (1913), *LL.*, II, 143.
26 Douglas Hewitt, *op. cit.*, 73–6. [See Bibliography. Ed.]
27 'The Secret Sharer', *'Twixt Land and Sea*, 36.
28 *Ibid.*, 4.

and to answer charges of desertion. It is tempting to identify Conrad
with Leggatt and to see the implicit justification of Leggatt's action as
a justification of Conrad's own, which metaphorically had made[358]
him too 'a fugitive and a vagabond on the earth, with no brand of
the curse on his sane forehead to stay a slaying hand—too proud to
explain'.[29] It seems that in the twelve months which saw the com-
pletion of the reminiscences, the writing of 'The Secret Sharer' and
the finishing of *Under Western Eyes,* Conrad finally succeeded in
coming to terms with his sense of guilt with regard to Poland. It is
thus that the last sentence of 'The Secret Sharer' acquires an added
significance as an expression of Conrad's desire to be:

a free man, a proud swimmer striking out for a new destiny.[30] [359]

29 *Ibid.,* 35.
30 *Ibid.,* 36.

❖ ❖

"THE SECRET SHARER" AND HUMAN PITY*

Walter F. Wright

. . . *The Shadow Line* (1916) and "The Secret Sharer" (1909) differ from *Typhoon* in that each presents the achievement of solidarity [of mankind] by persons who at first distinctly lack it. . . .[46] . . . In "The Secret Sharer" the young captain knows what is wrong with himself when he steps on board his ship:

But what I felt most was my being a stranger to the ship; and if all the truth must be told, I was somewhat of a stranger to myself... I wondered how far I should turn out faithful to that ideal conception of one's own personality every man sets up for himself secretly. (4-5)

This could be Lord Jim stepping aboard. Each order to the crew reminds the captain of his proper position, and each time he timidly falls short. The rest must be whispering about him, and his own blunders are fast making his position intolerable. It is through his negligence in setting the watch that the "sharer" comes aboard. Like Jim with the pirate Brown, the captain reads his own weaknesses into this man, the mate of the *Sephora,* who has killed a rebellious sailor. Unlike Jim, he is correct. The mate has erred through lack of mastery of his responsibility. When the captain of the *Sephora* comes to inquire and remarks that the fugitive is[48] not the kind of man to be first mate, the hero feels that he, too, is being condemned as unqualified to be chief mate on the *Sephora.*

The presence of the stranger, hidden now in the cabin, further alienates the captain from his ship. The suspected whispering becomes actual. Everyone knows that the captain is not meeting his task. The awareness of his own inadequacy makes him sympathize with like human error in others, even as Hester Prynne's feeling that she herself is sinful makes her more deeply sympathetic to sinful humanity. But what causes the struggle here is that the very bond which should tie him to his fellowmen—the secret of man's emotional and impulsive nature, of his fear and irresolution, of his unpredictability to himself —this bond is pulling him further away from the kinship which he must achieve with humanity as the master of a crew and a ship.

---

* Reprinted with permission from Walter F. Wright, *Romance and Tragedy in Joseph Conrad.* Lincoln: University of Nebraska Press, 1949, pp. 46, 48–50, 112–113. [Title mine. Ed.]

He seems caught in one universe which keeps him from finding a place in the other. In *Lord Jim*, where the hero is similarly torn by conflicting bonds, the atonement for his mistake in judgment, profoundly human as it is, comes when Jim pays with his life for believing in Brown. We are likely to feel that tragedy, as in *Lord Jim*, can resolve all psychological struggles. It is possible that it could resolve the captain's, but Conrad's dénouement is simpler. The captain must help the mate to escape. With Jim's delicacy of conscience, he cannot condemn to punishment a man who is his *alter ego* without feeling that he has been a traitor to his own soul and has forever separated himself from any standard of decency which makes society tenable.[1]

As the reader will remember, under the excuse of saving time the captain takes his ship dangerously close to shore, actuated by a desperate concern that the mate shall escape. In a burst of tenderness he has given the man his hat, the meager token of his realization that the fugitive will be forever a "vagabond on the earth." When this is left behind in the water as the man swims ashore, the captain descries it and uses it as a mark by which to sail his ship. As he gives[49] the orders that recover the boat from the shoals and watches it respond, he knows that he has sailed it as none of the mates would have dared to do and that he is its master and theirs as well:

Nothing! no one in the world should stand now between us, throwing a shadow on the way of silent knowledge and mute affection, the perfect communion of a seaman with his first command. (36)

The motif of the kind act's saving the doer is at least as old as Christianity. Conrad objected to Tolstoy for making the Christian religion his basis; yet he himself not infrequently arrived at a resolution of a paradox in accord with Christian sentiments. . . .[50] . . . In "The Secret Sharer," the captain is actually torn by his fellow-feeling and is a worse officer for it. It is only after he has gained command of the ship that he can have peace of mind and realize that his kind act rescued him. In Christian tragedy the hero achieves expiation when his own sin makes[112] him pity others. In "The Secret Sharer" the hero could not have achieved peace without such pity. . . .[113] . . . Since the particular choice of a hat as a gift, appropriate though it was, and its loss in the water rather than before, possible though that was, must conspire to help the captain find himself, the

1 Miss Muriel Bradbrook (*Joseph Conrad*) and Professor Zabel ("Joseph Conrad: Chance and Recognition") point out the possible significance of the sharer's being dressed in sleeping clothes: he becomes the representation of the captain's unconscious self. Such an interpretation is in accord with Conrad's statement that a work of art is not limited to any one meaning.

incident certainly assumes symbolic importance. If the incident be
accepted—otherwise, despite Conrad's assertion, the reader will put
the ship high on the shoals—then one form of solidarity, the kinship
of the suffering heart, has brought about the second, the submergence
in the tradition to which a captain must belong. This is a tradition
which, in the language of Stein, serves for him as a dream, a world
in which, in Conrad's own terms, the captain can believe.

From Conrad's writing, quite apart from the tragic scenes, many
other examples can be found to support those that have been given.
Solidarity was obviously, for Conrad, no light acquiescence in society.
It was certainly not arrived at by one's intellectually deciding what
would be most helpful to one's fellows and then exerting will power
to do one's duty. It came when a man apprehended the mysterious
nature of human personality and destiny and found a dream that gave
his world a center. When he did this, however far he might be
estranged from actual men, he was true to the life of man.[50]

MORALITY AND PSYCHOLOGY
IN "THE SECRET SHARER"*
Royal A. Gettmann and Bruce Harkness

Basil Lubbock's account of the incident upon which Conrad based
"The Secret Sharer" may profitably be used in various ways to sharpen
one's reading of the story. More significantly it raises the question of
historical as differentiated from artistic truth, and provides some insight into the creative process.

In one sense there is but little invention in "The Secret Sharer."
In respect to the world of external appearances—the world of things,
places, and actions—there are numerous parallels between the short
story and the actual events aboard the *Cutty Sark* as narrated in Lubbock's "A Hell-Ship Voyage." The same is true of the possible source
material from the London *Times*. Among the most prominent like-
nesses are the following:

1. The mutinous spirit of Wallace's men (after the mate has
escaped) seems to be transformed into the suspicion with which the
mates and the steward view the Captain in "The Secret Sharer."

2. The troublesome, inefficient qualities of John Francis seem to
be translated into the noxious qualities of Leggatt's victim, thus help-
ing to secure the reader's sympathy for Leggatt. And the good qualities
of Smith as emphasized in the *Times* items are echoed in the admirable
traits in Leggatt.

3. Lubbock describes in detail the running of the *Cutty Sark*
before a gale, during which the men had to go aloft to bend the topsail.
Does not this incident, combined with the earlier fight between Francis
and Smith, remind one of the extreme difficulty Leggatt had in getting
the sail reefed, as he relates in "The Secret Sharer"?

4. In Lubbock the gale is followed by good breezes, but the *Cutty
Sark* is later becalmed "in under the shadow of Krakatoa" and her
rival, the *Titania,* glides into Anjer ahead of her. Are not this and the
three-day calm after Smith's escape reminiscent of the nerve-twisting

* This article represents an expansion by the present editor of a note first
published by the authors in the *Teacher's Manual* for *A Book of Stories*
published by Rinehart & Co., Inc., New York, 1955, pp. 41–46. It is reprinted by
permission of Holt, Rinehart and Winston, Inc., and Royal A. Gettmann.

calm which Conrad so heavily emphasizes? (It is "one of my two Calm-pieces," he said in his "Author's Note.")

5. Numerous details of the actual events may be echoed in "The Secret Sharer." Perhaps Thwarttheway or the rocks in the Sunda Sea which the *Cutty Sark* skirted are the source of the Koh-ring episode in the short story.

These parallels and echoes should not be pressed very far for the obvious reason that Conrad's years at sea must have made known to him numberless episodes which he might have drawn upon in the writing of "The Secret Sharer." Nevertheless, one is bound to confess to the impression that the historical event of the murder in the *Cutty Sark* is the source of more Conradian details than at first might be supposed.

But in another and more important sense "The Secret Sharer" is quite independent of the analogue and is wholly the creation of Conrad's imagination. Indeed, the contrast of the two versions is a good illustration of Aristotle's doctrine that poetry—creative writing—is higher than history:

> ...Poetry is something more philosophic and of graver import than history, since its statements are of the nature rather of universals, whereas those of history are singulars. By a universal statement I mean one as to what such or such a kind of man will probably or necessarily say or do—which is the aim of poetry, though it affixes proper names to the characters; by a singular statement, one as to what, say, Alcibiades did or had done to him.

In other words, Lubbock is writing a particular, and is content to supply the simplest of motives for Wallace's suicide—namely, worry over the scandal and fear of losing his job. But to Conrad the moral and psychological issues raised by the events in 1880 on the *Cutty Sark* are far more complex and cause him to shift the focus of the story entirely.

To put it simply, Conrad begins his story where Lubbock's account left off: he is telling not the story of a murder but the story of what happened after the escape of the mate. What happened, furthermore, was not a crime that could be adjusted by laws and juries and indemnities but an inward problem in morals, which required the utmost in self-scrutiny and complete personal responsibility. Conrad passes over Wallace and shifts the interest to the Captain of the ship to which the mate escaped. By making Leggatt symbolically the Captain's double, Conrad makes the moral issues all the greater, since *our* Captain faces the problems of all three men—Smith, Wallace, and the Captain of the American ship, *Colorado*. (Symbolically, he joins Leggatt in the killing, Wallace in arranging the escape, the other Captain in harboring a murderer.)

Indeed, Conrad deepened the moral issues even further, for he radically altered the moral problem to the concept of joint guilt—the guilt of one is the guilt of all. In these "philosophic" terms, Lubbock's accomplishment was a modest one—to record how in the 1880's a particular man, Sidney Smith, struck one John Francis and how his blow affected the men immediately connected with the two. Conrad felt obliged to penetrate much more deeply: to show that the universe and human nature are so constituted that any man innocently passing the time of night anywhere may have thrust upon him a moral dilemma that can be resolved only at the cost of a bitter struggle.

"The Secret Sharer" is of a class of stories all too rare. It has, as so many modern stories do not, a sustained and combined appeal. It offers the immediate appeal of an action or adventure story as well as the aesthetic pleasures of symbolic, psychological, and moral investigation. Most commentaries on the story, though often excellent, tend to concentrate on the technical beauties of the piece as it presents the theme of the "double" man—the psychological aspect. Although clearly recognizing that the story's symbolism has a moral as well as a psychological content, many critics have fixed their discussion on Conrad's presentation of Leggatt as the Captain's hidden self, his alter ego. This critical concentration has led Marvin Mudrick (in the article reprinted in this volume) to an attack on the critics—and on the story—as a labored and wordy statement that man has an inner self and that the inner self is not so good as it might be.

In the final analysis, Conrad's greatest interest is in the moral aspect of the story. At the level of action he adds little to Lubbock's account; likewise the possible social issues are played down—Conrad, for example, has no reference in civil or maritime law for his conclusion, nor does he bring in the point that the victim, John Francis, was a Negro, which could have been used to give an entirely different and social focus to the story. What Conrad adds to Lubbock are the psychological and the moral elements. And our interest in the psychological should be counterbalanced by an analysis of the story's moral range. What is Conrad saying about moral problems *through* what he is saying about psychological facts? For that seems to us the proper stress of one's reading.

When the Captain states the theme early in the story, saying "I wondered how far I should turn out faithful to that ideal conception of one's own personality every man sets up for himself secretly," he is talking about more than psychology: he is worried about his moral state. That the story is primarily moral is brought out clearly later on in the tale. It is, for example, a matter of *conscience* for the Captain to bring the ship closer into shore than he need for so strong a swimmer as Leggatt.

Guerard implies that the story, insofar as we interpret it according to the Captain-narrator's motives for sheltering Leggatt, is essentially psychological: "the reasons for the narrator's act are defined as 'psychological (not moral)'" (p. 66, above). This evidence, however, can be taken to have a very different significance. Guerard is referring to the scene in which Captain Archbold confronts our Captain. "I could not, I think," says the narrator, "have met him by a direct lie, again for psychological (not moral) reasons. If he had only known how afraid I was of his putting my feeling of identity with the other to the test" (p. 21.39)!

But what Conrad is saying here is that the psychological aspect of the story is *settled;* it is the moral issue that is still operating. "A mysterious communication" exists between Leggatt and the Captain from the first moment they meet. That psychological issue is resolved long before Archbold arrives, but the moral problem still exists. It is this side of the situation, not the psychological, that gives the shape and drive of the story. In other words, one suspects that Guerard takes the narrator to mean that he had no moral qualms about lying to Archbold, but for psychological reasons he couldn't—and he knew he couldn't—give the direct lie. Perhaps the sentence would bear this meaning, but in context, and as it relates to the plot of the story, the meaning is very nearly the opposite: the psychological problems have been solved, but the moral ones remain and are those which are being struggled with—though often in terms of the psychological. At the very least, the sentence cannot be said to "define" the reasons for the Captain's decision to harbor Leggatt.

We suggest, then, not only that the basic theme of "The Secret Sharer" is a moral one, but that emphasizing this aspect of the story will minimize such questions as Guerard's on the last paragraph of the tale. In his "Direction One" monograph on Conrad, Guerard feels that the ending does violence to the symbolism:

...The story is ... surely a study of the preconscious and the subconscious.... Leggatt is not a fragment of the Captain's imagination but a created symbol.... The marked advantages of lucid definition through the body of the story more than compensate for the wrenching of the symbol at the end. Theoretically, Leggatt should have remained on the ship, "locked up" perhaps... —unless we argue that once we have faced and conquered our dark potentialities we have conquered them for good and all. But to have Leggatt remain in the ship would of course have ruined the first and purely adventurous level of the story.[1]

Guerard, in other words, considers Leggatt as primarily a psycho-

[1] Albert Guerard, Jr., *Joseph Conrad*, "Direction One"; New York, 1947, pp. 40–41.

logical symbol, and is forced to refer the ending to the level of the adventure story (as well as, earlier, to grant as barely acceptable Gustav Morf's theory that the story is another example of the theme of *Lord Jim*: "paralysis through identification with guilt").

There are at least two responses called for here. First, to question whether all details in the story—or any such story—are equally significant in all its aspects of meaning. For example, is the "young cub" of a second mate equally significant in the adventurous, psychological, and moral strands? Clearly not. Second, to point out that the psychological problem (or error on Conrad's part) which Guerard raises is considerably less significant in the moral reading of the story. It seems to us that only if one takes the tale to be essentially psychological can he interpret the last paragraph as a wrenching of the symbolism of "The Secret Sharer."

To develop this point, the general significance of Leggatt must first be determined. His own story in the background of "The Secret Sharer" has often been overlooked. In the killing of the man, and in the weeks of contemplation, Leggatt has discovered that he, although not a "murdering ruffian," does have a streak of violence within him. The killing itself was no accident, although the crime is mitigated by the storm and the wave that struck the *Sephora* at that moment. The truth is that Leggatt completely lost control of himself—a *fit* of temper. "It's clear I meant business, because I was still holding him by the throat when they picked us up [after more than ten minutes]...." "When I came to myself," he adds later—which can only mean that he was unconscious with anger, for there seems no indication in the passage that Leggatt had passed out from near-drowning. This fit, furthermore, lasted even after the wave had passed—"It *seems* they rushed us forward," Leggatt had said of the crew. (Our italics.)

Although it is not a crime in the sense that Leggatt intended or premeditated a murder, and although Leggatt is not a "murdering ruffian" as Conrad might very possibly have applied the term to Smith of the *Cutty Sark*, Conrad is clearly portraying a man who does have a streak of violence within him. This Leggatt, even before he meets our Captain, admits to himself. It is this he has learned. The Captain, so obviously identified with Leggatt, hence learns that he too has this criminal instinct. Furthermore, Leggatt in the terms of *Lord Jim* is "one of us" and so is the Captain—the criminal instinct is in every man. To Conrad—the rebel as well as the aristocrat—a man's knowledge of his criminality is a private concern: neither the church (represented by Leggatt's father, who is a Norfolk parson, and Captain Archbold of the *Sephora*) nor the law ("an old fellow in a wig and twelve respectable tradesmen") can understand, judge, or help a man. Perhaps later the issue can be referred to a social level, but it is essentially private.

This, then, is what Leggatt symbolizes: the instinct for violence in the Captain; his acknowledging Leggatt as his double means just that, for to acknowledge Leggatt is to acknowledge violence.

When Leggatt comes to the ship, the issue shifts to that of guilt. He at first confesses no guilt whatever: "I can't see the necessity [of standing trial]. . . . An angel from heaven [would have killed the troublemaker]." He partly had accepted the mark of Cain when he asked Archbold to let him swim to the Java Coast, and he accepts it more fully later. He will become a wanderer. But only he knows the nature of his guilt. "What can they know whether I am guilty or not—or of *what* I am guilty, either? That's my affair" (p. 29.15). All of this the Captain of course shares. But only he, not Leggatt, fully accepts the word "guilt" (p. 24.13). From Leggatt, then, the Captain gains self-knowledge by sharing his climactic experience—just as Marlow does from Kurtz in "Heart of Darkness." It is again knowledge of inner savagery.

At the end of "Heart of Darkness," while winning his way back to civilization, Marlow lies to Kurtz's Betrothed, though he hates a lie. Just as Marlow feels he owes Kurtz that Lie, so does the Captain in "The Secret Sharer" feel that he owes Leggatt something. Leggatt has had to go through intense pain to win his knowledge and his freedom —most obviously, through the imprisonment and the swimming. For the Captain, the knowledge has come too easily—despite the more than four days of anxiety caused by Leggatt's presence. And that is why the Captain must shave so closely the sides of Koh-ring. He deliberately puts himself in pain and danger because he thus will "pay" Leggatt, pay for his self-knowledge and "lay Leggatt's ghost" as Marlow had laid Kurtz's.

Furthermore, this dangerous act is an atonement for a "sort of cowardice" earlier in the story. When Leggatt first suggests that he be abandoned on the Cambodje shore, the Captain refuses. But he immediately realizes that this was an indulgent pity, a "sham sentiment" through which he himself wished to escape punishment. In momentarily wishing to spare his double the punishment of being marooned, he was really trying to avoid the consequences of his own self-knowledge.

Finally, Conrad is making a point about the morality of action. It is a point concerned with the instinctive, impulsive side of man, represented primarily by Leggatt. We tend to return to the motive in order to judge good or ill of an act. Conrad reminds us that in doing so we must not ignore the result: "The same strung-up force which had given twenty-four men a chance, at least, for their lives [when Leggatt had reefed the foresail of the *Sephora*] had, in a sort of recoil, crushed an unworthy mutinous existence."

Leggatt, the evil, impulsive side of the Captain, had saved the *Sephora;* both a murderous act and a good one have the same source in impulse. Leggatt's second impulsive act is in jumping overboard from the *Sephora* when he escapes. ("I don't know that I meant to do anything. . . . Then a sudden temptation came over me.") His only other impulsive act is in leaving the hat as he swam from the Captain's ship—"It must have fallen off his head . . . and he didn't bother." It is symbolically, then, the dark, inner side of the Captain which saves the ship in both instances.

Or, rather, it is the *hat* which saves the ship. And the hat is a double symbol—first, of Leggatt, the impulsive man (and it can be seen by the Captain only because Leggatt passes under it in "a phosphorescent flash," just as he had first appeared as "a faint flash of phosphorescent light"); second, of the Captain's pity for the human, fallen condition—giving the hat to Leggatt is just about the only impulsive act of our Captain in the whole story: "a sudden pity for his [Leggatt's] mere flesh," as he saw himself [Leggatt, in the *MS*] "wandering barefooted, bareheaded, the sun beating on" his head on the stark land of Cochin-China, moved the Captain to this act.

The hat then combines the expression of the Captain's pity and the dark impulse of Leggatt. It is, finally, a symbol of integration. It saves the present ship by permitting the Captain to navigate his ship safely past the rocks. The dark side of man saved the *Sephora,* as well as all hands aboard the new ship. In the world of ships at least, in Conrad's basic world of confidence, restraint, and trustworthiness, the savage [Leggatt] within a man has a place.

That savagery is part and parcel of an attribute lacked by such men as Heyst in *Victory.* Heyst lacks the readiness to act without thinking; he falters in the moment that may save all. "Heyst in his fine detachment," Conrad said of him in the "Author's Note" to *Victory,*

had lost the habit of asserting himself. I don't mean the courage of self-assertion, either moral or physical, but the mere way of it, the trick of the thing, the readiness of mind and the turn of the hand that come without reflection and lead the man to excellence in life, in art, in crime, in virtue and for the matter of that, even in love. Thinking is the great enemy of perfection. The habit of profound reflection, I am compelled to say, is the most pernicious of all the habits formed by the civilised man.

For Heyst, in trying to be entirely good, has ceased to be a man. A man must act, must be in part impulsive, instinctive—and this side of him is in a sense amoral. It may produce good (the giving of the hat) or evil; but the basic point is that it is essential for life and action. "A certain order should spring to his [a seaman's] lips without thinking;

a certain sign should get itself made, so to speak, without reflection," says the Captain in "The Secret Sharer." A kind of amoral spectrum is set up, in which Conrad recognizes the moral importance of vast differences of degree: at one end of the spectrum is the criminal instinct, which imperceptibly merges through the instinct for right action and the giving of certain orders to the other extreme of pity. The management of this spectrum—where there is no logical way of drawing a dividing line—is the art of life. Conrad is saying that there is no difference in moral kind between the making of a certain sign and the killing of a man; the attribute of impulsive action contains within it the seeds of savagery. To deny it is at best foolish, to be unaware of it (the Captain at the beginning of the story, or the early Leggatt) is to imperil all. If this attribute contains savagery, that is a fact to recognize and be wary of: but it is a fact to swim and sail on from, in the self-confidence and manhood won by pain of recognition.

◆ ◆

ECHO STRUCTURES: CONRAD'S "THE SECRET SHARER"*
Louis H. Leiter

For the most part critics agree that the narrator of Joseph Conrad's *The Secret Sharer* is a double for the protagonist, that actions and gestures of this newly appointed captain are reflected in the movements and behavior of the recently escaped Leggatt, and that each man echoes the most private thoughts and sentiments of the other. A series of echoes established by means of image, metaphor, symbol, and mime consistently suggest to the reader the manner in which he should interpret the roles of Leggatt and the captain-narrator. Although they are one person figuratively, the inner and the outer, the unconscious and the conscious, they are split for didactic and aesthetic reasons into two characters. What has escaped notice, however, is that echo structures similar to those which portray character have been employed for other reasons as well as this throughout the short novel. Structures not only of character but also of narrative action, parable, metaphor, and the like, become a fundamental means for achieving aesthetic and thematic effects.[1]

The echo structure: An echo structure implies one or more structures similar to itself. The tautology which is the echo structure may be a repeated symbol, metaphor, scene, pattern of action, state of being, myth, fable, or archetype. If viewed within the perspective of Biblical story or classical myth, either directly stated in the text of the story or implied, that perspective may suffuse the echo structures of similar

* Reprinted from "Echo Structures: Conrad's 'The Secret Sharer,'" *Twentieth Century Literature,* V, No. 1 (January 1960), 159–175. By permission of the author. [The quotations from "The Secret Sharer" in this article are taken from the 1912 Doubleday edition. Ed.]

1 All quotations are from *'Twixt Land and Sea* by Joseph Conrad, 1912, Doubleday & Company, Inc. For the most perceptive analyses of *The Secret Sharer* I refer the reader to R. B. West and R. W. Stallman, *The Art of Modern Fiction* (New York, 1949), pp. 490–500; Albert J. Guerard's introduction to *Heart of Darkness* and *The Secret Sharer* (New York, 1950), pp. 7–15; Winifred Lynskey's provocative questions and statements in *Reading Modern Fiction* (New York, 1952), pp. 147–149. All italics are mine except the title of the novel and the name of the ship.

I am grateful to Robert Creed and George Monteiro of Brown University for their encouragement and criticism.

construction with additional meanings. If seen from the vantage of imagery alone, an echo structure is what has been called the principle of reflexive reference.[2] It evokes thematic meaning when the total pattern of images has been examined in the context in which it appears. The thematic significance of echo structures will be demonstrated in the course of this essay.

Image cluster as echo structure: In this essay an image is any word which creates a relatively concrete "picture" in or presents some configuration[159] to the reader's mind. Almost any word may be used for this purpose. Clusters of images occur when certain groups of words fall together recurrently so that we identify them as somehow significantly related. Thus Conrad's short novel opens with these lines:

> On my right hand there were *lines of fishing-stakes* resembling *a mysterious system* of *half-submerged bamboo fences, incomprehensible in its* division of the domain of tropical fishes, and *crazy of aspect* as if abandoned forever by some *nomad tribe of fishermen now gone to the other end of the ocean;* for there was no sign of human habitation as far as the eye could reach.

In isolation these opening lines accomplish little more than the establishing of an appropriate atmosphere of mystery and the underlining of the narrator-captain's solitude as a stranger to his ship, to his men, and to himself. A few hours later, however, as the narrator paces the deck of his first command after sending all his men to rest, he suddenly discovers the ladder hanging over the side:

> Then I reflected that I had myself peremptorily dismissed my officers from duty, and by my own act had prevented the anchor-watch being formally set and things properly attended to.... Not from compunction, certainly, but, as it were mechanically. I *proceeded to get the ladder in myself.* Now a side-ladder of that sort is *a light affair* and comes in easily, yet my *vigorous tug,* which should have brought it flying on board, merely recoiled upon my body in *a totally unexpected jerk.* What the devil! ... I was so *astonished* by the immovableness of that ladder that I remained stock-still, trying to account for it myself *like that imbecile mate of mine.* In the end, of course, I put my head over the rail.... I saw at once *something elongated and pale floating very close to the ladder.* Before I could form a guess a faint flash of phosphorescent light, which seemed to issue suddenly from the naked body of a man, flickered in the sleeping water.... *As he hung by the ladder,* like a resting swimmer, the sea lightning played about his limbs at every stir; and he appeared in it *ghastly, silvery fish-like. He remained as mute as a fish, too.*

---

[2] I am referring to Joseph Frank, "Special Form in Modern Literature," *Sewanee Review,* 53:221–240 (Summer, 1945), 53:433–456 (Autumn, 1945), 53:643–653 (Winter, 1945).

In this passage the imagery cluster of the opening lines is echoed. However, the original cluster has been modified into another cluster which resembles the first one but with certain significant changes. What is described as a seascape in the first passage is echoed in the second, and we shall see it once more in a third, with a more personal significance for the narrator. The "half-submerged bamboo fences" for catching fish suggest the "ladder," that "light affair," which the narrator, annoyed with his own negligence, "proceeded to get in." The "tug" and "jerk" of the second passage further suggest the idea of the narrator's fishing with something like a bamboo fence which has undergone a transformation into a ladder. "Mysterious" of the first passage echoes in "astonished"[160] of the second, while "crazy of aspect" in the first appears as "imbecile mate" in the second. And "fishermen" of the former echoes in "fish-like" of the latter, reinforced by Leggatt's being "mute as a fish."

This first cluster of images along with the second, somewhat modified cluster appears once more in *The Secret Sharer*. Toward the end of the story when the narrator relates that he must rid himself and his ship of Leggatt, he thinks:

Whoever was being driven distracted, it was not he. He was sane. And the proof of his sanity was continued when he took up the whispering again. "It would never do for me to come to life again. . . . What does the Bible say? *'Driven off the face of the earth.' Very well. I am off the face of the earth now. As I came at night so I shall go."*

Once more the cluster of images echoes in this passage. We perceive that the two earlier structures are here somewhat shortened, some elements eliminated, and others echoed more strongly in modified form. "Distracted" and "sane" and "sanity" echo one set of images, while the Biblical quotation, "Driven off the face of the earth," transforms the image of "nomad tribe" into something more mysterious and frightening.

What the second and third passages accomplish is to charge the first passage with meanings which it does not possess when first read. Only after reading the second passage, and especially after reading the third, do we see that the first is a symbolic seascape corresponding point by point to the central thematic tensions of the novel and to the narrator's lack of knowledge of his own untested psyche. What we perceive through the narrator's eyes as he describes the setting is the projected, unexplored, unknown seascape of his own mind plucked, as it were, inside out and superimposed on the sea and land; but neither the narrator nor the reader becomes fully aware of this until much later. For the reader this occurs at the moment he perceives that the imagery clusters in the two widely separated echo structures have already appeared in the introductory passage.

The setting at the beginning is mysterious, atmospherically strange and unknown. Gradual revelation of and coming to terms with self throughout the novel is accompanied by a gradual change in and transformation of the imagery clusters parallel to the awakening to self-knowledge. The bamboo fence belonging to the strangers becomes the narrator's own ladder, the means by which he "hooks" and brings to the surface his own secret self, that strange being who seems to live beyond the pale of human laws and who does indeed circumvent human punishment. The imagery in "fishing-stakes . . . . crazy of aspect" echoes in the narrator's being "astonished" when he pulls at the ladder with the creature, "mute as a fish," at its end, and in his description of his Chief Mate as an "imbecile." What this identification by means of imagery suggests is that somehow the three men, Leggatt-narrator-mate, are one person, or that certain aspects of their personalities are to be identified as similar.

Leggatt performs the role of the narrator's inner self, the possibility[161] of the defections of the unconscious mind, its lawless (libidinous) forces breaking forth and overpowering law and order. Since they are identified through the imagery cluster, however, a specific aspect of the narrator's personality must be embodied in his Chief Mate. The narrator becomes more and more certain throughout the novel that he is losing his mind, that he is insane, that perhaps he is only imagining that he shares his cabin with Leggatt whom no one else has seen. In this way he gradually drifts toward the "imbecility" which he attaches so violently to his Chief Mate. Then in the third echo structure, the narrator confirms his own dangerous psychic condition when he seriously hints at his gradual loss of sanity, "Whoever was being driven distracted, it was not he. He was sane. And the proof of his sanity was continued when he took up the whispering again."

Conrad, I believe, wants us to see here that both men are indeed different aspects of the narrator's personality. The Chief Mate in many respects is just as dangerous as Leggatt. It is he who goes to pieces during the narrator's supreme test. Like Leggatt and like Captain Archbold of the *Sephora* he loses control of himself when in danger. Unlike Leggatt but still like Captain Archbold, the Chief Mate is obtuse. This very insensitivity, lack of trust, unawareness of the possible strength of personality, leads to his breakdown. But it also contributes to the narrator's demonstration of control over that very weakness of his own personality during the final trial scene in which he seizes the blubbering Chief Mate and transfers his strength to that man. Through this gesture (a mime repeated from the sail locker scene where he had gripped Leggatt just before consigning him to the deep) the narrator symbolically conquers the obtuseness of his own personality. The imagery cluster identifies the three men as one person and imagistically suggests that "insanity" and "imbecility" are symbolic of weakness or obtuseness. That part of the first cluster which is not echoed in the second cluster but appears in the third cluster of images, "some nomad tribe of fishermen now gone to the other end of the ocean," suggests the fate of Leggatt and the fate of the narrator himself. The Biblical echo, "Driven off the face of the earth," is identified throughout *The Secret Sharer* with the Cain and Abel story, to which I shall return later in this essay. The first time the imagery appears, it is impersonally attached to "nomad tribe"; it does not affect the narrator in any way, although when we glance back at it we see it as part of the symbolic construction in that first passage to which "meanings" may be attached. Then suddenly a stranger, a wanderer, a swimmer really, appears at the ship's side. The absence of this part of the cluster of images in the second echo passage suggests the absence of knowledge as to who the stranger is or what he represents. But when the cluster appears again in the third echo passage, the narrator-captain has already gained knowledge of himself, of Leggatt, of his Chief Mate, and of the perilous situation on board his ship; he knows that he must help Leggatt, the Cain aspect of his personality, escape back into the sea (come to terms with or repress his inner self). The imagery cluster[162] consequently from its introduction (nomad tribe) to its final echo (the Cain as wanderer reference) describes a movement from the superficial to the profound, from lack of knowledge of personality to penetrating awareness of what that part of the personality is capable of accomplishing—victory over moral disorder and victory over obtuseness.

Parable as echo structure: Parable, a short, simple story or observation, usually but not always an allegory, may serve as an echo structure. In the beginning of *The Secret Sharer,* as the narrator stands on the deck of his first command, watching the departing tug, which brought him to the harbor, he observes:

Here and there *gleams as of a few scattered pieces of silver* marked the windings of the great river; and on the nearest of them, just within the bar, *the tug steaming right into the land became lost to my sight, hull and funnel and masts, as though the impassive earth had swallowed her up without an effort, without a tremor.* My eye followed the light cloud of her smoke, now here, now there, above the plain, according to the devious curves of the stream, but always fainter and farther away, till *I lost it at last behind the mitershaped hill of the great pagoda.* And then I was left alone with my ship, anchored at the head of the Gulf of Siam.

This parable of the tug is echoed later in the novel when Conrad expands it into a major action, the most important one of the novel. As the tug steams into the land, so does the narrator's ship steam into the land when he sails in shore to rid himself of Leggatt. The identity of the echoed structures is made clear through the use of corresponding images. The water in both passages is silvery; a tug appears in one, a ship in the other; the "mitre-shaped" hill in the first, the mountain "Koh-ring" in the second. This is strengthened in the echo structure at the moment of climax when the narrator says of his ship, "Already she was, I won't say in the shadow of the land, but in the very blackness of it, already swallowed up as it were, gone too close to be recalled, gone from me altogether." The "silver" marking the passage of the river from the land into the sea will be reversed in the final structure into the "white hat" which marked the passage of Leggatt towards the land, with a reversal of the action included in the structures "from land to sea" to "from sea to land."

The major difference between the parable and its tautological echo in the latter structure is one of expansion and substitution; the dozen lines of the parable become the half dozen pages of the dilated action. Similarly that which the twenty-seven year old narrator impassively narrates in the first structure becomes that in which he is intimately, even passionately, involved in the echo structure. He speaks in the parable of the land as "impassive"; but in the structure of the echoed parable, the land becomes a place of "unrest" and "disquiet." The echo suggests, consequently, not only a structural principle operative in the novel, but also the result of "involvement" in experience, an experience[163] which the narrator, untried in his new command, has never undergone previously, one which he observes in the parable's structure and one which he suffers through most intimately in the echo structure. The echoed, symbolic parable suggests that impassivity becomes disquietude when impersonality, lack of dedication to knowledge of self, becomes conscious dedication to a course of behavior leading to self-knowledge. "I wondered how far I should turn out faithful to that ideal conception of one's own personality every man sets up for himself secretly." As such this echoed parabolic structure establishes thematic meanings.

One more example of this principle will contribute to our understanding here. When thinking of his new Chief Mate, the narrator describes him in these terms:

He was of a painstaking turn of mind. As he used to say, he "liked to account to himself" for practically everything that came in his way, down to *a miserable scorpion he had found in his cabin a week before. The why and wherefore of that scorpion—how it got on board and came to select his room rather than the pantry (which was a dark place and more what a scorpion would be partial to), and how on earth it managed to drown itself in the inkwell of his writing desk*—had exercised him infinitely.

The extended actions of Leggatt in *The Secret Sharer* are an echo structure of the parable of the scorpion. As a matter of fact, the parable is almost a brief allegory of the entire action of the novel itself. The scorpion appears from the sea and enters the Chief Mate's cabin only to fall into the ink. Leggatt rises from the sea, enters the narrator's cabin, and then returns to the black waters of Koh-ring. Both scorpion and Leggatt are identified with light. The latter appears beside the ship all flashes of fire and phosphorescence; the former seeks the light of the Chief Mate's cabin. And Captain Archbold of the *Sephora*, repeating the allegory once more, appears over the side of the ship in daylight and disappears over her side a short time later with his red whiskers twitching.

As in the instance of the tug-ship parable, the scorpion-Leggatt parable structure is expanded into many times its former, brief form and is modified and told in human terms. The echo structure of the scorpion parable appears a fourth time when after Captain Archbold of the *Sephora* departs, the narrator's Chief Mate tells him that the crew of the *Sephora* suspected Leggatt was aboard:

"There was some little dispute about it. Our chaps took offence. *'As if we would harbour a thing like that,'* they said. *'Wouldn't you like to look for him in our coal-hole?'* Quite a tiff. But they made it up in the end. *I suppose he did drown himself. Don't you, sir?"*

Comparison of the scorpion parable and the echoing structures suggests the significance of the echo technique. Thematically the parable symbolizes something about the echoing action. The scorpion, mysterious, poisonous, inexplicable,[164] provides meanings for Leggatt's actions, meanings for the consequences of those actions, which are not explicitly stated. Leggatt's arrival on the ship is as mysterious as that of the vermin and as dangerous to the narrator if he remains on the ship. The deadly quality of the scorpion is precisely that danger the captain experiences in his intercourse with Leggatt, the gradual but continuous poisoning of his relationship with his crew. Thus in another brief echo of the scorpion parable, Leggatt tells the narrator of the steward and second mate of the *Sephora* who hated him "like poison." And in still another the poison is at work in the narrator's ship:

I was not wholly alone with my command; for there was that stranger in my cabin. *Or rather, I was not completely and wholly with her. Part of me was absent. That mental feeling of being in two places at once affected me physically as if the mood of secrecy had penetrated my very soul.*

Drowning of the scorpion signified not only the return of Leggatt to the black waters of Koh-ring but also the metaphorical death of the captain's "secret-sharer," the inner, uncontrollable, unconscious self, which verminlike, must return into the great sea of the unconscious from which it arose.

As the consequence of the use of parable as a structure which is echoed again and again in the novel, multiple thematic and symbolic dimensions are created which contribute to total meaning.[3]

Action as echo structure: Action may also create echo structures. When Leggatt tells the young narrator of the man he has murdered, he says:

There are fellows that an angel from heaven—And I am not that. He was one of those creatures that are just simmering all the time with a silly sort of wickedness. Miserable devils that have no business to live at all. He wouldn't do his duty and wouldn't let anybody else do theirs.... *He gave me some of his cursed insolence at the sheet.* I tell you I was overdone with this terrific weather that seemed to have no end to it. Terrific, I tell you—and a deep ship. *I believe the fellow himself was half crazed with funk. It was no time for gentlemanly reproof. So I turned round and felled him like an ox. He up and at me. We closed just as an awful sea made for the ship.* All hands saw it coming and took to the rigging, but *I had him by the throat, and went on shaking him like a rat, the men above us yelling 'Look out! look out!'* Then a crash as if the sky had fallen on my head. They say that for over ten minutes *hardly anything was to be seen of the ship*—just the three masts and a bit of the forecastle head and of the poop all awash driving along in a smother of foam. It was a miracle that they found us, jammed together behind the forebits. *It's clear that I meant business, because I was holding him by the throat when they picked us up.* He was black in the face.

Later when the narrator takes his untried ship into shore, ostensibly[165] to catch the land breezes, the following transpires between him and his Chief Mate hard upon a description of the "very blackness" of the mountain Koh-ring:

---

[3] West and Stallman in their sensitive analysis of *The Secret Sharer* suggest that the novel might be read as an allegory of the artist and his coming to terms with himself and his materials. If we accept this, then we may read the parable of the scorpion as an epitomization of the writer's situation. The mysterious and dangerous materials which rise from the sea-unconscious are symbolized by the scorpion. His entering the lighted cabin suggests a bringing into consciousness if we see the cabin as created, ordered, civilized place, the home of the meticulous "Chief Mate." The scorpion's drowning in "ink" further suggests the transformation these forces must undergo from poison to ink, the sublimation of those forces into written form. There are also a number of provocative hints in the novel as Leggatt and the narrator pour over charts, books, and the like.

Then stillness again, with the great shadow gliding closer, towering higher, without a light, without a sound. Such a hush had fallen on the ship that she might have been *a bark of the dead floating in slowly under the very gate of Erebus.*

"My God! Where are we?"

It was the mate moaning at my elbow. He was thunder-struck, and as it were deprived of the moral support of his whiskers. He clapped his hands and absolutely cried out, "Lost!"

"Be quiet," I said sternly.

He lowered his tone, but I saw the shadowy gesture of his despair. "What are we doing here?"

"Looking for the land wind."

He made as if to tear his hair, and addressed me recklessly.

"She will never get out. You have done it, sir. I knew it'd end in something like this. She will never weather, and you are too close now to stay. She'll drift ashore before she's round. O my god!"

I caught his arm as he was raising it to batter his poor devoted head, and shook it violently.

"She's ashore already," he wailed, *trying to tear himself away.*

"Is she? . . . . Keep good full there!"

"Good full, sir," cried the helmsman in a frightened, thin, child-like voice.

I hadn't let go the mate's arm and went on shaking it. "Ready about, do you hear? You go forward"—shake—"and stop there"—shake—"and hold your noise"—shake—"and see these head sheets properly overhauled"—shake, shake—shake.

And all the time I dared not look toward the land lest my heart should fail me. *I released my grip at last and he ran forward as if fleeing for dear life.*

The dramatic actions of the two passages are analogous: both Leggatt and the narrator, caught in perilous situations, attempt to save their ships; both have an encounter with someone who opposes their will; both come to grips with that person; both save their ships; but both face tests which they solve differently. Clearly the second of the two structural units is an echo of the former with certain very important changes. Thus in the latter structure, it is not the disobedient sailor's face which is black, that miserable devil "who had no business to live at all." That color has been transferred to the threatening land. Likewise, Conrad transfers in the echoed passage Leggatt's epithet for the recalcitrant sailor to the land, "the very gate of Erebus."

What Conrad achieves by shifting images from the sailor to the land is a transference of symbolic meaning, so that instead of the Chief Mate's being the threat, it is the land which threatens the ship and crew with evil and annihilation. To come to knowledge of self is a hellish business; the seeking of the winds of self-knowledge and recon- ciliation with self and the world is full of terror, fraught[166] with danger to life and soul. The new captain's Chief Mate does not resemble the murdered sailor in action as we might expect; for the land, because it assumes the epithet, symbolizes cursedness, hellishness, and deadliness, the meaning also of the storm of the original passage in which Leggatt was involved in murder. In the echo structure, it is not a noisy typhoon which releases destruction; it is the silence of the ship and land and the Chief Mate's fear of the narrator's lack of experience, youth, and strange behavior, which unsettle him. Similarly, as Leggatt makes clear, the roles in the echo structure are a reversal of those of the earlier structure. Speaking to the narrator, Leggatt says of Captain Archbold during the typhoon:

I assure you he never gave the order. He may think he did, but he never gave it. *He stood there with me on the break of the poop after the main-topsail blew away, and whimpered about our last hope—positively whimpered about it and nothing else—and the night coming on! To hear one's skipper go on like that in such weather was enough to drive any fellow out of his mind.*

The meaning of the technique of the echo action in these passages is somewhat elusive but not impossible to establish. Analogous scenes suggest by means of similar images and similar mimeing that the two scenes are essentially the same scene, something like archetypal initiations or tests. The first of the two scenes creates a kind of order, for good or for evil, against which the second tautological structure must be judged and evaluated. The differences between the two scenes, those dissimilarities which appear in the echo structure, when evaluated within the framework of the former scene, suggest the meaning of the latter scene. Both men, Leggatt and the young captain, undergo the same experience; Leggatt seizes the man by the throat at the climax of his archetypal trial by storm and kills him in a fit of uncontrolled passion; the narrator also seizes his Chief Mate under similar circumstances, his archetypal trial by silence, but by controlling himself, controlling the frightened, disbelieving man, he controls the ship and consequently saves her from destruction, while saving his reputation and winning the respect of his crew. The action of the echo structure implies, it seems to me, a moral judgment of Leggatt, although it does not state the judgment openly. It dramatizes it and by doing so makes the reader psychologically aware of it. At the same time the echo scene declares the moral superiority of the consciously aware narrator-captain who has come to face his secret inner self, to conquer it, and to control it.

Archetype, myth, or Biblical story as echo structure: A course of action, a metaphor, a symbol, an image, and the like, repeated often enough to assume traditional meanings and to be recognized as ritualistic, is what is meant by archetype or archetypal pattern. The life and death of Christ is archetypal in these terms. It has certain similarities to the life, death, and resurrection of pagan gods, Dionysus, Tammuz, Adonis, the passing of the seasons, the rising and setting of the sun, and the phases of the moon, all recognizable as archetypes.[167] The cross is an archetype which contains in it the entire Christian story. "Miserable devils," "hellish spell of bad weather," and "gate of Erebus" are conceivable as archetypes of the demonic in *The Secret Sharer*. Archetypes may be obvious at once if they have not undergone complex disguise, or they may be distorted, disguised, fragmentary, inverted, or merely implied.[4]

In Conrad's novel several direct references to the Cain and Abel archetype draw our attention to its relation to the Leggatt story. Leggatt describes his experience to the narrator-captain in these words:

Devil only knows what the skipper wasn't afraid of (all his nerve went to pieces altogether in that hellish spell of bad weather we had)—of what the law would do to him—of what his wife, perhaps. Oh, yes! She's on board. Though I don't think she would have meddled. She would have been only too glad to have me out of the ship in any way. *The "Brand of Cain" business, don't you see. That's all right. I was ready enough to go off wandering on the face of the earth—and that was price enough to pay for an Abel of that sort.*

Later the captain reminds us of the story when he thinks, "The very trust in Providence was, I suppose, denied to his guilt." And once more it is echoed when the narrator and Leggatt search the map of the Gulf of Siam for an appropriate place for Leggatt's escape:

He looked thoughtfully at the chart as if surveying chances and distances from a lofty height—*and following with his eyes his own figure wandering on the blank land of Cochin-China, and then passing off that piece of paper clean out of sight into uncharted regions.*

This is re-echoed in the structure of Leggatt's words when he decides to return to the sea, "What does the Bible say? *'Driven off the face of the earth.'* Very well. I am off the face of the earth now. As I came at night so I shall go." The obvious references to the Cain and Abel archetypal structure are paralleled, as Leggatt suggests, in his relationship with the murdered sailor. As such they dictate a major structure of the novel, a ritual of murder, guilt, judgment, banishment or escape, and wandering, corresponding to the narrative course of Leggatt's story. But that

---

[4] These remarks are based on Northrop Frye's *Anatomy of Criticism* (Princeton, 1957), pp. 131–239. I have attempted to extend Professor Frye's theory of archetypes in two directions, practical and aesthetic.

is not all because the brother-murder-banishment-wandering archetypal structure echoes most of the principal relationships in the story. Leggatt and the murdered man; the narrator and Leggatt; the captain of the *Sephora* and Leggatt; the narrator and his Chief Mate and crew. Although Leggatt suggests the archetypal relationship between himself and the murdered man and the Cain and Abel story, the archetype is not complete because the captain of the *Sephora* also becomes the Cain figure who wants to kill Leggatt by turning him over to the law for trial. Because he is jealous of Leggatt's having saved the ship with the reefed sail, the *Sephora's* captain plays in an ironic reversal the Cain role to Leggatt's Abel. The Cain-Abel archetype circumscribes the[168] narrator-Leggatt relationship as well, the longest pattern of action and most important relationship of the novel, for the narrator, in a role comparable to that of Cain, figuratively kills his Abel-Leggatt when he consigns him to the sea. But the meaning of this archetypal action is symbolic and thematic because this Cain recognizes that he must destroy his Abel personality, an inversion of the Abel role, by sending him back to the sea. That the narrator will wander the face of the earth like Cain is made clear in the last sentence of the novel. But by shifting our perspective slightly, we observe that the relationship of the narrator to his Chief Mate and crew and ship is also a fragment of the echoing Cain and Abel archetype. The narrator may have killed the hysterical Chief Mate, as Leggatt killed the mutinous sailor, and as Cain killed Abel, but he does something else. By transcending and controlling the Abels on the ship, Leggatt, the chief mate, the crew, he avoids the Cain role and, incidentally, transforms the archetype even as he completes it.

The echoed archetypal structures suggest the multiplicity of similar experiences. They suggest that every man may be his brother's killer wittingly or unwittingly. The captain of the *Sephora*, for instance, wishes to preserve law and order by turning Leggatt over to the courts, but how much of jealousy and shame lie behind his decision he never admits. To what degree does he maintain morality and responsibility and to what degree does he demand the death of Leggatt to free his own conscience from accusations of cowardice during the typhoon? How strong is the narrator's Chief Mate who likes to account for everything, and how much of the Cain does he have in him when he goes to pieces under the blackness of Koh-ring? Precisely this kind of ambivalence characterizes the use of the echoed archetypal structure in *The Secret Sharer*. Thus the narrator as Cain *must kill* Abel-Leggatt in order that he may come to mature moral terms with his ship, crew, and self; and as Abel he *must not kill* or shame his first mate and crew in order that the trial be successfully passed.

The echo structure, by identifying various members of the ship's company now as Cain and now as Abel, suggests that all men in the ship-world are both Cain and Abel, that the Cain-Abel personality dwells in every man. "I wondered," says the narrator, "how far I should turn out faithful to that ideal conception of one's own personality every man sets up for himself secretly." And as the final structure in the novel suggests, the narrator meets his Cain personality in the form of Leggatt and in the form of his own blubbering Chief Mate and conquers both, dramatically answering his own question. Seeing Leggatt's phosphorescent flash pass under the white hat he wears into the water, the narrator thinks, "But I hardly thought of my other self, now gone from the ship, to be hidden forever from all friendly faces, *to be a fugitive and a vagabond on the earth, with no brand of the curse on his sane forehead to stay a slaying hand . . . . too proud to explain."*

Less explicit than the Cain-Abel archetypal structure is that of the Jonah archetype which appears in somewhat shadowy form in *The*[169] *Secret Sharer* but which creates an echo structure nevertheless. During the fierce typhoon Leggatt kills the mutinous sailor, as he reminds us, a "miserable devil." Then he describes the mounting fury of the storm which follows hard upon his act:

And the ship running for her life, touch and go all the time, any minute her last in a sea fit to turn your hair gray only a-looking at it. I understand that the skipper, too, started raving like the rest of them. The man had been deprived of sleep for more than a week, and to have this sprung on him at the height of a furious gale nearly drove him out of his mind. *I wonder they didn't fling me overboard after getting the carcass of their precious ship-mate out of my fingers.* They had rather a job to separate us, I've been told. A sufficiently fierce story to make an old judge and a respectable jury sit up a bit.

This first part of the structure is about one half of the Jonah archetype: the fierce storm, the cursed or pursued or immoral person whose actions are intimately connected with the howling typhoon, the breach of a moral code, the suggestion of being thrown overboard, the hint at judgment. The final half of the archetypal pattern appears many pages later when at the end of the novel the echo structure completes the archetype. The narrator-captain has made a decision to put Leggatt overboard:

"Now" I whispered, loudly, into the saloon—too loudly, perhaps, but I was afraid I couldn't make a sound. He was by my side in an instant— *the double captain slipped past the stairs—through the tiny dark passage . . . a sliding door. We were in the sail locker, scrambling on our knees over the sails.* A sudden thought struck me. *I saw myself wandering barefooted, bareheaded, the sun beating on my dark poll.* I snatched off my floppy hat and tried hurriedly in the dark to ram it on my other self. He dodged and fended off silently. I wondered what he thought had come to me before he understood and suddenly desisted. Our hands met gropingly, lingered united in a steady, motionless clasp for a second. . . . No word was breathed by either of us when they separated.

Returning to the deck, the narrator looks about on the sea for some marker which will indicate the position of the ship as it begins its turn from the land:

All at once my strained, yearning stare distinguished a white object floating within a yard of the ship's side. White on the black water. A phosphorescent flash passed under it. What was that thing? . . . I recognised my own floppy hat. It must have fallen off his head . . . . and he didn't bother. Now I had what I wanted—the saving mark for my eyes.

Thus at the last moment before the turn toward resolution in the novel, the second half of the echo structure is completed when Leggatt leaves the ship so that she may save herself and he himself. But[170] the novel suggests more than this. Since Leggatt is to be saved from immediate death, since the suggestiveness of the sail locker scene evokes the atmosphere of the belly of the whale into which Jonah descended and from which he was to be released, since the ship releases him into the waters of freedom, and since the narrator himself is released from his Cain (Leggatt) personality in the sail locker scene ("I saw myself wandering barefooted, bareheaded, the sun beating on my dark poll"), the echo part of the structure seems to identify the ship as an archetypal image of Jonah's whale. At the same time the Cain-Abel archetype passes through the Jonah archetype when the narrator thinks of himself as wandering unprotected over the face of the earth. The significance of this crossing of archetypes lies, I believe, in the identification of common elements between Jonah as wanderer and Cain as wanderer. The former refused to carry out the commands of his God; the latter broke the commandments of his God by killing his brother.

What, then, is the significance of the Jonah archetype which we have seen is split into several parts, the first appearing near the beginning of *The Secret Sharer*, the second part, the echo structure, appearing on the last page of the novel? The archetype, for one thing, gives meaning to experience, those traditional meanings which cluster about the Cain and Abel story and, in the immediate situation, the Jonah story. The echoed archetype especially gives a kind of continuity to fragmentary, splintered, or shattered actions, movements, or partial patterns of behavior. It makes sense out of the meaninglessness of disparate experiences by giving recognizable form to discontinuous, perhaps chaotic experiences. The Biblical archetypes establish a moral climate within whose atmosphere the actions of the story may be judged. The archetype ritualizes, congeals, makes cohere, for instance,

those scattered, almost senseless actions of men. To this, however, it
brings its own meaning from the tradition of which it is a part. The
way Leggatt is significantly identified as Jonah and the way the narrator
is also identified as Jonah must now be examined.

Aboard the narrator's ship, Leggatt gradually poisons the relationship between the narrator and his crew. In the becalmed sea, a direct
reversal of the typhoon scene, the threat of the presence of this Jonah
to the narrator and his ship is as great as the threat to the *Sephora* and
Captain Archbold in the howling storm. Jonah's moral weakness arose
from his disobedience; Leggatt's moral defection lies in his murderous
disposition, his inability to live within the strict confines of a moral
atmosphere, and his essentially nihilistic attitude toward inferiors:
"Miserable devils that have no business to live at all." Jonah flees his
Lord; Leggatt flees from the captain's retribution and from the threat
of law. Jonah, after spending three days in the whale, is coughed up
and reconciled with his God; Leggatt, after spending a number of days
in the narrator's cabin, bathroom, and sail locker, is lowered into the
water signalizing the reconciliation of the narrator with that other part
of himself, the moral, controlled, ethical forces with the threatening,
amoral forces of his personality.[171]

The Jonah archetype like the Cain-Abel archetype contributes
another dimension to the novel and reinforces its central thesis by suggesting in "other words" the very same thing that the Cain-Abel archetype suggested. Every man potentially *is* Cain and *is* Abel or every man
is Jonah (Cain and Abel in one configuration); every man must come
to terms with the other personality lurking within the human flesh.
But, and this is most important, the Cain-Abel archetype suddenly
crosses or is superimposed on the Jonah archetype in the sail locker
scene. As suggested, this correspondence of archetypes seems to hint
that essentially the two are one archetype told in different terms. Thus
murder and disobedience are deliberately confused by means of the
fusion of the archetypes, and they become, in terms of the thematic
development of the novel, symbolic of any moral weakness which would
not permit man to know his most secret self and the constant threat
which that inner self imposes on personality. Leggatt does not have the
brand of Cain on him, the echo structure suggests and the narrator
says at one moment near the end of *The Secret Sharer*, "with no brand
of the curse on his sane forehead to stay a slaying hand." Leggatt does
swim from the ship-whale, however, identified as the Cain who is condemned to wander the earth even if incognito "now gone from the ship
to be hidden forever from all friendly faces, to be a fugitive and a
vagabond on the earth." At the moment the two archetypes cross, while
the men are in the darkened sail locker, Leggatt assumes his role once
more in the Cain-Abel archetype; and the narrator assumes the role of

Jonah in the second archetype. Symbolically this transference is achieved when the narrator claps his hat on the head of the reluctant Leggatt and when their hands meet for a final identification and farewell. The narrator arises to pace the deck of his ship-world no longer the disobedient Jonah within the punishing whale. He returns to the deck in the symbolic role of the obedient Jonah from that sail locker-belly to assume full command of himself, of his men, and of his ship.

Anyone familiar with archetypal structures will observe immediately that another archetype complicates the two discussed here by overlaying them with suggestions of Leggatt as scapegoat. As Kenneth Burke describes the archetypal function of this device, the scapegoat is "the 'representative' or 'vessel' of certain unwanted evils, the sacrificial animal upon whose back the burden of these evils is ritualistically loaded.... the tendency was to endow the sacrificial animal with social coordinates, so that the goat became replaced by the 'sacrificial King.' " The conditions for becoming the archetypal scapegoat are any of these:

> (1) He may be made worthy legalistically (i.e., by making him an offender against legal or moral justice, so that he "deserves" what he gets).
>
> (2) We may make him worthy by leading towards sacrifice fatalistically (as when we so point the arrows of the plot that the audience comes to think of him as a marked man, and so prepares itself to relinquish him). . . .[172]
>
> (3) We may make him worthy by a subtle kind of poetic justice, in making the sacrificial vessel "too good for this world," hence the *highest* value, hence the *most perfect* sacrifice (as with the Christ theme, and its secular variants, such as little Hanno Buddenbrooks, whose exceptional sensitivity to music made him worthy to be sacrificed to music).[5]

Clearly Leggatt is the scapegoat for Captain Archbold and for the narrator as well. In the case of the captain of the *Sephora* Leggatt fulfills the first of the three conditions. By offending against legal justice when he kills the devilish sailor, Leggatt becomes "worthy legalistically" for sacrifice. But his guilt is complicated and mitigated because of his relation with Captain Archbold, for the captain uses him as a "vessel" for his own lack of bravery, for his own going to pieces when the ship appeared lost, and for his sense of guilt in front of his crew and wife. In the latter sense, then, the damning legal condemnation must be ameliorated and Leggatt, the legal murderer, must be seen as something less than a criminal. This scapegoat does, after all,

---

[5] Kenneth Burke, *The Philosophy of Literary Form* (New York, 1957) pp. 34–35. I am indebted not only to this book but also to all Professor Burke's work for constant stimulation.

save the *Sephora* and the lives of everyone on board including that of Captain Archbold, who performs the sacrifice of his scapegoat by putting him down a suicide.

For the narrator Leggatt serves as a scapegoat by fulfilling the two final conditions of the archetypal structure. Leggatt is led "towards sacrifice fatalistically" because the reader is constantly reminded that he represents Cain, that he destroys the harmony of the narrator's ship, that he prevents order from being established, and that he is the metaphorical scorpion threateningly present. It is not guilt or a sense of guilt or jealousy or evil which the narrator transfers to him as he places his hat on his head in that sail locker scene. It is something more subtle and more elusive. This scapegoat is a reminder to the narrator at the outset of his taking command of his first ship that all men have within them the very great possibility of another "presence" which in times of trial will defeat the outer self, the social mask constructed for our relationships with other men, unless the presence and its threat is met and conquered. The "secret self," Leggatt, struggles for a moment in the darkness of the sail locker (whale's belly), trying to fend off the hat, but the narrator defeats him there and places it firmly on his head. In the same way he will defeat his own threatening obtuseness when he returns to deck and seizes and shakes strength into his bewhiskered Chief Mate.

As a fulfillment of the final condition, Conrad draws Leggatt as worthy of the sacrifice, with overtones of great reluctance on the part of the narrator. First, he is identified with the narrator whose own personality we admire. Then through a piling up of detail, Conrad builds a case for our admiration of Leggatt, and this in spite of the murder. He is, for instance, "a strong soul"; his father is "a parson"; he and the narrator are "Conway" boys. The narrator thinks, "And I knew well enough also that my double there was no homicidal ruffian." Leggatt does not despair nor does he think of[173] suicide when he is certain that he is lost, although Captain Archbold will make him a suicide to clear his records and conscience. Leggatt refuses to try to break out of the *Sephora* in a violent manner because, "somebody would have got killed for certain, and I did not want any of that." The narrator marvels "at that something unyielding in his character which was carrying him through so finely." And, finally, the last statement of the novel, a deliberate ambiguity referring to both the narrator and Leggatt, "A free man, a proud swimmer *striking out* for *a new destiny*." In this way and because he frees the narrator from the threat of defections of self, Leggatt is the most perfect sacrifice, the scapegoat of the highest value.

The sail locker scene is crucial to an understanding of the functioning of archetypal patterns. Here the three patterns suddenly coalesce and when they separate thematic relevance has been resolved. Until the transfer of the hat, Cain, Abel, Jonah, and scapegoat relationships are mingled and fused into each other. Then the hat is pushed down on Leggatt's head, the three archetypes separate, and the story plunges toward its climax, each archetypal role clearly distinguishable from all others.

The fundamental thematic tensions in *The Secret Sharer* are embodied in and conveyed by these overlapping archetypal patterns. The knowledge which the narrator must gain, that he has lurking within the possibilities of moral corruption, represented by Leggatt and his attitude towards humanity, and the narrator's being tested, is carried in the Cain-Abel archetype which creates for the narrator a situation similar to that created for Leggatt. But by failing to pass his initiatory test successfully, Leggatt remains a Cain figure. By passing his test successfully the narrator faces his Cain characteristics and subjects them to his will. The Jonah archetype is introduced to suggest reconciliation by showing the two figures re-united in one person who carries with him the moral background of the Biblical tradition from which the archetype came. The possibility of danger and threat to those intimately related to Jonah as he seeks to flee is suggested by Leggatt's flight from the *Sephora* and his gradual disruption of the narrator's relationship with his men. But the possibility of salvation through a period of suffering and willingness to admit to and rid oneself of certain defections, and the possibility of undergoing a test of the reintegrated personality is portrayed in and symbolized by the narrator's shifting to the leading role in the Jonah archetype. As the reborn Jonah arose from the belly of the whale successfuly reconciled with his God, so too the fully reintegrated narrator climbs from the sail locker a new person to face and pass his test victoriously. [174]

TEXTUAL NOTE

Contrary to the general impression, the status of Conrad's texts is far from clear. "The Secret Sharer" is, however, aside from accidentals —punctuation, spelling, and the like—the cleanest of Conrad's texts that I have examined. The notes that follow apply only to "The Secret Sharer," though presumably other works of Conrad follow the same pattern.*

Previous editors of Conrad have followed the lead of Richard Curle, Conrad's biographer and friend, who said that though many forms of the fiction exist, Conrad concerned himself with one only— "the collected edition book form." (See *The Last Twelve Years of Joseph Conrad*, p. 64.) It is also clear that Conrad, in general, paid more attention to his English editions than to his American. The editor is then left with the question of which collected edition to reprint. General practice has been to print from the Dent (English) or Doubleday (American) general collected edition. The present edition is the first of "The Secret Sharer" to be based on a collation of the authoritative texts. These are as follows (in book form, of course, in the *'Twixt Land and Sea* volume):

MS. Manuscript. Now owned by Professor S. Sterling McMillan of Western Reserve University.†

HM. Serial version. "The Secret-Sharer." Published in *Harper's Monthly Magazine*, CXXI (August and September 1910), 349–359; 530–541. These installments correspond to the parts of the story in book form.

---

*See the Textual Note in *Conrad's "Heart of Darkness" and the Critics*, Belmont, California, Wadsworth Publishing Company, Inc., 1960, for a discussion of the text of that tale by the present editor, a discussion in the main of the collected editions of the story. The present note deals more generally with all editions.

† Professor McMillan, to whom my thanks are due, has permitted me to study the manuscript and reproduce some (but by no means all) of its variants. Professor McMillan is planning later to publish a study of the growth of the text, but he has kindly permitted me free use of the *MS* to help establish Conrad's final intention as to his text. Thanks are also due for reprinting rights to the Trustees of the Joseph Conrad Estate, Doubleday & Co., Inc., New York, and J. M. Dent and Sons, Ltd., London; and to *Harper's Magazine* for permission to quote from the serial.

E.   English edition. In the *'Twixt Land and Sea* volume. Dent. Collated are the issues of 1912, 1913 (University of Toronto Library copy), 1920 (University of Pennsylvania Library copy), and one copy of the "cheap" edition from the Wayfarer's Library, n.d. (Western Reserve University Library copy). I have not been able to obtain a copy of the November 1918 issue. (The cheap edition was published in 1914, 1918, and 1920, but apparently without distinguishing features. Two other copies have been spot-collated.) The text of the story is identical in all issues of *E*, the same type or plates being used throughout.

A.   American edition. In the *'Twixt Land and Sea* volume. Collated are the issues of 1912 (Hodder and Stoughton [then associated with Doran] and George H. Doran), the Library of Congress second copyright copy; 1912 (Doubleday, Page & Co. [which Doran joined], which thereafter published Conrad in the U.S. in his lifetime); 1917 (Princeton University Library); 1920 (Princeton University Library).* Perhaps other issues of the edition exist, but I have been unable to locate them. The text of the story is identical in all issues of *A*, the same type or plates being used throughout.

CS.   Collected limited American edition, "Sun-Dial," 1920–25. (First five volumes, 1920; last two, 1923 and 1925; the rest, 1921. *'Twixt Land and Sea* in 1921.)

CD.   Collected general American "edition," "Kent." This, like the "Malay" and others, was issued by Doubleday beginning in the middle twenties. It is made from duplicate plates of *CS*, and has seven variants from it. Not a true edition—that is, not a separate setting up of the story in type.

CU.   Collected, general English "edition," the Dent "Uniform," beginning in 1923. It is made from duplicate plates of *CS*, and the text of the story is identical (except for one comma) in both. Not a separate edition in the strict sense. (The current Dent Collected, 1946, is from the same plates.) This is probably accepted generally as the best copy-text, though in many respects it is faulty.

CH.   Collected, limited English edition, by Heinemann, beginning in 1921 (last two volumes are 1926, 1927). This is the copy-text for the present edition (1921).

ST.   "The Secret Sharer" as printed in *The Shorter Tales of Joseph Conrad*, Doubleday, Page & Co., 1924, pp. 41–95. Doubtless the last issue of the story in Conrad's lifetime, and identical with *CD*—it has seven variants from *CS*, and is made from duplicate plates of it.

These are the only authoritative editions of the story; all impressions I have been able to locate (as noted above) have been collated and are included in these notes.†

---

*I wish to express here my thanks to the above libraries for lending their copies. Unless otherwise specified, copies are from the University of Illinois Library.

† The Tauchnitz edition of 1912 may have variants, but I have been unable to examine a copy.

Preparation of the present text has led to several conclusions which are supported by a textual study of "Heart of Darkness," but must still be treated as tentative until more of Conrad's letters are published, or until publishers' files may be consulted. *CH* is taken as copy-text for many reasons. It is here reprinted for the first time. These reasons have a cumulative effect, though no one is conclusive:

1. *CS* was made in a foreign country, and perhaps the author did not revise fully for it.

2. *CU*, though the last issue of the collected works in Conrad's lifetime and widely publicized, is a reissue of *CS* by duplicate plates. The very nature of the reprinting would preclude major changes.

3. It follows that *CH* in a sense represents the last separate printing of Conrad's complete works in his lifetime, and may therefore be the edition he spoke of to Curle.

4. There is the negative evidence that Conrad's published letters nowhere speak of revising for *CU*. On the contrary, his letter of 3 Sept., 1920 (*Life and Letters*, II, 247–248), to the Heinemann firm, shows very careful editing on the part of that firm and Conrad, for the *CH Nigger of the "Narcissus."* Perhaps like care went into the preparation of the other novels and tales.

5. *CD* and *ST*, when they vary from *CU* and *CS* in substantives, agree with *CH*.

6. A study of the *MS* shows that even in accidentals—spelling, punctuation, etc.—*CH* is closest of all editions, even *A* and *E* (*HM* has more Americanisms than any other form). This unusual situation (which also obtains for "Heart of Darkness") has led me to follow *CH* in accidentals except when clearly contradicted by *MS*. Space forbids much illustration of variation among accidentals; but the word *sui–cide* [with a dash] in *MS* and *CH* contrasted to *sui-cide* [with a hyphen] in all other forms, will demonstrate the point. (See note to pp. 21.17.)

Perhaps some evidence should here be cited for the assertion that all impressions of *A*, all of *E*, and all collected editions except *CH* constitute in fact only three editions. A glance at almost any page is sufficient, but especially these:

E. Page 137, second line from foot, where the words *the reference to* are imperfectly justified in all issues.

A. Page 124, line 15, where the words *the inspecting* are overinked in all issues.

Collected editions other than *CH.* Page 103 (55 of *ST*), third line from foot, where the *h* in the word *the* is oddly and identically turned in all issues.

It is to be regretted that the collation notes that follow cannot be given in full. For the *MS* variants we eagerly await Professor McMillan's study, but the following are listed here:

1. All substantive variations in the book form of "The Secret Sharer." (Hence, only samples of *MS* and *HM* substantive variants, and none of the variants in the title-page and "Author's Note.")

2. All cases of substantive changes I have made from the copy-text, *CH;* in all but one instance, with *MS* authority.

3. All places where collected editions other than *CH* vary among their impressions.

4. A selection of typical variants of accidentals.

A second table gives a few interesting readings from *CH, MS,* and *HM* only.

The student may ask why changes from early editions are not to be considered authorial. A glance at virtually any unauthoritative reprint will demonstrate the freedom many editors and publishers allow themselves—some, for example, completely Americanize Conrad's spelling.

The word *all* is used to indicate that all editions other than those specified have the same reading. The numeral following the decimal point indicates the line on the page, and all page references are to the present text. The asterisk notes a departure from the copy-text, *CH,** in which case the text followed is put in parentheses.

Page Line

3.17	Meinam *all*	Mekong *HM*	Menong *MS*
4.20*	main-deck *all*	main deck *(MS)* [so throughout]	
4.21*	poop-deck *all*	poop deck *(MS)* [so throughout]	
4.23*	supper-table *CH*	supper table *(all)*	
4.29	, "Bless *CH*	: "Bless *all*	"Bless *MS*
5.4	[blank space on page] *all*	[¶ only] *MS*	
5.21	mate suddenly *CH, MS*	mate, suddenly *all*	
5.37	anchor-watch *all*	anchor watch *MS*	
6.1	anchor-watch *all*		
6.25*	sleeping-suit *all*	sleeping suit *(MS)* [so throughout]	
6.25	warm, breathless *CH*	warm breathless *all*	
7.15*	guess, a *CH*	guess a *(all)*	
7.29	past too. *CH, MS*	past, too. *all*	
8.19*	resolute—a *CH*	resolute. A *(all)*	
9.25	suggested confidently. *CH, MS*	suggested, confidently. *all*	
	[So throughout with adverbs qualifying the tone of voice already implied in the verb.]		

---

* In transcribing the *MS*, I have used italics to indicate words Conrad deleted in the manuscript; words surrounded by carets (∧,∧) were added above the manuscript line; words surrounded by plus signs (+ , +) were added in the margin (usually to the left), perhaps with arrows to indicate position.

9.34* too—" *all*   too . . ." *HM, (MS)*
[In *MS*, Conrad seems to reserve the dash in such construc-
tions for interruptions—whether by another or the speaker.]

9.39 saying: [¶] "My *all*   saying: [no ¶] "My *CD, CS, CU, ST*

9.41 charge? . . . There *all*
        charge. For myself I can stand it. There *MS*

9.42* heaven——and *CH*   heaven——And *(all)*
        heaven . . . And *HM, MS*

10.3* cur—" *all*   cur. . . ." *HM*
        cur . . . *(MS* [except for quotation mark])

10.22 yelling, 'Look out! Look out!' Then *CH*
        yelling, 'Look out! look out!' Then *A*
        yelling, "Look out! look out!" Then *E*
        yelling, Look out! look out!" Then *CS, CU*
        yelling, 'Look out! look out!' " Then *CD, ST*
        yelling. Then *HM, MS*

10.30 'Murder!' *all*   "Murder!" *E, HM*   Murder! *MS*

10.37 shipmate *CH, MS*   ship-mate *all*

11.10* witchcraft; *all*   witchcraft: *(MS)*

11.12 undertone: [¶] "My *CH*   undertone. [¶] "My *all*
        undertone: [no ¶] "My *MS*

11.16* state-room *CH*   stateroom *(all)* [so throughout]

11.21 assented sleepily *CH*   assented, sleepily *all*
        answered ∧assented∧ sleepily *MS*

11.30 ship's *all*   ships' *A*

11.38 L, the *CH, HM*   L the *all*   L. the *MS*

11.44 such-like *CH*   such like *all*

12.1 bathroom *CH, MS*   bath-room *all* [so throughout]

12.15* seven weeks. *all*   nine weeks. *(HM)*   six weeks. *MS*

12.17* bed-place *all*   bedplace *(MS)* [Conrad may possibly have in-
        tended two words.]

12.40 halter round *all*   halter around *A*

12.43* Angier *all*   Anjer *(MS)*

13.21 Oh yes! *CH*   O! yes! *MS*   Oh, yes! *all*

13.24 see? *CH*   see. *all*

14.21* was . . . narrative, or *all*
        was *something in his narrative* +something+
        that made comment impossible, in his narrative, or *(MS)*

14.24 whisper, "So *CH*   whisper: "So *all*
        +whisper+ "So *MS*

14.29 thousand feet *CH, MS*   thousand-feet *all*

15.37 asked, with *CH, MS*   asked with *all*

16.12 now, and *CH*   now and *all*

16.27   crew washing   *all*   hands washing   *HM, MS* [so virtually throughout]

16.35*   doorway, and   *CH*   doorway and   (*all*)

17.23   executed too.   *CH MS*   executed, too.   *all*

17.27*   breakfast-/time,   *CH*   breakfast time,   *all*
          breakfast ⋏time⋏ +eating nothing myself+ I (*MS*, [but comma added])

17.41   I then   *all*   then I   *CD, CS, CU, ST*

18.3   stood drawn bolt upright in   *CH*
          stood drawn up bolt upright in   *all*
          stood +*perfectly*+ *motionless* ⋏drawn up very still⋏ in   *MS*

18.21   me, out   *CH, A, E*   me out   *all*

18.25   there, . . . stool,   *all*
          there sitting bolt upright on the low stool   *MS*

18.37   him?   *all*   him.   *MS*

18.39   [*MS* has indication of a paragraph only, not a part-division.]

19.14   , though.   *all*   tho'.   *MS* [Spelled thus virtually throughout.]

19.20*   mumbling, and   *CH*   mumbling and   (*all*)

19.23*   his smeary blue,   *all*   his *hard*, ⋏smeary⋏ blue,   (*MS*)

19.24*   What . . . disease?   *all*
          "What . . . disease?"   *CD, HM*, (*MS*, for quotes), *ST*

20.1*   seven-and-thirty   *all*   seven and thirty   (*MS*)

20.9   uttered impressively,   *CH*   uttered, impressively,   *all*
          uttered impressively   *MS*

20.11   that." He   *all*   that. [¶] He   *MS*

20.44   went on, groping   *all*   went groping   *HM, MS*

21.3   on. He looked   *all*
          on. Our senior partner spoke to me himself *And h* He looked   *MS*

21.5   chief mate   *all*   chief-mate   *MS* [So virtually throughout]

21.17   "Sui—cide!   *CH, MS*   "Sui-cide!   *all*

21.39   not, I think,   *all*   not, I think   *MS*

21.42   enough (I thought of it only afterward),   *CH, MS* [*MS* lacks comma]
          enough—(I . . . afterwards)—   *CD, CS, CU, ST*
          enough—(I . . . afterward)—   *all*

22.9   Necessity, they say, is mother of invention, but fear, too, is. . . .   *all*
          [But *MS* has not a single comma in the sentence.]

22.13   saloon,   *all*   cabin,   *HM, MS*

22.34*   item: mate's room,   *CH*   item; mate's room,   *all*
          detail; ⋏item⋏ mate's rooms,   *MS* [Text here item: mates' rooms,]

22.35*   store-rooms,   *A, CH*   storerooms,   (*all*)

22.35   sail-locker, which   *CH*   sail-locker which   *all*

23.9   had an idea   *all*   had no idea   *HM, MS*

23.11*   mystified,   *CH*   mystified   (*all*)

24.12*	suppose *all*	supposed (*MS*)
24.17	everything *all*	anything *HM*
24.33*	bo's'n *all*	boss'en (*MS*)
24.38	coal-waggon *all*	coal-wagon *CD, CS, CU, HM, ST*
24.42	lives had, *CH, MS*	lives, had, *all*
25.8*	him, and *CH*	him and (*all*)
25.31	, as instinctively, as *CH*	, as instinctively as *all*

, *as the winking of* as [*illegible word*] instinctively as   *MS* [*MS* fairly commonly omits the second comma of a parenthetical element.]

25.45	asked, astonished *all*	asked astonished *MS*
26.24*	paté de foie gras *all*	pâté de foies gras *HM*

pâté de foie-gras (*MS* [but not for hyphen])

27.3	whiskered *all*	mustachioed *HM, MS* [So through *MS;* changed

to *whiskers,* etc., in book form.]

28.2*	eyes, I asked *CH*	eyes I asked *all*	eyes? I asked *HM*

eyes? *I thought.* ∧I asked∧ (*MS*)

28.36	his arm . . . same—" *all*	his head . . . same..." *HM*

his hand . . . same...."   *MS* [*MS* followed for ellipses only.]

29.7	Cambodje *all*	Cambodge *CD, ST*
29.20*	Judgment *all*	Judgement (*MS*)
29.28	as I know *all*	as you know *HM, MS*
30.8	look out *CH, MS*	look-out *all*
30.9*	islands before *all*	islands long before (*MS*) [*long* is an after-

thought, squeezed into line.]

30.21*	telescope. I *CH*	telescope I (*all*)
30.33	"Well, if *CH, MS*	"Well—if *all* [The *MS* comma often re-

sembles a hyphen.]

31.20*	way on to the *CH*	way on the (*all*)
31.29	tell *all*	told *HM, MS*
31.29	opened wide *CD, CH, ST*	open wide *all*
31.40	I shall *all*	I will *CD, CS, CU, ST*
32.2	you shall have *all*	you will have *CD, CS, CU, ST*
32.18*	slowly against *all*	slowly *against* ∧amongst∧ (*MS*)
32.19	more distant *all* [more *distinct* would be a possible emendation.]	
33.16	He fled up *all*	He flew up *CD, CS, CU, ST*
33.41	"She will *all*	"She may *CS, CU*
34.4*	I had shut *all*	I *closed* ∧had to shut∧ (*MS*)
34.8	Koh-ring *all*	Koh-rong *MS* [Spelled thus only once.]
34.11*	toward *all*	towards *CD, CS, CU,* (*MS*), *ST*
34.26	together, "We *CH*	together: "We *all*

together "We *MS*

34.28	without a light *all*	without light *CS, CU*
34.29*	barque *CH*	bark (*all*)
35.8*	toward *all*	towards *CD, CS, CU,* (*MS*), *ST*

36.13   remark, "She's *CD, CH, ST*   remark "She's *all*
         remark *one sea [?] in a relieved tone* "She's *MS*
36.20*   affection, *all*   affection; *(MS)*
36.27   water . . . punishment: a *all*   water . . . punishment, a *HM*
         water—a *MS*

Manuscript and Serial

The study of an author's revisions from manuscript through serial to book form is an illuminating critical experience, but it is not within the aim of this volume. The following notes are intended merely to give the flavor of the manuscript. More than that must await Professor McMillan's study of the growth of the text.

Of the manuscript, this much may be said here. Up to page 33 of the present text, the *MS* agrees quite closely in final wording: there are a few differences in wording, but by and large, the manuscript is interesting in showing the numerous revisions *within its* stage as Conrad worked toward his final text. From pages 33 to 36, the substantive variations in *MS* from the above text are considerably more numerous.

Written in November (and perhaps part of December), 1909, "The Secret Sharer" *MS* is relatively straightforward—for Conrad. The revisions in it, and after it, are almost entirely matters of rewording, not the wholesale reworking of material that Conrad went through, for example, with *The Secret Agent*.

Limitations of space prevent the giving of many examples, but some typical kinds of changes follow, showing only the texts of *CH, MS,* and *HM*—the last being the most Americanized of all versions. (Italicized words in *MS* indicate deletions by Conrad; words surrounded by carets [ʌ,ʌ] indicate additions above the line or overwritings; words surrounded by plus signs [+,+] indicate additions in the margin or inserts between the manuscript lines.)

Page Line
5.14   infinitely. The ship *CH*
         infinitely. We had been having scorpion at every meal, and the
              second mate's lip had been kept on the quiver all the time.
              The ship *HM, MS*
7.22   head. A headless corpse! The *CH*   head. The *HM, MS*
15.10   And as . . . I said. *CH, HM*   And as to *them* +the+
              ʌcrewʌ all they knew was that I *was* +came on board+
              ʌwas appointedʌ ʌ[illegible word]ʌ to take *them* ʌthe shipʌ
              home. For the rest I was *[illegible]* ʌalmostʌ as *complete*
              ʌmuch of aʌ stranger *to them* on board as himself—I said.
              MS
17.5   say nay to me *CH, HM*   say me nay *MS*

17.22   first particular order   *CH*   first general order   *HM, MS*

19.6   ashamed . . . name   *CH, HM*   ashamed of *himself* what he was
         saying; declined his name   *MS*

33.21   I saw myself . . . poll. I   *CH, HM*   I saw him wandering bare-
         footed, bareheaded the sun beating on his *head.* ∧dark poll∧.
         I *MS*

34.3   The strain . . . still?   *CH, HM*   The strain of watching the
         ∧dark∧ loom grow was too much. I *closed* ∧had to shut∧
         my eyes. She must go closer. Must. The stillness *of* grew
         intolerablye. were we standing still?   *MS*

In sum, then, it can be said that *CH* is a very good copy-text. I
have followed it in all substantive readings except those noted above.
In accidentals, I have also followed *CH* in nearly all readings. The
ideal copy-text for accidentals, one supposes, would be the corrected
typescript (if it survived) sent to the printer—though that form also
would be incorrect in some details, because the typist's usage would
be reflected in it. I have often not followed *MS* for accidentals because it is clearly wrong in matters such as we might expect an author
to ignore in the throes of composition. (See the question mark in the
note to 18.37, above, for example.) Furthermore, *CH* is a particularly
good text to follow because it is pointed according to the same
philosophy of style as is *MS*. That is, it uses "open" or "light" pointing—not the heavier punctuation that reflects house-practice of the
publishers. The comparative rarity of *CH* (780 copies were made before
the type was distributed) has caused our estimate of the style of "The
Secret Sharer" to be set mainly (and erroneously) by *CD* and *CU*.

Of the editions in general, this comment should be added. The
proper line of descent—by internal evidence as well as Conrad's
various statements about preferring the English editions to the
American—is *MS*, [*TS*], *E*, through the various impressions to *CH*.
As the above collation notes show, *CH* is hitherto the best available
edition, with *CD* (followed by *CU*) next.

Finally, it should be said that the present edition is not intended
as definitive, though it does present all substantive variants in book
form. For there are no explanatory notes, no emendations although
some seem called for, and copy-text has a few times silently been
departed from—but in accidentals only. (Aside from a half-dozen instances the accidentals silently changed have been the less meaningful
kind, as changing a dash to a series of dots at the close of a speech.)
Furthermore, I have of course not been able to print all the variants
found in the *MS*: even though many of these variants never found their
way into print, they are exceedingly illuminating. *Conrad's "Secret
Sharer" and the Critics*, then, gives a text which is as close as I can
make it to the final one Conrad wished. It gives a good reading edition
of "The Secret Sharer" for study.

Here follows a transcript of the first page of the manuscript.

DN/1   The Secret Sharer   [in blue crayon]

                              I   [ink]

                                  I.   [in crayon; the text is in ink]

                          On my right hand there were
                            some fishing stakes like a *submerged* ∧mysterious∧
                            fence system of ∧half∧ submerged fences;
                            to my left a group of islets
                            incomprehensible in its division of
                            the domain of *fishes out* [?] tropical
                            fishes and crazy of aspect as
                            if belonging to no one.

            if   abandonned[?] by ∧some∧ nomad tribe
      of brown *of*   fishermaen now removed to
                          the other end of the earth.
                          To my *right* ∧left∧ a group of
        ruined   islets as perfectly stony as if
      piled up   *built* [?] there by the hand of man
                          had its foundations set in
                          in a *blue* [?] blue sea that
                            itself looked as smooth and hard
                            as a polished stone.
                            itself looked solid so still
                            it was and so perfectly smooth
                            and when I turned my head
                            to take a parting glance

[*Reduced Facsimile of MS, Page 1*]

On my right hand there were
some fishing stakes like a mysterious
system of half submerged fences,
incomprehensible in its division of
the domain of tropical
fishes and crazy of aspect as
if abandoned by some nomad tribe
of fishermen now removed to
the other end of the earth.
To my right a group of
ruined islets as perfectly stony as if
piled up by the hand of man
had its foundations set in
in a blue sea than
itself
as a polished stone.
itself looked solid so still
it was and so perfectly smooth
and when I turned
to take a passing glance

STUDY QUESTIONS, THEME AND PAPER TOPICS

"The Secret Sharer" is so rich a story that a wealth of issues is raised by it, even after one has read a selection of the best criticism. The questions that follow are in no way exhaustive, nor are they intended to direct the student or the teacher toward a particular approach to the tale. Rather, they are sample questions which the instructor will probably modify to meet the needs of his particular class. Although their organization is flexible, three basic kinds of questions are included: questions on the story itself; questions which compare and contrast the criticism reprinted in the volume; and questions which require outside reading and research on the part of the student. Needless to say, questions intended by the editor as paper topics might well be used for themes or for essay questions on examinations; and in a sense all questions are study questions.

Study Questions

1. Many critics feel that one should begin by annotation of the work of art. Look up such technical terms and phrases as "deadened in stays," "mainsail haul," "hard alee," "sail-locker." What is a "Conway boy"? Similarly, on the Lubbock analogue, to what catastrophe at Krakatoa is the author referring?

2. Do you fully understand the nautical problem faced by the Captain as he takes his ship in close to Koh-ring?

3. Conrad at two points lavishly describes the saloon and cabin— the famous letter L shape. Can you diagram these rooms and their relation to the whole ship? Is the shape of the cabin significant?

4. Stallman says the voyage can be sketched on a map. Do so. The location of the river Meinam is a problem. Can you make use of manuscript readings in drawing your map? Note that the river Menong (*MS*) or Mekong (*HM*) is *not* at the head of the Gulf of Siam, and that it is also called the Maenam Khong. There is a Koh-Rong in the Gulf, but apparently not a Koh-ring. (See John D. Gordan's book, *passim*, for illustrations of the way Conrad often used factual names in his *MS*, but then disguised his source with a fictional name in the printed version. Is that pattern followed in "The Secret Sharer"?)

5. Learn to check your critics on matters of fact. Stallman (p. 103 above) comments that "It is said that this story was written in order to resolve a personal crisis." Where was it said? By whom? (See also Benson, p. 91 above.)

6. Look up Conrad's letter to Richard Curle, which Stallman uses on page 95. Has Stallman interpreted Conrad's words in their proper context, or not?

7. To Guerard, Leggatt is a poor seaman; to Baines, an exemplary seaman; to Leiter, a good seaman. This would seem to be an issue of fact. Is it? How do you interpret Leggatt as a seaman?

Similarly, Gettmann and Harkness see the killing as an act of murderous rage; Curley, as Leggatt's act of self-preservation. Which interpretation, if either, does the story confirm?

8. Is Leiter right in saying that as the story progresses the Captain becomes more and more convinced that he is insane?

9. Read the story of Cain and Abel in the Bible. Why did God set a mark upon Cain? In one's interpretation of Leggatt and of "The Secret Sharer," how much should one stress Conrad's statement that Leggatt will *not* bear the "brand of [Cain's] curse on his sane forehead to stay a slaying hand"?

10. How would you complete Captain Archbold's sentence, "You don't think that—?" Does the way you would end the sentence affect the meaning of the next few lines (p. 23.6)?

11. Characterize the tone and style of the Captain-narrator. In reference to question 9 above, is it technically the Captain or Conrad who refers to the mark of Cain?

12. Characterize the secondary personages in the story—the officers, the steward, and so on. Has Conrad presented them fully enough? Skillfully enough? Can these questions be answered in the abstract, or should they be related to the story's theme? Why does the Captain fear the steward the most?

Theme Topics

1. Using the Textual Note in this volume, can you catalogue the kinds of changes made in the text through the years? Do the variant readings substantially help your understanding of the story, or of Conrad as an artist? What does the facsimile of the first page of the *MS* tell you of Conrad's habits of composition? How important do you feel the recovery of the typescript of the story might be?

2. In comparing "The Secret Sharer" to "A Hell-Ship Voyage," consider Basil Lubbock's statement that Conrad's version of the mate's escape from the *Cutty Sark* is absurd, because Leggatt would have been eaten by sharks as he swam. Most readers would

reject the comment as itself absurd—but can you explain in a concise essay why it is?

3. Do you agree with what the critics have said in general about "The Secret Sharer" and its analogues? Write an essay centered on the comparison and contrast of the "versions"—on the significance of Conrad's "changes."

4. As you read criticism, compare one commentary with another. What, for example, do Benson and Wright say about the significance of pity in "The Secret Sharer"? In an essay, comment on the importance of the theme of pity in the story.

5. Benson and Guerard arrive at opposite judgments on the relative merits of "The Secret Sharer" and *The Shadow-Line*. Why? What principles of evaluation does each use? Write an essay evaluating the two fictional pieces, or write an essay on the problem of evaluation.

6. "The Secret Sharer" is a story built in large part on the idea of a "double"—a character who represents some aspect of the major character, as Leggatt represents a part of the Captain. Many authors other than Conrad have used this device: write an essay comparing Conrad's usage to that of Dostoevsky (in *Crime and Punishment*) or Poe (in "William Wilson"), or as your instructor may assign.

7. Specifically, compare Leggatt and the Captain as doubles to Kurtz and Marlow in Conrad's "Heart of Darkness." How closely related are the meanings of the two stories? Write an essay concerning the relationship of subject matter and meaning in fiction.

8. Perhaps the most basic technical decision an author must make concerns "point of view": from what angle will the story be told? What are the advantages of the point of view used in "The Secret Sharer"? How does it enable Conrad to meet questions of exposition, of transition, of management of minor characters? Would the story be successful if told from another point of view? As an exercise, rewrite the opening section (down to the words "Meantime the chief mate . . .") using the omniscient point of view. What is lost? What is gained? Discuss Conrad's management of point of view in the story.

9. As you can tell from the criticism here reprinted (as well as from your reading of other stories and novels), Conrad is a conservative. "The Secret Sharer," at first reading, seems to be radical and rebellious in significance. Do you see it (as do many of the critics) as fitting ultimately into a conservative position, or do you feel that it stands apart from much of Conrad's fiction? Be sure to define your terms.

10. Notice that Conrad is very detailed and explicit about certain things, vague about others. Why? Is it significant, for example, that we never learn the Captain's name or the name of his ship? Is

Conrad implying that this could be *any* ship or *any* man? (But observe that there are many other people whose names we do not learn.) How does one decide which inclusions and which exclusions are important to an interpretation of a story?

11. How often has the criticism reprinted in this volume turned on the interpretation of a small section of the story? Note that the critics may be in agreement about the over-all meaning or importance of the story, but disagree at length about some aspect of it. With this comment in mind, can you decide how to interpret in detail the story's last paragraph? Or, in your view of the over-all story, where should the stress be put in its title: "The *Secret* Sharer," or "The Secret *Sharer*"?

12. What do you take the over-all shape and meaning of "The Secret Sharer" to be? The critics represented in this volume regard it, variously, as a story of initiation, a story of the night journey, a story of a growth toward self-mastery, a story of a growth toward solidarity, and so forth. Note that many critical issues are involved in forming a concise statement of the purport of a story. The critics are not even agreed on the most basic issue of all —that of which character is the central one; for, while nearly all agree that it is the Captain, Baines implies that it is Leggatt.

Can you state the story's growth, unity, meaning, in a single sentence? Write an essay defending your statement.

Longer Essays and Term Papers

1. Basil Lubbock's comment in "A Hell-Ship Voyage" about the probability of sharks eating the escaped mate raises the question of an author's intentions in making changes from his "raw materials." What advantages did Conrad achieve in making Leggatt swim to the new ship?

Further, what is the relationship of an author's intention to the meaning of a story? Curley, in his essay, makes a definite use of Conrad's intention; Baines apparently would restrict the meaning of a story to just that (p. 118)—it could mean only and whatever the author intended. Do you agree?

2. On the issue of an author's intention, remember that sometimes the evidence seems contradictory. For example, Jessie Conrad in one of her books about her husband, *Joseph Conrad and His Circle,* testifies that Conrad told her that "The Secret Sharer" "is pure fiction. I don't know where the idea came from, but I've taken you in beautifully [in making her think that the tale was autobiographical]. Hurrah" (p. 77). Compare this statement to those in Conrad's "Author's Note" to *'Twixt Land and Sea.* How important are we to consider the author's comments? (By the way, as an extension of the study question 6 above, check the context of the lines from Mrs. Conrad, cited just above.)

3. The whole issue of meaning and intention is a big one, with an extensive bibliography—beginning in recent times with W. K. Wimsatt, Jr., and M. C. Beardsley, "The Intentional Fallacy," available among other printings in *Modern Literary Criticism*, ed. Ray B. West, Jr. (New York, 1952), pp. 174–189. In an essay, discuss either Conrad's intention and the meaning of "The Secret Sharer" or the general issue of intention versus meaning. Wimsatt and Beardsley argue that the two are entirely divorced, but later critics often modify that position. (Your instructor will assign later articles; or, see *Literary Symbolism*, ed. Maurice Beebe, in this series of Guides to Literary Study, pp. 11–17.)

4. The critics of "The Secret Sharer" have directed their primary attention to these aspects of the story: the significance of Leggatt, the significance of the Captain's going so close to Koh-ring, the significance of the Captain's hat on the water, and the story's mythic or allegoric meaning. Are you convinced that these are the important elements, the significant issues. Are there others equally or more significant?

5. Furthermore, after reading these critics are you convinced of their interpretations of these four elements? Do they agree—or are their views reconcilable? For example, to Guerard, Leggatt is the evil aspect of the inner, instinctive man; to Curley, he is the ideal inner man; to Stallman, he is also the ideal; to Leiter, he is (primarily) a scapegoat; but to Baines, he is not the Captain's double at all! Write an essay on the significance of Leggatt.

6. Consider the question of why the Captain sails so close to Koh-ring. To Guerard and in a different way to Gettmann and Harkness, it is in "payment" to Leggatt; to Benson, it is to show his power and authority and to prove to himself that he can measure up to Leggatt (and perhaps because he forgot temporarily how fine a swimmer Leggatt is). Other critics take different views. Can you agree with any?

7. Similarly, the hat on the water signifies a bringing together of all the archetypes to Leiter, "fidelity" to Stallman, the personality to Guerard, the joining of the instincts of violence and pity to Gettmann and Harkness, and so on. Is any one view "right"? Will this detail in the story bear such a weight of meaning? Write a paper on the import of the hat.

8. Several critics see the story as more than symbolic—as mythic, archetypal, allegoric. Yet their interpretations vary: the allegory of the artist (among others) to Stallman, the night journey to Guerard, many different myths to Leiter. Can these views be reconciled? Should one discard some of these mythic readings? Is there a "super myth" which contains them all?

9. Note that Mudrick seems to reject any such reading of the story, and prefers to concentrate on plot, event, character, narrative. Evaluate his criticism. (He is, by the way, referring primarily to a

different article by Stallman. See the Bibliography at the end of this volume.)

10. Or, to come at the issue from another angle, what does it mean to say that a story has different "levels" or "aspects" of meaning? Can a story at once be one of action, of psychology, of morality, of myth, of allegory? Most of the critics imply that it can: but what does this mean?

11. Examine the theory that fiction can have levels of meaning, both in a general sense and in relation to details. For example, what does it add to one's understanding of the *meaning* of "The Secret Sharer" to say that the sail-locker is an image of Jonah's whale's belly (Leiter, p. 146)?

12. Compare the problems of the Captain and Leggatt to those of the characters in Herman Wouk's *The Caine Mutiny*, which is probably the most recent fiction closely related to "The Secret Sharer" in meaning and subject matter. Another interesting comparison is that of Melville's *Billy Budd*: Leggatt's innocence-in-killing is somewhat like Billy's, while the problems of Captain Vere and the Captain in Conrad's story are strikingly similar. Compare and contrast the views of Melville and Conrad on these issues. (In this connection, it will be helpful to read *Melville's "Billy Budd" and the Critics*, ed. William T. Stafford, in this series of Guides to Literary Study.)

Finally, "The Secret Sharer" can interestingly be placed in the whole tradition of nautical tales, and an assessment of its values made. Not only can this be done for Joseph Conrad (as in a comparison to *The Nigger of the "Narcissus,"* for example) but also for English and American literature in general—*Moby-Dick, Two Years Before the Mast,* and *Roderick Random* are but three of many possibilities. Such a comparison can be very illuminating in showing the different uses to which the sea can be put by an author, and also in showing the extreme differences in complexity and tightness which are possible in good fiction.

How highly do you rank "The Secret Sharer" in the tradition?

BIBLIOGRAPHY OF WORKS FOR
FURTHER STUDY

The student might do well to start by reading the full articles or books from which the critical selections of this volume are taken. Over the years Conrad has received great critical attention, and consequently this note is divided into two sections—(1) a list of works on "The Secret Sharer," although virtually all books on Conrad have commentaries on the story, and (2) a brief list of works on Conrad in general. It should be emphasized that not all studies of Conrad and the story are listed here.

"The Secret Sharer"

(Critical selections included in this volume are not repeated.)

Robert O. Evans. "Conrad: A Nautical Image," *Modern Language Notes,* LXXII (1957), 98–99.

Albert Guerard, Jr. *Joseph Conrad.* "Direction One"; New York, 1947, pp. 38–42.

Albert J. Guerard. Introduction to *Heart of Darkness and The Secret Sharer.* New York (Signet Classic), 1950, pp. 7–15.

Robert F. Haugh. *Joseph Conrad: Discovery in Design.* Norman, Oklahoma, 1957, pp. 78–82.

Douglas Hewitt. *Conrad, A Reassessment.* Cambridge, England, 1952, pp. 70–79.

E. Arthur Robinson. "Conrad's 'The Secret Sharer,'" *Explicator* (1960), item 28.

Robert W. Stallman. "Life, Art, and 'The Secret Sharer,'" in *Forms of Modern Fiction,* ed. William Van O'Connor. Minneapolis, 1948, pp. 229–242.

Charles C. Walcutt. "Interpreting the Symbol," *College English,* XIV (1953), 452–454.

Paul L. Wiley. *Conrad's Measure of Man.* Madison, 1955, pp. 94–97.

Joseph Conrad

BIOGRAPHICAL

Jocelyn Baines. *Joseph Conrad.* London, 1960.

Jessie Conrad. *Joseph Conrad and His Circle.* London, 1935.

Joseph Conrad. *The Mirror of the Sea*. London, 1906.

Joseph Conrad. *A Personal Record*. London, 1912.

Joseph Conrad. *Life and Letters*, ed. G. Jean-Aubry. London, 1927.

Joseph Conrad. *Conrad to a Friend*, ed. Richard Curle. London, 1928.

Joseph Conrad. *Letters from Joseph Conrad*, ed. Edward Garnett. Indianapolis, 1928.

Joseph Conrad. *Lettres Françaises*, ed. G. Jean-Aubry. Paris [1930].

Joseph Conrad. *Letters to William Blackwood and David S. Meldrum*, ed. William Blackburn. Durham, 1958.

John D. Gordan. *Joseph Conrad: The Making of a Novelist*. Cambridge, Mass., 1940.

Gustav Morf. *The Polish Heritage of Joseph Conrad*. London [1929].

BIBLIOGRAPHICAL

Maurice Beebe. "Criticism of Joseph Conrad: a Selected Checklist," *Modern Fiction Studies*, I (February 1955), 30–45.

George T. Keating. *A Conrad Memorial Library*. New York, 1929.

Kenneth A. Lohf and Eugene P. Sheehy. *Joseph Conrad at Mid-Century: Editions and Studies, 1895–1955*. Minneapolis, 1957.

CRITICAL

Joseph Warren Beach. *The Twentieth-Century Novel*. New York, 1932. Esp. pp. 337–365.

Joseph Conrad. *Conrad's Prefaces to His Works*. With an introduction by Edward Garnett. London, 1937.

Edward Crankshaw. *Joseph Conrad*. London [1936].

Donald Davidson. "Joseph Conrad's Directed Indirections," *Sewanee Review*, XXXIII (1925), 163–177.

Frederick R. Karl. *A Reader's Guide to Joseph Conrad*. New York, 1960.

Thomas Moser. *Joseph Conrad: Achievement and Decline*. Cambridge, Mass., 1957.

R. W. Stallman, ed. *The Art of Joseph Conrad: A Critical Symposium*. East Lansing, 1960.

Robert Penn Warren. Introduction to *Nostromo*. New York (Modern Library), 1951.

M. D. Zabel. Introduction to *The Portable Conrad*. New York, 1947.

M. D. Zabel. In *Craft and Character in Modern Fiction*. New York, 1957.

The current bibliographies in *PMLA* (April issues), and *Abstracts of English Studies*, will list new additions to the critical studies on Conrad and "The Secret Sharer."

M